One Dream or Two?

One Dream or Two?

Justice in America and in the Thought of Martin Luther King, Jr.

Nathan W. Schlueter

LEXINGTON BOOKS
Lanham • Boulder • New York • Oxford

LEXINGTON BOOKS

Published in the United States of America
by Lexington Books
A Member of the Rowman & Littlefield Publishing Group
4720 Boston Way, Lanham, Maryland 20706

PO Box 317
Oxford
OX2 9RU, UK

Copyright © 2002 by Lexington Books

All rights reserved. No part of this publication may be reproduced, stored in a retrieval system, or transmitted in any form or by any means, electronic, mechanical, photocopying, recording, or otherwise, without the prior permission of the publisher.

British Library Cataloguing in Publication Information Available

Library of Congress Control Number: 2002114247

ISBN 0-7391-0469-1 (cloth : alk. paper)

Printed in the United States of America

∞™ The paper used in this publication meets the minimum requirements of American National Standard for Information Sciences—Permanence of Paper for Printed Library Materials, ANSI/NISO Z39.48–1992.

For my wife

Elizabeth Marie Schlueter

Amor vincit omnia et nos cedamus amori

Contents

Acknowledgments	ix
Prologue	xi
Chapter One: I Have a Dream	1
Chapter Two: The Foundations of Liberalism in America and in King	31
Chapter Three: Racial Discrimination	59
Chapter Four: Political Economy	89
Chapter Five: Civil Disobedence	125
Conclusion	151
Bibliography	153
Index	167
About the Author	173

Acknowledgments

I would like to express a special thank you to all of those who assisted me in bringing this work to completion, especially the following: Thomas G. West, who as the first reader of my dissertation provided invaluable insight and guidance; John Paynter, whose wonderful courses in American government and political theory provided the inspiration to tackle such an ambitious topic; John Alvis, for his steady encouragement and diffusive love of literature and politics; George Martin and Liberty Fund for giving me the opportunity to explore the nature of liberty with many great minds and for providing me the leisure to complete this project; Shane Tucker and Gabriel Harris for their scrupulous review of the manuscript and many useful comments; and above all, my wife Elizabeth, to whom this book is dedicated, for her thorough and painstaking editing of the manuscript, and for her constant love, support, and encouragement.

Prologue

> And I tell you this morning, my friends, the reason we got to solve this problem here in America: because God somehow called America to do a special job for mankind and the world (Yes, sir. Make it plain). Never before in the history of the world have so many racial groups and so many national backgrounds assembled together in one nation. And somehow, if we can't solve the problem in America the world can't solve the problem, because America is the world in miniature and the world is America writ large. And God set us out with all of the opportunities. (Make it plain) He set us between two great oceans; (Yes, sir) made it possible for us to live with some of the great natural resources of the world. And there he gave us through the minds of our forefathers a great creed: "We hold these truths to be self-evident, that all men (Yes, sir) are created equal."
>
> —Martin Luther King, Jr.[1]

> The whole future of America will depend upon the impact and influence of Dr. King.[2]
>
> —Rabbi Abraham Heschel

On 2 November 1983, in a ceremony at the White House, President Ronald Reagan signed into law the King Federal Holiday Act, establishing the birthday of Martin Luther King, Jr. as a federal holiday.[3] Consequently, King's birthday has become one of only ten national public holidays legally recognized in the United States Code. This distinction is magnified by the fact that it is shared by only one other American, George Washington, whose birthday was not made a federal holiday until 1879, eighty years after his death.[4] Not even Abraham Lincoln, the "Great Emancipator," whose firm leadership purged America of the sin of slavery and brought it through its bloodiest war, and whose magnificent oratory called it back to the principles of the Declaration of Independence, has been given this status.[5]

Since that time, King has attained an almost unparalleled, though not uncontroversial, place in the American political pantheon. Every state celebrates his birthday; large cities across the United States possess major thoroughfares bearing his name; and school children spend substantial amounts of time in class studying and celebrating his contributions to America. This adulation is not limited to those on the left—a number of conservatives have also jockeyed for position in the King craze[6]—a craze which hardly seems to have been tarnished by revelations regarding his marital infidelity, and more recently, his plagiarism.[7]

Still, despite his national recognition and evident popularity, King has not achieved a corresponding status in the hearts and minds of all Americans, many of whom are reluctant to offer him the devotion and reverence due a national hero. A 1993 report by the now defunct Martin Luther King, Jr. Federal Holiday Commission concluded that, despite the fact that the King holiday had gained recognition in most states,[8] "Unfortunately, the King holiday continues to be viewed by many as a holiday for black Americans alone."[9] For many, King still remains in the shadow of Lincoln, beneath whose memorial he delivered his historic "I Have a Dream Speech."[10]

While this fact might be attributed to the lingering effects of white racism, or to concerns about King's moral life, part of the explanation may rest in the fact that many Americans are not persuaded by King's legal status as an exemplar of American principles. After all, King is a man remembered in part for his popular encouragement of civil disobedience, his advocacy of unpopular causes (e.g., his opposition to the Vietnam War), and above all, for his often impassioned invectives against American hypocrisy. None of these are formula for civic popularity.

And where King has achieved mythic popularity, this has perhaps come at the expense of truth. This phenomenon of "collective amnesia" was the subject of Vincent Harding's book *Martin Luther King: The Inconvenient Hero*.[11] Harding subtitled his book after the lines from a poem written by Carl Wendell Himes, Jr. in 1969: "Now that he is safely dead / Let us praise him / build monuments to his glory / sing hosannas to his name. / Dead men make / such convenient heroes: They cannot rise / to challenge the images / we would fashion from their lives / And besides, it is easier to build monuments / than to make a better world."[12] Harding argued that the King federal holiday was part of an effort to tame King, to make him "harmless" by focusing on the unitive and optimistic elements of his "I Have a Dream" speech in 1963, and neglecting the more radical elements of his life, the "post–March-on-Washington" King. Harding called for a "re-calling," a "second coming of Martin Luther King" that would recover the radical and controversial dimensions of King's dream. A more recent book, *I May Not Get There With You: The True Martin Luther King, Jr.* by Michael Eric Dyson continues and extends Harding's argument.[13]

In large part King's rhetorical power and appeal rest in his use of the jeremiad, the prophetic form of the American civil religion. The jeremiad is a genre of literature taking its name from the prophet Jeremiah. It usually refers to a prolonged lamentation or complaint about some unfortunate circumstance, combined with an augury of imminent destruction or calamity. America, however, has developed its own distinctive style of jeremiad, inherited from Puritan covenant theology, which takes the following form of promise, declension, and prophecy: (1) America consists in dedication to certain fundamental principles of justice (promise). (2) We have neglected those principles of justice (declension). (3) If we do not return to those principles, catastrophe awaits us. And perhaps (4) if we do return to those principles, peace and prosperity are in store (prophecy).[14]

King's life was an extended jeremiad. In his speeches and writings he quoted the Declaration of Independence and the Constitution more than any other text except the Bible, a fact that is too often overlooked by King scholars. According to him, the principles expressed in these documents constitute a comprehensive vision of justice toward which America has an obligation to strive. Thus in 1957 he helped found the Southern Christian Leadership Conference (SCLC) with the explicit mission "to save the soul of America."

King's jeremiad was best expressed in his "I Have a Dream" speech, delivered in 1963 beneath the symbolic shadow of the Lincoln Memorial in Washington, D.C. "I Have a Dream" is arguably the most famous American speech of the century. This is due at least in part to King's extraordinary oratory (and one must indeed *listen* to the speech to appreciate its brilliance). But the delivery alone is not what is best remembered. Best remembered is a trope, a simple metaphor attesting to the vast power of the spoken word, and the continuing political relevance of the imagination. This trope is that for which the speech is named, King's Dream, a Dream he claimed was "deeply rooted in the American Dream, that one day this nation will rise up and live out the true meaning of its creed—we hold these truths to be self-evident, that all men are created equal." The Dream, which King often called "Beloved Community," was King's "City in Speech" (to use the term of Socrates in Plato's *Republic*) if not his City of God, in which all the virtues, and especially Justice, would be effectively realized. Thus King's speech and Dream was not the innocuous stuff suggested by Harding: it was a comprehensive idea, concerning itself not only with segregation and racial discrimination, but also with poverty, war, and other social, moral, and political issues. To ignore or minimize this fact, as Harding, Dyson, and others rightly observe, contracts the idea of justice for which King gave his life and thus does him and us a great disservice.

Of course, the "Dream" metaphor had been in use long before King's famous speech. In the late nineteenth century Horatio Alger had celebrated and popularized "the American Dream" in his fiction, and in 1951 African American poet Langston Hughes had written the poem "A Dream Deferred," which powerfully foreshadowed King's conception of the Dream. But King's Dream revived the metaphor in the popular imagination and gave it increased force by attaching it to the American jeremiad.

The Congressional debates on the King Federal Holiday Act attest to the prevalence and force of King's jeremiad. For example, Representative Thomas ("Tip") P. O'Neill, the once powerful Democrat from Massachusetts, stated that King "asked America to be as good as its Declaration of Independence, to be as good as its Bill of Rights. He asked all of us to take the words of our Founding Fathers and make these words come alive for all people."[15] And then New York Republican Representative Jack Kemp stated that the purpose of the holiday was to commemorate "the idea, that dream that all people have all over this country and indeed the world, to live in freedom, justice, dignity."[16] Representative Arlen Specter, a Republican from Pennsylvania, asserted that the civil rights movement "for which Dr. King was largely responsible, was built on distinctly American principles" and that King's words "reflect his commitment to American ideals: equal opportunity, freedom and justice." According to Specter, "The motivation of his movement was to have these ideals realized in their truest and most exalted form." Specter concluded that "Dr. King personified the American sense of justice and appealed to that basic American ideal as part of his movement for civil rights."

These appeals to King's Dream share a common defect: They fail to consider the character of their claim that King's Dream and the American principles of justice are identical. Nor did opponents of the federal holiday attempt to supply this defect, choosing instead to focus on procedural issues. Certain persons in Congress did indeed question King's involvement with Communists, and less often his views on civil disobedience and political economy, but these episodes were sporadic, and rarely attempted to engage the larger question of how King's Dream fit into the American political tradition.[17] No less typical was a question posed on a radio talk program aired during a recent celebration of the King federal holiday: "Are we closer today to realizing King's Dream?" None of the callers dared the irreverence of questioning the various presuppositions: How does King's Dream compare to "The American Dream"? Does it differ?

But if the potential tension over the validity of King's claims remains latent, it is present. Consider for example the report from the Committee on Post Office and Civil Service which accompanied H.R. 3706. According to that report, King "gave to this great country a new understanding of equality and justice for all" and that the holiday would "act as a national commitment to Dr. King's vision of an ideal America."[18] What is meant by a "new understanding of equality and justice for all?" What is the relation of this new understanding to the old understanding, and what is the flaw in the old understanding? And what is meant by "Dr. King's vision of an ideal America"?

What is that vision, and does it follow from American principles?

One finds this same ambiguity in the statements made by Democratic Senator Edward Kennedy. According to Kennedy, King "dedicated his life—and then gave his life—to complete the unfinished business of the American Revolution and the Civil War." Then Kennedy goes further: "In a very real sense, he was the second father of our country, the second founder of a new world that is not only a place, a piece of geography—but a noble idea, a set of ideals."[19] Senator Kennedy suggested his meaning later in the debates when he pointed out that the famous March on Washington, where King delivered his "I Have a Dream" speech, was not simply for the elimination of segregation, but for "recognition that the elimination of segregation was going to be tied to the achievement of jobs and the cause of social justice."[20]

The words of Senator Kennedy are almost self-contradictory, and reflect the same confusion as the Committee Report: On the one hand he suggests that King was finishing the business of the Revolution and the Civil War, and on the other he suggests that King is a "second father to our country, the second founder of a new world that is not only a place . . . but a noble idea, a set of ideas." What idea, or ideas, is Senator Kennedy speaking of?

Nearly all the statements in support of King share a common theme: First, America from its founding has espoused, and consists of, a commitment to a noble ideal. Second, Martin Luther King, Jr., dedicated his life to realizing that ideal. If the former statement about America is true, what is the ideal to which America is committed? Repetition of high sounding concepts and fine utterances like "equality" "liberty," "justice," and "dignity" may be an exigency of American political rhetoric, as they have a timeless capacity to touch every patriotic and justice loving heart in America, but they cannot replace hard thinking about their meaning. Liberty and equality are potentially both the lodestar, and also the Scylla and Charybdis of American politics, depending on their intended meaning, and a certain precision about that meaning is the necessary responsibility of every statesman worthy of the name. Thus, the mere fact that King appealed to the principles of American justice does not in itself establish a meaningful claim. Perhaps King misunderstood those principles, or perhaps he deliberately infused them with a different meaning. The latter is suggested in an essay by Cornel West, who argues that King "creatively" extended the tradition of American jeremiads. West writes that "King was convinced that despite the racism of the Founding Fathers, the ideals of America would be sufficient if they were only taken seriously and lived in practice." Moreover, "[King's] understanding of what the Declaration was about had tremendously progressive and prophetic implications."[21]

West's argument shows greater clarity than that of the committee or Kennedy about the nature of King's claims. Still, West's King appeals to the Declaration as the source of American principles while at the same time denouncing the authors of the Declaration as racist. The only way out of this difficulty is to divorce the meaning of the Declaration from the intention of those who wrote it, and to tease out its "progressive implications," which are presumably beyond the understanding and intention of the framers. But the legitimacy of this exercise in interpretation is questionable on both historical and political grounds, and it is telling that even King is not progressive enough for West. As he writes in *Race Matters*, leaders must learn to question "King's sexism and homophobia and the relatively undemocratic character of his organization."[22] As an initial inquiry, we might ask West where the "ideals" of the Declaration come from, if not from the "racist" founding fathers? Moreover, where precisely is the flaw in the understanding of the Founding? Finally, where has our dedication to the principles of the Declaration been formally rescinded and the new meaning formally ratified?

Thus, ultimately, West reflects the same ambiguity on these questions as the Committee Report and Senator Kennedy's speech above: On the one hand, the "ideals of America" are sufficient if they are "taken seriously." On the other hand, there is considerable suggestion that King's understanding of these ideals is new, or that there is some discrepancy between the American understanding and King's understanding. This suggestion is born out later in West's essay when he states that "King did not support or affirm the bland American dream of comfortable living and material prosperity," but rather "put forward his own dream, grounded and refined in the black church experience, supplemented by liberal Christianity, implemented by Gandhian ideals." Thus, according to West, King did not affirm the American Dream, but went "beyond" it "to those despised people who have been locked out."[23] What does it mean to "go beyond" the American Dream? The very suggestion seems to indicate that in the process the fundamental Dream (the "roots" of the Dream) will be changed. In other words, according to West's King, the American conception of justice is wrong, and has been flawed from the start. King's purpose is to give America a "new" understanding. If this interpretation is true, does it not follow that the King federal holiday implicitly recognizes a revolution?

One might respond that the King holiday is symbolic, that it is not about the individual achievement of King so much as it is about the achievement of the Afro-American race. As Lerone Bennett, Jr. remarked in article entitled "The Real Meaning of the King Holiday," "On King Day, Americans of all races, backgrounds and political persuasions, segregationists as well as integrationists, will be forced to take official notice not only of Martin Luther King, Jr. but also of the maids, the sharecroppers, the students and the Rosa Parkses who made him what he was." According to him, the King holiday tells us "that a people who could produce a King has no need for fears or apologies or doubts." Yet in the same article Bennett declares that the Holiday signifies "the national task of continuing the struggle for the fulfillment of King's

Dream." He continues:

> It is a day set aside for measuring ourselves and America against the terrible yardstick of King's hope. And if we ever loved him, we will use this time to mobilize against he evils he identified in his last article—the evils of racism, militarism, unemployment and violence. It is on this deep level, and in the context of personal responsibilities, that the King holiday assumes its true meaning. For it is not enough to celebrate King; it is necessary also to vindicate him by letting his light shine in our own lives.[24]

As Bennet rightly observes, the King federal holiday cannot simply be written off as a symbolic celebration of Afro-American achievement. It demands a confrontation of Americans with the vision of justice of the man for whom the Holiday is named. Such a confrontation has yet to be realized. This study seeks to undertake such a confrontation, through a critical examination of King's Dream from the perspective of the American political tradition to which he appealed for the legitimacy of his causes. For such a study, it is important to anticipate and address several objections and establish certain parameters.

First, the term "American political tradition" refers to the primary political documents, institutions, symbols, and events which have shaped American political life. The reader may be disturbed by the author's use of the singular "tradition" rather than "traditions": Not only are there multiple and intersecting political (northern, southern, populist, progressive, etc.) and cultural traditions (ethnic, gender, etc.), these multiple traditions often offer competing interpretations of the same events and symbols. Thus it would seem that there are as many views of King as there are traditions. This obstacle, however, is not insuperable. After all, King himself did not scruple to positively identify American principles of justice and to locate them in the central documents, symbols, and events of American history. In so doing King was speaking to an American audience who, despite their great differences, shared a common history, a common culture, common political institutions, and in most cases, common values. It is that shared understanding which will provide the material for this study.

Nevertheless, in making a case for the "common understanding" it would be naïve for the reader to expect—and dishonest for me to claim—"objectivity" in the following study, as that term is commonly understood. The subject necessarily involves competing orthodoxies, about which evaluative judgments must be made even as they touch such sacred pieties as race relations in America. But insofar as objectivity involves making judgments based upon reasonable evidence, I have sought to be as objective is possible. Still, because it is likely that this study will be identified as "conservative"—most probably without any of the attendant distinctions that make such an appellation meaningful—the amazing fact should be pointed out that of the abundant writings on King *there has not been a single book length study of King from a conservative perspective.* As late as 1988 Michael O'Brien, in summarizing scholarship on King, had written the following:

> The King scholars strongly endorse the radicalism of King's last years. There is not a conservative among them. Conservatives have mostly ignored King and the civil rights movement, conceding the field to their political opponents. In January, 1987, the Public Broadcasting System aired the six-part television series, "Eyes on the Prize," an account of the civil rights movement. Earlier, PBS had gathered scholars who specialized in the movement to preview a session. Concerned with fairness, PBS tried to recruit a conservative authority but without success. "None of us could think of someone who was a knowledgeable academic [on civil rights] who we would call a conservative," said Garrow.[25]

It is almost unbelievable (and perhaps a bit telling) that Garrow and others *could not find a single conservative scholar on civil rights.* "The King scholars share leftist political views—either liberal or democratic socialist," O'Brien continued, pointing out that Garrow is himself a "paper member" of the Democratic Socialists of America, and quoting King scholar David Cone as saying, "Yes, I would be learning towards democratic socialism."[26] Since O'Brien wrote these remarks, the field for conservative scholars on King has remained open.

If by conservative is meant one who has strong reservations about King's more radical proposals—while giving full approval to his liberal proposals—then the author of this study qualifies as a the first candidate in the nonexistent pool of conservative King scholars. Still, I do not seek the title, but only a new and critical perspective on King's thought and legacy that resonates with America's founding principles, political/Constitutional institutions, and rhetorical/historical symbols. Where King stands in the American political tradition can be considered and judged from the evidence (so long as we remember with Aristotle that "it is the mark of an educated man to seek as much precision in things of a given genus as their nature allows"). How we evaluate that tradition and that stand is left to the reader to decide.

Second, it is imperative to point out at the beginning of this study that King was foremost a preacher, and that he viewed his Christian vocation as the vital center of his activity. This fact has important consequences that must be treated over the course of the study, the most important being the relationship between Christian revelation and American liberal principles. Because the jeremiad can only be understood within the context of American civil religion, this study requires treatment of American civil religion throughout. Indeed, American civil religion is the underlying thread that ties together this whole work.

Third, the reader might also be troubled by the argument that King had a definite, concrete idea of what his Dream would entail.[27] Carolyn Calloway-Thomas and John Louis Lucaites, for example, in their treatment of King's rhetoric assert that "King was neither so much a philosopher nor a theologian as he was a public advocate, and while his Dream of a beloved community was motivated by a spiritual transcendence of this-worldly, secular differences, it was never static." Calloway-Thomas and Lucaites contend instead that King's Dream "revealed a dynamic vision of what American society could become, and it changed as King recognized and adapted to the social and political exigencies of time and place."[28]

This point merits a longer treatment. In its relatively brief life King historiography has already experienced what amounts to the early stages of a cycle of historical interpretive perspectives. This cycle, like most historical interpretive cycles, has been driven as much by political as by academic motivations. It can be characterized in the following way. The earliest treatments of King focused on his public presentation, which for most Americans meant his presentation to mainstream "white" culture. Following his murder, great attention was given to his published speeches and writings, his formal education, and to the effect of his message on mainstream American institutions and traditions.[29] But from the race-conscious politics of the seventies and eighties—and partly as a response to revelations of his plagiarism—a revisionist historiography has emerged which seeks to recover the "true" King behind the public persona, the authentic King of southern, black culture.[30] In this revision the previous treatments of King's thought have been minimized, and occasionally denigrated. Lewis Baldwin, for example, in his introduction to *There is a Balm in Gilead* argues that previous treatments of King "reflect a narrow, elitist, and racist approach that assumes that the black church and the larger black community are not healthy and vital contexts for the origin of intellectual ideas regarding theology and social change." "The consequence of that approach," he argues, "has been to abstract King's intellectual development from his social and religious roots—family, church, and the larger black community—and to treat it primarily as a product of white Western philosophy and theology."[31] And Keith Miller argues that while King's "magisterial image as a philosopher and his consummate political skill disproved white's patronizing and stereotypical views of black preachers as uneducated souls ranting in the pulpit to wildly emotional followers," his "philosophical image was an utterly necessary fiction" that is "no longer necessary or useful."[32]

Why this "fiction" of King is no longer necessary or useful, Miller does not say, but he does point to a potential problem in the revisionist scholarship. While it would seem that Miller overstates his case, there is no question that his treatment has enriched our understanding of King and corrected the narrow tendencies of earlier King scholarship. But at what expense? Miller's King is no longer a thoughtful, prophetic King consumed with a vision. He is little more than an eloquent, creative imitator. This limitation of Miller's approach might explain the more recent attempts to recover the more radical dimensions of King's political ideals while still presenting them from the framework of the Afro-American sermonic tradition. Finally, Miller simply fails to appreciate the philosophical dimensions of King's personality, that he had a tremendous intellectual curiosity that persisted into the last stages of his life, and that he found great meaning in the western philosophical tradition. Thus, when asked in an interview in 1965 the proverbial question of what one book, excluding the Bible, he would take on a desert island, King replied,

> I think I would have to pick Plato's Republic. I feel that it brings together more of the insights of history than any other book. There is not a creative idea extant that is not discussed, in some way, in this work. Whatever realm of theology or philosophy is one's interest—and I am deeply interested in both—somewhere along the way, in this book you will find the matter explored.[33]

The burden is certainly on Miller and others to prove that King here was simply responding to the expectations of his white audience rather than expressing his true opinion. To those who have studied Plato's *Republic*, however, King's remarks reveal a thoughtful individual who understood a great book.

Not so easy to dismiss is a fourth difficulty: We are not exactly sure what King's works really are. As James M. Washington writes, "I discovered in my research that King's staff often either actually wrote or made heavy contributions to some of the published writings."[34] Washington gets around this difficulty by agreeing with Stephen B. Oates, who, writing on one such piece says "the language, style, and sense of history are King's."[35] In reference to his collection of King writings, Washington concludes:

> The documents in this anthology . . . were primarily written by King, whose arduous schedule limited the amount of time available for the intricate work involved in carefully producing texts. They reflect the view that King and his close associates agreed should be given to the American public. As such, these published documents represent the public stance of King as president of the Southern Christian Leadership Conference.[36]

As much as one might wish to presume that a vicariously written piece captures King's "language, style, and sense of history," the fact remains that the words are not his, and that it is deception to give him the full credit for them. This same criticism does not necessarily apply to those speeches which were written with the help or consultation of others, an acceptable and long-standing practice. We all occasionally need "midwives" for our thoughts. Advice and authorship, however, are not the same thing.

The criticism, if not avoided, is somewhat mitigated by several factors: First, King was an intelligent man and able speaker, capable of producing the kinds of work with which he is credited. Second, one can be fairly confident that his greatest pieces, e.g., "Letter from Birmingham Jail" and the "I Have a Dream" speech, were written by him.[37] Third, there is a good deal of continuity in King's thought from the first of his public writings to the last. Finally—and perhaps this is dispositive for the purposes of this study—since the documents published in his name were done by and with the consent of King, it is right to hold him responsible for their content, *as if* he wrote them himself. It should be emphasized that this study is not concerned with finding the "real" King beneath the various voices of his published and unpublished writings, as important and interesting as such a study might be. It is eminently concerned with the "public" King, the King Americans read about and watched and listened to, the King who challenged and confronted America to realize its ideal. Ultimately this is the only King that matters.

All of the works thus far written on King share a common failure to carefully consider King's Dream from within the context of the American political tradition. Smith and Zepp, for example, note the fact that the Declaration of Independence and the Constitution are "the two documents quoted by King more often than any others except the Bible,"[38] yet remarkably they don't assign them very much importance in King's understanding (this is one of only two references in the entire book), nor do they give these documents the critical attention expended upon the other influences on King's thought. And while John Ansbro acknowledges that King "sought to arouse the conscience of the nation to return to the sublime principles proclaimed in the Declaration of Independence," not only does he fail to discuss what those sublime principles are, he barely mentions the Declaration twice, and fails to mention the Constitution even once. The revisionist scholars, for the reasons already stated, also make this mistake. Even writers like Dyson, who celebrate the more radical elements of King's philosophy, fail to recognize the tension.[39] Indeed, Dyson quotes with approval jazz musician Wynton Marsalis: "When I think of King, I think of a man who was the single person in the 20th century who did the most to advance the meaning and feeling of the Constitution, the Declaration of Independence and the Bill of Rights. He is the single most important person in the fight that America has to be itself."[40]

Finally, it may be useful to point out that this study seeks to integrate two principles that are in some tension. The first principle holds that the proper object of politics is deliberation about justice. In other words, it assumes with Aristotle that speech is what distinguishes human beings from other animals, and that speech "serves to reveal the advantageous and the harmful, and hence also the just and the unjust."[41] The second principle holds that politics is also about persuasion, and that effective persuasion, because of the limitations of human nature, requires more than simple logic; it requires rhetoric, or the wrapping of logic into an imaginative and stylistic clothing which suits the exigencies of circumstance and occasion. In other words both politics and political speech are about the pursuit of justice within the limitations of circumstance and condition. The premise of this study, then, is that King had a concrete understanding of justice, and that he often presented that understanding in a rhetorical fashion. It considers his words with a careful, critical eye, not dismissing them as mere rhetoric, nor necessarily taking them as the definitive statement of his principles, but negotiating them in a way that illuminates the principle and appreciates the presentation.[42]

King's rhetoric was extraordinary; his fusing of religious imagery with social concerns was marvelous, and they are attended to in this book; but his persuasiveness cannot be attributed to these factors alone. King's message resonated with not only with the religious beliefs of his listeners, but also with their civil religion, the body of quasi-religious political principles and symbols directing their understanding of justice. Thus the "I Have a Dream" speech is the fitting point of departure for this study (chapter 1). From here the study will turn to the philosophical/theological foundations of King's liberalism (chapter 2), attempting to understand those principles in light of the principles of the American founding. From these foundations, the study moves to the substantive content of King's Dream by addressing what King argued were the three fundamental obstacles to its realization, racism (chapter 3), poverty (chapter 4), and militarism (with special attention to nonviolent direct action, chapter 5).

Notes

1. Clayborne Carson and James Holloran, eds., *A Knock at Midnight: Inspiration from the Great Sermons of Martin Luther King, Jr.* (New York: Warner Books, 2000), 92.

2. Quoted in Stephen B. Oates, *Let the Trumpet Sound: A Life of Martin Luther King, Jr.* (New York: Harper & Row, 1982), 473.

3. Public Law 98-114 [H.R. 3706]. See U.S. Code, vol. 5, secs. 61-63(a) (1983).

4. The other (national) legal public holidays are: New Year's Day, January 1; Washington's Birthday, the third Monday in February; Memorial Day, the last Monday in May; Independence Day, July 4; Labor Day, the first Monday in September; Columbus Day, the second Monday in October; Veterans Day, the fourth Monday in Oc-

tober; Thanksgiving Day, the fourth Thursday in November; Christmas Day, December 25.

5. I believe the closest effort to recognize Lincoln's birthday as a (national) legal public holiday (and thus a paid federal holiday) was defeated in the Senate in 1920. In the Congressional debates Senator Humphrey offered an amendment which would substitute Abraham Lincoln for Martin Luther King, Jr. His proposal was rejected without debate. See 98th Cong., 1st sess., Congressional Record (19 October 1983) vol. 129, pt. 20, 28343.

6. For positive conservative appraisals of King, see Dinesh D'Souza, *The End of Racism* (New York: Free Press, 1995), especially 163-99; William J. Bennett, "The Conservative Virtues of Dr. Martin Luther King," *The Heritage Lectures* (Washington, D.C.: Heritage Foundation), 481; Harry V. Jaffa, "Martin Luther King, Jr. Remembered," *Public Research Syndicated* (23 March 1983).

7. For a controversial account of King's plagiarism, see Theodore Pappas, *Plagiarism and the Culture War: The Writings of Martin Luther King, Jr., and Other Prominent Americans* (Tampa, Fla.: Hallberg Publishing, 1998). See also Peter Waldman, "To Their Dismay, King Scholars Find a Troubling Pattern," *Wall Street Journal*, 9 November 1990, 1ff; Anthony DePlama, "Plagiarism Seen by Scholars in King's Ph.D. Dissertation," *New York Times*, 10 November 1990, 1ff; Clayborne Carson, "Documenting Martin Luther King's Importance—and His Flaws," *Chronicle of Higher Education*, 16 January 1991, A52; David J. Garrow, "King's Plagiarism: Imitation, Insecurity, and Transformation," *Journal of American History*, 78 (1991): 89. To see the dissertation along with the citations of plagiarism, see Clayborne Carson, ed., *The Papers of Martin Luther King, Jr.*, vol. 2, *Rediscovering Precious Values July 1951– November 1955* (Berkeley: University of California Press, 1994), 339-544. Evidence for King's marital infidelities are recounted in nearly every biography of King written since 1984. See especially the controversial accounts in Ralph Abernathy, *And the Walls Came Tumbling Down: An Autobiography* (New York: Harper & Row, 1989).

8. New Hampshire became the last state to recognize King with a holiday in 1999.

9. King Holiday and Service Act of 1993, report: Y1.1/8:103-418/PT.1.

10. In 1984 the Martin Luther King, Jr. Federal Holiday Commission was established by law to "assist in the first observance of the Federal legal holiday honoring Martin Luther King, Jr." by encouraging "appropriate ceremonies and activities throughout the United States on the first observance of the Federal legal holiday." This commission was intended to express "a national commitment to the work and ideals of Dr. King must be perpetuated." See Congress, House, Committee on Post Office and Civil Service, Martin Luther King, Jr. Federal Holiday Commission, report to accompany H.R. 5890, 98th Congress, 2nd sess., 1984 [Y1.1/8:98-893]. The observation of the minority should be pointed out: "There is no precedent for making a commission of this type permanent, much less the appropriation of federal funds for its operation. No other federal holiday has ever had anything similar." Contrast this response to Washington's birthday: Though Washington's birthday, February 22, did not become a legal holiday until the late nineteenth century, it was widely celebrated even during his lifetime. "After 1832, celebrations of Washington's birthday were firmly established" around the country. See Jane M Hatch, ed., *The American Book of Days*, Third Edition

(New York: H. W. Wilson, 1978), 197-203.

11. Vincent Harding, *Martin Luther King: The Inconvenient Hero* (New York: Orbis Books, 1996).

12. Carl Wendell Himes, Jr., "Now That He Is Safely Dead," in *Drum Major for a Dream* (Thompson, Conn.: InterCulture Associates, 1977), 23, quoted in Harding, *Inconvenient Hero*, 3.

13. Michael Eric Dyson, *I May Not Get There With You: The True Martin Luther King, Jr.* (New York: Free Press, 2000). See also Kenneth L. Smith, "The Radicalization of Martin Luther King, Jr.: The Last Three Years," *Journal of Ecumenical Studies* (26 September 1989): 270-88.

14. For more on the American jeremiad, see Sacvan Bercovitch, *The American Jeremiad* (Madison: University of Wisconsin Press, 1987); Robert Bellah, *The Broken Covenant: American Civil Religion in a Time of Trial* (New York, Seabury Press, 1975). An informative treatment of the use of the jeremiad by professional historians can be found in David Noble, *The End of American History: Democracy, Capitalism, and the Metaphor of Two Worlds in Anglo-American Historical Writing, 1880-1980* (Minneapolis: University of Minnesota Press, 1985). The argument has been made that within the American jeremiad tradition exists a specific Afro-American form according to which the redemption of white America (the oppressor) will come through the speech and action of Afro-Americans (oppressed minority). See for example Dean Howard-Pitney, *The Afro-American Jeremiad: Appeals for Justice in America* (Philadelphia: Temple University Press, 1990); Lewis Baldwin, *There is a Balm in Gilead: The Cultural Roots of Martin Luther King Jr.* (Minneapolis: Fortress Press, 1992), 229-72; and Wilson Jeremiah Moses, *Black Messiahs and Uncle Toms: Social and Literary Manipulations of a Religious Myth.* (University Park: Pennsylvania State University Press, 1982).

15. 98th Cong., 1st sess., Congressional Record (2 August 1983), vol. 129, no. 112, H6263.

16. 98th Cong., 1st sess., Congressional Record (2 August 1983), vol. 129, no. 112, H6256.

17. 98th Cong., 1st sess., Congressional Record (18 October 1983), vol. 129, pt. 2, 28114. A summary of stages and deliberation leading to the King Federal Holiday Act can be found in William H. Wiggins, Jr., *O Freedom! Afro-American Emancipation Celebrations* (Knoxville: University of Tennessee Press, 1987), 134-51.

18. Congress, House, Committee on Post Office and Civil Service, Designation of the Birthday of Martin Luther King, Jr. as a Legal Public Holiday, House Report No. 98-314 accompanying H.R. 3345, Report Together with Minority Views, 98th Cong., 1st sess., (26 July 1983) [Y1.1/8:98-314]. The rest of the report reads: "The committee concurs that a national commitment to the work and ideals of Dr. King must surface in the form of a national holiday whereby every American will be reminded of his great struggles and contributions to mankind. In honoring Dr. King, the committee does not intend to foreclose consideration of legislation to honor other distinguished Americans. The committee's action with respect to this bill is based solely on its examination of Dr. King's monumental contributions to the Nation."

19. 98th Cong., 1st sess., Congressional Record (18 October 1983), vol. 129, pt.

2, 28367. In his remarks Kennedy draws a revealing parallel between King and George Washington: "George Washington was the first in rank among the founders of the Nation. Martin Luther King, Jr., was the first in rank among the founders of a newer and fuller American freedom—of a nation truly dedicated to 'Liberty and Justice for All.' In a very real sense, Martin Luther King is a second father of our country, for he led us to pursue our own fundamental ideals and our own best destiny" Senate, Kennedy, 28110.

20. 98th Cong., 1st sess., Congressional Record (18 October 1983), vol. 129, pt. 2, 28094, (italics mine).

21. Cornel West, "The Religious Foundations of the Thought of Martin Luther King, Jr." in *We Shall Overcome: Martin Luther King, Jr., and the Black Freedom Struggle*, ed. Peter J. Albert and Ronald Hoffman, (New York: Da Capo Press, 1993), 127-28.

22. Cornel West, *Race Matters* (New York: Vintage Books, 1994), 70. Dyson voices the same objection to King's conservative views on sexuality. See Dyson, *I May Not*, 165 and 305.

23. West, *Race Matters*, 70.

24. Lerone Bennett, Jr. "The Real Meaning of the King Holiday," *Ebony* (January 1986): 31.

25. Michael O'Brien, "Old Myths/New Insights: History and Dr. King," *History Teacher* 22 (November 1988): 61.

26. O'Brien, "Old Myths," 61.

27. Most works that have been written on King fail to take a critical perspective on his ideas, settling instead for summation. Perhaps with the completion of Taylor Branch's massive tome *America in the King Years* this trend will reach some semblance of an end. Branch's three-volume work is still in progress. The first two volumes have been completed. Taylor Branch, *Parting the Waters: America in the King Years 1954-1963* (New York: Simon and Schuster, 1988). *Pillar of Fire: America in the King Years, 1963-65* (New York: Simon and Schuster, 1998). This fascination with King's biography began during his life with the publication in 1959 of Lawrence Reddick's *Crusader Without Violence: A Biography of Martin Luther King, Jr.* (New York: Harper, 1959), a thoughtful treatment of King's early years through the Montgomery protest, and written with a respectful deference to King's care as a speaker and thinker. *Crusader* was followed by Lerone Bennett's *What Manner of a Man: A Biography of Martin Luther King, Jr.* (Chicago: Johnson, 1964), which updated Reddick's work. Not long after King's death, David Lewis wrote *King: A Critical Biography* (New York: Praegen, 1970), which doesn't offer much more than the preceding biographies except for its more comprehensive treatment. A more recent biography, still written before the King federal holiday, is *Let the Trumpet Sound: A Life of Martin Luther King, Jr,* by Stephen B. Oates (New York: Harper & Row, 1982). Oates had previously written a number of other biographies, including one on Lincoln, *With Malice Toward None: The Life of Abraham Lincoln* (New York: Harper & Row, 1977), which offers him a unique perspective on King. One of the most well supported (almost one hundred pages of citations from newspapers, books, articles, interviews, and government documents), comprehensive and less hagiographic biographies on King is David Garrow's *Bearing the Cross: Martin Luther King, Jr., and the Southern Christian Leadership Conference*

(New York: Vintage Books, 1988). While tracing a theme on the tragic dimensions of King's life, Garrow does not compromise on his selection of material. I have relied heavily on this book as a historical and biographical resource.

28. Carolyn Calloway-Thomas and John Louis Lucaites, eds., *Martin Luther King Jr. and the Sermonic Power of Public Discourse* (Tuscaloosa: University of Alabama Press, 1993).

29. The most notable works in this regard are Kenneth L. Smith and Ira G. Zepp, Jr., *Search for the Beloved Community: The Thinking of Martin Luther King, Jr.* (Valley Forge, Pa.: Judson Press, 1974), and John Ansbro, *Martin Luther King, Jr.: The Making of a Mind* (Maryknoll, New York: Orbis Books, 1982).

30. Studies which emphasized King's roots in the black church antedate revelations of his plagiarism, but the approach was not developed extensively until after the revelations. For "pre-plagiarism" accounts, see Baldwin, "Understanding," footnote 1. For "post-Revelation" accounts, see Lewis V. Baldwin's two companion books *There is a Balm in Gilead: The Cultural Roots of Martin Luther King, Jr.* (Minneapolis: Fortress Press, 1992) and *To Make the Wounded Whole: The Cultural Legacy of Martin Luther King, Jr.* (Minneapolis: Fortress Press, 1992). See also Keith D. Miller, "Alabama as Egypt: Martin Luther King, Jr., and the Religion of Slaves," in Carolyn Calloway-Thomas and John Louis Lucaites, eds., *Martin Luther King, Jr., and the Sermonic Power of Public Discourse* (Tuscaloosa: University of Alabama Press, 1993). See also Keith D. Miller, *Voice of Deliverance: The Language of Martin Luther King, Jr., and Its Sources* (New York: Free Press, 1992).

Some scholars have attempted to bridge this divide. Cornel West, for example, while giving credit to the historical conditions surrounding King's leadership, and his cultural and religious background, asserts that "King reveled in ideas, he took the life of the mind seriously . . . Never before in our past has a figure outside elected public office linked the life of the mind to social change with such moral persuasiveness and political effectiveness." According to West there are "four principle intellectual and existential sources . . . preeminently religious in character and prophetic in content—that informed King's thought." These are (1) "the prophetic black church tradition," (2) "prophetic liberal Christianity," (3) "the prophetic Gandhian method of nonviolent social change," and finally (4) "prophetic American civil religion, which fuses secular and sacred history and combines Christian themes of deliverance and salvation with political ideals of democracy, freedom, and equality." See Albert and Hoffman, *We Shall Overcome*, 116.

31. Baldwin, *There is a Balm*, 3.

32. Miller, *Voice of Deliverance*, 141.

33. James M Washington, *Testament of Hope: The Essential Writings of Martin Luther King, Jr.* (New York: Harper San Francisco, 1991), 372.

34. Washington, *Testament*, introduction, xxii. In the Senate debate on the King Federal Holiday Act, Mr. Helms produced FBI file 100-5506, which demonstrated that King directly placed suggestions of his friend Stanley Levison, a well-known Communist, into a speech. 98 Cong., 1 sess., Congressional Record (18 October 1983), vol. 129, pt. 2, 28106. See also Garrow, *Cross*, 73.

35. Washington, *Testament*, xxii.

36. Washington, *Testament,* xxii.

37. Although see E. Culpepper Clark, "The American Dilemma in King's 'Letter From Birmingham Jail,'" in Calloway-Thomas and Lucaites, *Sermonic Power,* 33-49, especially notes 3, 4, and 13.

38. Calloway-Thomas and Lucaites, *Sermonic Power,* 88.

39. Dyson's book (*I May Not Get There*) is full of statements such as the following: "Beyond his speech, King proved his tenacious fidelity to American ideals"(247). Harding, to his credit, does imply that King later in his career sought to re-found America, not simply reform it.

40. Jet, 25 January 1999, 9; quoted in Dyson, *I May Not,* 8.

41. Aristotle, *Politics,* 1253a10, 37.

42. Stanley Fish identifies the common understanding of rhetoric as "opposite the Real, the Substantial, or the Essential, and accordingly, rhetoric stands for the inauthentic, the ephemeral, and the superfluous." Stanley Fish, "Mission Impossible: Settling the Just Bounds Between Church and State," *Columbia Law Review* 97:8 (December 1997): 2319. Of course, this study does not accept that understanding, nor does it accept Fish's ultimate effort to reduce all matters of principle to rhetoric.

Chapter One

I Have a Dream

The Historical Legacy of "I Have a Dream"

If it is true that a man can make a speech, it is almost as true that a speech can make a man. Like Odysseus, Martin Luther King, Jr., was a small man with a great voice and a powerful gift of speech. Alongside Lincoln's Gettysburg Address, his "I Have a Dream" speech has justly taken its seat in America's small but distinguished hall of rhetorical monuments. Arguably the most famous American speech of the twentieth century, it has come to be understood as one of the fundamental moments in American history. Evidence the words of President Reagan on the occasion of signing H.R. 3706 into law: "If American history grows from two centuries to twenty, his words that day will never be forgotten."[1] References to "I Have a Dream" in the Congressional debates over the King holiday, both direct and indirect, are more numerous than all the other references to King's speeches or writings combined. Some of these references are quite personal, as when Rep. Jerry Patterson from California remarked that the speech "had a profound effect on me and contributed to my embarking on a public service career to work toward these American ideals."[2]

According to King biographer David Garrow, it was the March on Washington that finally brought the race issue to the "front of the American political agenda."[3] Garrow argued that "the speech had been the rhetorical achievement of a lifetime, the clarion call that conveyed the moral power of the movement's cause to the millions who had watched the live national network coverage." Garrow concluded that "Now, more than ever before, even more than when the footage of Bull Conner's Birmingham had horrified thousands, white America was confronted with the undeniable justice of blacks' demands."[4] In Garrow's account, King's speech was the epitome, the perfecting moment, of the March.

The *New York Times* described the march as a "pilgrimage," which was "merely a spectacle" until King brought alive the audience with "a peroration that was an anguished echo from all the old American reformers." According to the *Times*, each instance in which King cried out "I have a dream" was "a promise of our ancient articles of faith: phrases from the Constitution, lines from the great anthem of the nation, guarantees from the Bill of Rights, all ending with a vision that they all might one day come true." "He was full of the symbolism of Lincoln and Gandhi, and the cadences of the Bible. He was both militant and sad, and he sent the crowd away feeling that the long journey had been worthwhile."[5] The *Times* perceived immediately that "I Have a Dream" would become an historical treasure.

In light of its enormous influence and popularity, it is surprising how little careful attention "I Have a Dream" has received. Close, careful rhetorical treatments of King's "Letter from Birmingham Jail"—King's most anthologized work—are abundant, but there is not a single comparable treatment of "I Have a Dream."

Moreover, since the passage of the King Federal Holiday Act the "I Have a Dream" speech has come under increasing criticism from King scholars *precisely because of its success*. According to Kenneth Smith,

> Dr. King's feet have been frozen to the steps of the Lincoln Memorial *because it has not been recognized that, between that speech and the time of his assassination, King had broadened both his vision of the kind of society required to eliminate racism and achieve justice for everyone and his view of the tactics necessary for the actualization of such a society. King's dream was not fulfilled by the Civil Rights Act of 1964 and the Voting Rights Act of 1965* [italics in original].[6]

Smith's remarks illustrate what has become a chorus of lamentation by King scholars: Americans, by celebrating a sanitized—and thus incomplete and distorted—idea of King and his Dream, continue to anesthetize themselves to injustice. As stated above, King scholars point out that King's thought went through a significant transformation in the last three years of his life, embracing a more radical program for change which included "a fundamental redistribution of wealth and power, full employment legislation, a guaranteed annual wage, massive expenditures to renew central cities and to provide jobs for ghetto residents, a national health insurance, a more equitable tax system, and more effective affirmative action programs."[7] They find King's turn to radicalism exemplified in his much publicized "Riverside Address" in which he declared that "we as a nation must undergo a radical revolution of values" in order to overcome "the giant triplets of racism, materialism, and militarism."[8]

More recently Michael Eric Dyson has attempted to reclaim the "I Have a Dream" speech for the left by pointing out its more radical implications, and by showing the ways in which King stretched the Dream metaphor in his later years to include the more radical elements.[9] This approach to "I Have a Dream" seems more promising and more true to King's own understanding (especially in showing the continuity of his thought),[10] but it also raises some significant difficulties that King scholars—perhaps as a result of their own radical bias—have not entirely faced. In excoriating Americans for neglecting the vision/agenda of the radical post-1965 King they engage in a sleight of hand, assuming a moral equivalence between both phases of King's career that a large number of thoughtful and well-intentioned Americans reject. By attaching his radical agenda to his more liberal agenda against discrimination and segregation, King scholars are setting up the problem in a way that may be true to King's Dream, but may not be true to American principles. In short, there is tremendous support in the American liberal tradition for opposition to segregation and discrimination (much of which will be offered in chapters three and four of this study), whereas there is very little support in that tradition for the principles of democratic socialism (chapter 5). When King scholars interpret this lack of support in America for King's radical agenda as an illustration of the same entrenched racism, classism, sexism, etc. which drove some Americans to oppose desegregation, they are disingenuously simplifying and conflating very different moral and political traditions.

The confusion over King's Dream and American principles, which continues to haunt King scholars as well as popular perceptions of King, is doubtless a result, at least in part, of King's own ambiguity on the matter. As will be discussed in later chapters, King most often appealed to American principles for his causes, but occasionally—and increasingly toward the end of his career—he suggested that it was necessary to go beyond American principles, to transform them into something new and different.

In light of this double claim, and especially in light of King's legal status as a national hero, Americans must again ask a question which heretofore has been avoided, "What does the King federal holiday mean for America?" In other words, in celebrating the King federal holiday are we committing ourselves as a nation to the full dimensions of his Dream, including its radical elements, and thus significantly altering our inherited political tradition, or are we only celebrating the pre-1965 King and his more traditional liberal principles? If the latter, how are we to understand the post-1965 King in the context of his national honor? How do we respond to King scholars who accuse us of neglecting, ignoring or rejecting the more radical elements of the Dream of the very man we have honored? Is it really fitting to honor King in this way, if we disapprove of that final purpose (or at least the means he advocated to achieve that purpose) to which he dedicated his life?

Most Americans will probably not lose sleep over these difficulties. So long as they continue to have that extra vacation day every third week of January they are content. But for those who take politics seriously, who understand that what we honor is in large measure who we are and what we will become, these questions are of the utmost importance. For this reason also, a study of King's thought from within the American political tradition must begin with that speech and action which, for good or ill, is the point of reference for the popular understanding of King in America, King's "I Have a Dream" speech. This is *not* because "I Have a Dream" perfectly or completely expresses King's Dream, which it surely does not (although it contains more radical implications than King scholars usually acknowledge, as will be seen below), but because it must be the necessary point of departure for such an understanding. Study of the speech will serve to help explain King's enormous influence on America, as well as uncover implicit tensions in his thought.

It is important to understand that "I Have a Dream" is both a speech and an action. Although it is obvious to most people that action is a critical component to all endeavors, it is less often observed that effective action usually requires speech. The men who fought and died at Gettysburg engaged in a most salutary and necessary action, but it was Lincoln's address that gave the battle its immortality. In the same way, King's languishing in Birmingham jail was an action, but it was his letter written from that jail that refined and captured the moment in the American imagination. In both cases, the much celebrated words could not have existed without courageous action, but it is highly doubtful the actions would have survived without the words. As Keith Miller writes in *Voice of Deliverance,* the cause for King's magnificent success as civil rights leader "can be stated in a single word: language."[11]

But language, especially political speech, is not unambiguous. As Tocqueville suggested, democratic peoples are suspicious of words. They expect sincerity, not subtlety and nuance.[12] Thus, the term rhetoric has developed a pejorative and disingenuous connotation, as when one is simply "being rhetorical," e.g.,, not direct or sincere. While this democratic prejudice often contains an element of truth and can be politically salutary when it warns citizens against irresponsible speech, it also betrays a certain naiveté about human nature and the subsequent limitations of political life. In brief, it assumes that there is a perfect harmony between knowledge of truth and appetite for the good. One of the many paradoxes of human nature is that we can know the truth and choose to disregard it. This discrepancy between reason and appetite makes rhetoric, or the art of persuasion, necessary. The classical and medieval writers understood this point very clearly, and thus they elevated rhetoric, along with grammar and logic, to the status of a liberal art.[13] It is a telling fact that the study of rhetoric, once a principle component of primary education, has disappeared from modern education altogether, with the exception of preacher training in seminaries.

King's Rhetorical Strategy

As a black leader in America King faced a number of nearly impossible difficulties, the most important of which has been summarized by Wilson Moses:

A great black leader would be expected to assume the mutually antagonistic roles of racial crusader and "Uncle Tom." He would have to be, at once, a symbol of aggressive militancy and social change, but, simultaneously, a subtle, manipulative seeker of good will from white American society. He would have to represent assimilative goals and the idea of full participation in American life but, at the same time, he would have to be combative and capable of inspiring black people to group solidarity and ethnic pride.[14]

This historical/racial challenge, requiring King to play two conflicting roles simultaneously, intersected with another challenging bifurcation: How to urge blacks to militant action while at the same time demanding from them the moderation of nonviolence? With respect to this latter challenge, a notable self-exploration of his strategy can be found in *Stride Toward Freedom*, where King offered a rare and revealing account of his deliberations in composing his first speech to the Montgomery Improvement Association (MIA), the speech that launched his career as a civil rights leader. King first described his dilemma:

With less than fifteen minutes left, I began preparing an outline. In the midst of this, however, I faced a new and sobering dilemma: How could I make a speech that would be militant enough to keep my people aroused to positive action and yet moderate enough to keep this fervor within controllable and Christian bounds? I knew that many of the Negro people were victims of bitterness that could easily rise to flood proportions. What could I say to keep them courageous and prepared for positive action and yet devoid of hate and resentment? Could the militant and the moderate be combined in a single speech?

The last question reveals a remarkable theoretical insight into human nature. King understood the opinions and passions of his audience, and thus discerned both the dangers of the moment, and also the precarious conditions for success.

I decided that I had to face the challenge head on, and attempt to combine apparent irreconcilables. I would seek to arouse the group to action by insisting that their self-respect was at stake and that if they accepted such injustices without protesting, they would betray their own sense of dignity and the eternal edicts of God himself. But I would balance this with a strong affirmation of the Christian doctrine of love.[15]

Here, in his very first public speech as civil rights leader, the young King revealed the principles which guided his rhetorical career, the combination of two apparently irreconcilable principles, moderation and militancy, through appeals to human dignity centered in Christ.[16] Indeed, it was only within the security of this last condition that King succeeded in being so immoderately militant in his demands for justice now. It was a difficult balance, a breathtaking walk of the tightrope that was eventually to falter due to the contending forces of human nature represented by the black nationalisms of the right and left.

In an early and much celebrated essay on King August Meier captured the paradox of King's success: "King can be described as a 'conservative militant.'"[17] According to Meier, it was King's "combination of militancy with conservatism and caution, of righteousness with respectability" that explained "the secret of King's enormous success." John F. Kennedy himself recognized the value of this moderation: "King's greatest virtue," Kennedy said, "was his relative moderation and his commitment to nonviolence. If King loses, worse leaders are going to take his place."[18] Kennedy's words were prophetic.

King's moderation in the first phase of his career was the key to his success, but it also had its cost. It is a now famous irony that after the famous arrest of Rosa Parks in Montgomery, the MIA did not demand desegregation, but only a fairer system of segregation. Only when even those moderate demands were rejected by the city council did the MIA decide they would be satisfied with nothing less than complete desegregation.[19] But King suffered criticism for supporting the Civil Rights Act "compromise" of 1957,[20] and again for proceeding with moderation in his dealings with President Eisenhower.[21] And when he "made a deal" rather than go to jail over criminal charges in Montgomery, he again lost prestige.[22] Again, he compromised in the Albany protests when he and others were prohibited by a federal injunction from participating in any mass demonstrations. Because this was the first time that the federal government had come out against him, this decision disturbed him greatly, but he still chose to obey it. This moderation caused King to suffer bitter criticism from within the black community by more radical groups like the Student Nonviolent Coordinating Committee (SNCC). "King's passive acceptance of the situation," they claimed, "was just one more example of his excessive moderation and was dampening the enthusiasm the black community had generated over the preceding week."[23]

In short, one could see the fissure in the black community widening even as civil rights victories multiplied, but it is reasonable to question whether this fissure was avoidable. Indeed, one of the important questions that must be asked is whether the enormous enthusiasm and massive expectations generated by King's own successful rhetoric largely contributed to the bitterness and despair of black nationalism and ghetto riots when those expectations were not immediately satisfied. Still, wonder abounds when one becomes aware of the magnitude of King's task and the degree of success he achieved, and this wonder finds its partial satisfaction in "I Have a Dream," a speech which met both of the rhetorical challenges in one complete action.

Historical Context of "I Have a Dream"

Every successful rhetorical performance is suited to the occasion and audience. Significantly, "I Have a Dream" was delivered from the Lincoln Memorial on August 28, 1963, on the hundredth-year anniversary of the Emancipation Proclamation. King's speech was the keynote address of the March on Washington for Jobs and Freedom. The crowd consisted of close to two hundred thousand people, about one quarter of which were white,[24] but it was broadcast to the entire nation via television. The original idea for the march came from A. Philip Randolph, the veteran civil rights leader and founder of the Brotherhood of Sleeping Car Porters (BSCP). It was Randolph's threat of a march in 1941 that first pressured President Roosevelt to issue Executive Order 8802, called by Juan Williams "the federal government's strongest civil rights actions since the post-civil war Reconstruction era."[25] Executive Order 8802, issued pursuant to executive war powers, prohibited racial discrimination in federal employment and defense contracts, and established the Committee on Fair Employment Practice (FECP) to help enforce the order.

While the primary purpose of the march was to pressure Congress to pass anti-discrimination legislation, the stated purposes of the March reflected the conviction of many civil rights leaders, including King, that civil justice and economic justice are closely related.[26] This fact suggests that the two Kings hypothesis—one moderate King who advocated traditional civil rights, and a more radical, post-March King who challenged the entire political and economic structure—is not entirely accurate.[27] The most important change in King—and the change was significant—was one of emphasis, not idea.

The first demand of the marchers was passage of a "comprehensive civil rights bill from the present Congress," which would include "provisions guaranteeing access to public accommodations, adequate and integrated education, protection of the right to vote, better housing, and authority for the Attorney General to seek injunctive relief when individuals' Constitutional rights are violated." They also sought the "withholding of Federal funds from all programs in which discrimination exists" and "desegregation of all public schools in 1963." In addition they demanded "a reduction in Congressional seats in states where citizens are disenfranchised" and "a stronger Executive order prohibiting discrimination in all housing programs supported by Federal funds." Finally, they demanded "a massive Federal program to train and place unemployed workers, an increase in the minimum wage to $2 an hour," an "extension of the Fair Labor Standards Act to include exempted fields of employment," and a "Federal Fair Employment Practices Act barring discrimination in all employment."²⁸

It is fair to say that the economic dimensions of the march—though considerably less radical than King's later demands—were not emphasized. Some feared the focus on economic issues would detract from the moderate and just attention that the pending civil rights legislation deserved. One such person was President Kennedy, who initially opposed the march, and then, as politicians are wont to do, supported it when he discovered that efforts to dissuade the leaders were futile.²⁹ In endorsing the March, the Kennedy administration sought to re-direct it in a more moderate direction. According to David Garrow this effort was successful: "[Attorney General] Robert Kennedy's and [Assistant Attorney General for Civil Rights] Burke Marshall's efforts to influence the March toward moderation and away from angry condemnations, toward a legislative focus and away from an economic one, had been an overwhelming success."³⁰ Part of the success of the Kennedy administration in changing the tone and emphasis of the March was due to King's own efforts. Nevertheless, as we shall see King managed to make his "moderate" speech more radical than is sometimes appreciated.

Some Remarks on King's Delivery and Style

As King understood, effective persuasion always works through the strongest opinions and beliefs of those who would be persuaded. Battles of rhetoric are conducted in person's souls, on the fields of passion, self-interest, imagination, and reason, all of which vie for superiority regarding the object of choice.³¹ The classical art of rhetoric strategically sought to fortify reason in such battles through three principle components, character (ethos), passion (pathos), and argument (logos).³² These three elements were incorporated into rhetorical arguments called enthymemes which according to Aristotle constituted the most important components of persuasion by avoiding propaganda (vulgar appeals to appetite and passion) and preserving the rational discourse proper to politics.³³ King's speeches continued this classical rhetorical tradition, popularized in the form of the "venerable three P's" ("proving an appeal to the intellect, painting an appeal to the imagination, and persuading by an appeal to the heart"³⁴) taught in most seminaries. One explanation of King's enormous rhetorical influence must be the way in which he continued and extended the classical rhetorical tradition while wedding it to the sermonic style, about which some brief remarks must be made.

It was stated in the introduction to this study that the necessary point of departure for any treatment of King must begin with the recognition that he was foremost a preacher, and that it was this vocation that informed the rest of his life and work.³⁵ As he stated in an interview in 1967, "I was a clergyman before I was a civil rights leader, and when I was ordained to the Christian ministry, I accepted that as a commission to constantly and forever bring the ethical insights of our Judeo-Christian heritage to bear on the social ills of our day."[36] From the very beginning it was clear that King's movement would be inspired by Christian teaching, as suggested both by the name of his organization, The Southern Christian Leadership Conference (SCLC), and by the sermonic form of his public addresses.

According to Calloway and Lucaites, the word sermon refers to "a form of religious exhortation in which the preacher admonishes a congregation to *understand* and to *act* in accord with a particular interpretation of the sacred values of their shared, religious community."[37] Calloway and Lucaites point out that sermonizing "does not serve an exclusively ecclesiastical function" and that "in one form or another sermonic discourse has assumed a significant and powerful role in the civil and secular lives of Anglo- and African-American society since at least the seventeenth century."[38] According to them, the sermonic rhetor played the role of "'leader' arguing a 'community' or order of collective being into existence" through three "separate but related rhetorical processes: the identification and definition of core communal values, the structuring of a values hierarchy, and the performative display of communal existence."[39]

More must be said later in this study about King's religious purposes within the context of American liberalism, but it is fair to say that King's close friend and associate Ralph Abernathy captured the significance of "I Have a Dream" best when he wrote: "Dr. King never tried to get away from his calling as a minister of the gospel, and at this moment I really think he felt that his congregation was the whole nation. He was speaking to the corrupt and unjust power structure, and to the oppressed people all over the country who needed to be given hope and courage."[40] Abernathy correctly identified the context for identifying King's ultimate significance to America as preacher and prophet of American civil religion, not of ecclesiastical faith, but that religion which "binds" together the American political community.[41]

It should go without saying that one cannot adequately appreciate the written form of "I Have a Dream" alone. King's delivery gives it a force far beyond what the literal text conveys.[42] The timbre of King's rich baritone enchants with a steady and almost lyrical rhythm, and his inflections give the speech a serious, somber, almost funereal tone. He avoids using meter, however, which while serving a mnemonic function can often have the effect of distracting the listener from the content of the speech.[43] His tone of voice is almost tremulous (perhaps a rhetorical device from the Baptist sermonic tradition), leaving the listener with the distinct sense that King is barely containing a tremendous force of passion and emotion which like an active volcano threatens to erupt at any moment. That he does not give in to that passion leaves one with the impression that he is a man of great discipline and self-control. This self-control in delivery exemplifies and imitates to his audience that delicate combination of militancy and moderation that form the substance of the speech. Finally, the oral pattern in the delivery composes a narrative of its own, as the pitch in King's tone makes a slow but steady ascent to its climax in the final lines of the peroration. One notices this ascent halfway through the speech, and waits anxiously as they are lifted to greater and greater heights of restrained yet powerful emotion.[44] The auditory effect of the speech is so great that one might well wonder whether the speech would have had the effect it did without King's unique delivery.[45] But the delivery was intended to serve as an adjunct and servant to the message. If one seeks to understand the extraordinary influence and popularity of King, the place to begin is a careful study of that message. Although it will not be an exhaustive study, hopefully what follows will be a complete study which seeks to capture the speech's essential elements, showing the means by which King "orders" America for action while at the same time examining the soundness of his claims.

The Argument of "I Have a Dream"[46]

Biographer Lawrence Reddick wrote that King was "methodical in his sermons and lectures." According to Reddick, "He likes to read up on his topic for a couple of days; outline it, then write out what he wants to say. He will then lay his manuscript aside, going back over it a few hours before it is to be delivered." This process allowed King to deliver lengthy sermons without the help of script or notes.[47] As might be expected, the structure of "I Have a Dream" reveals relatively careful planning. The speech can be divided into six parts. First there is the greeting (1), followed by an exordium (2-5). Next there is a militant plea for immediate action from the government (6-8) followed by a plea for moderation on the part of activists (9-11). In the fifth part (12-14) King responds to the question, "When will you be satisfied," and concludes with the first climax of the speech. Thus the body of the speech is roughly divided into three themes which each receive three paragraphs. Substantively, one notices that beginning with the exordium, each section roughly alternates between moderation and militancy. The remainder of the speech consists of a lengthy peroration (15-27) which constitutes nearly half of the speech.[48]

Greeting (1-2)

The effect of King's introductory sentence, which reminds his listeners of the significance of the March ("the greatest demonstration for freedom in the history of our nation"), is to elevate their pride and sense of purpose in participating in this great historic event. King indicates that *he* has joined *them*, and not that they have joined him. There may be something in this humility of Lincoln's ironic "the world will little note, nor long remember what we say here, but it can never forget what they did here." Certainly Lincoln's "shadow" at this March looms large.

Exordium (2-5)

The exordium breaks down into two parts, both of which make a similar syllogistic argument while shifting the major premise. The syllogism takes the form of (a) American consists of a promise of freedom, (b) the Negro in America still is not free, therefore, (c) America has defaulted on its promise. The major premise of the first argument is that the Emancipation Proclamation constituted a promise of freedom for Afro-Americans. The major premise of the second argument is that the American Founding as expressed in the Declaration of Independence and Constitution constituted such a promise. In both cases, King argues, the promise has not been fulfilled.

King's exordium already manifests what might be an implicit tension. Why does he appeal to *both* Lincoln and the American founding? Is the substantive argument identical in both cases, or does one contain something missing in the other? Indeed, many commentators on both the left and the right would immediately object to King's use of Lincoln, though for very different reasons. Therefore, a more careful look at his argument is in order.

King's opening diction ("Fivescore years ago") is intended to remind his listeners of the occasion for the March, the hundredth anniversary of Lincoln's Emancipation Proclamation. Yet it is significant that his words allude to the Gettysburg address rather than the Emancipation Proclamation, which Richard Hofstaedter somewhat unfairly criticized for having "the moral grandeur of a bill of lading."[49] This criticism betrays a fundamental misunderstanding of Lincoln's purpose, which was to preserve the Union. Lincoln believed that because the Union was founded primarily upon the principles of the Declaration of Independence ("fourscore and seven years ago our fathers brought forth on this continent a new nation") which hold that "all men are created equal," preservation of the Union was the necessary precondition for freedom (or eventual freedom in the case of blacks) for both blacks and whites.[50] Despite heavy criticism from both the right and left, Lincoln's historical argument that the founders of America viewed slavery as contrary to the principles of the Declaration, and only tolerated it as a "necessary evil" has been largely vindicated as the true conservative position, as contrasted with the innovations of Douglas and Calhoun.[51]

Lincoln was not seeking a "second founding," as Bradford claimed, nor was he attempting to establish "a new Jerusalem" in America. The legitimacy of the means Lincoln used to free the slaves (i.e., Emancipation Proclamation as a necessity of war, and coercive ratification of amendments to the Constitution), however, continues to be a subject of some controversy, especially for those who understand and appreciate the delicate balance the framers sought to establish and maintain between protection of rights and consent, and between national power and state power. While the controversy will undoubtedly continue, historian Herman Belz has made a strong case for a Lincoln who acted within legitimate and just constitutional and legal boundaries, and pursuant to a proper understanding of American principles.[52] But if changes under the Lincoln presidency were not quite a "second American revolution," as historian James B. McPherson and others have claimed, they still mark an extremely significant shift in American politics from state power to national power.[53] The extent and nature of that shift as it bears upon civil rights will be treated in a subsequent chapter.

King never developed his thoughts on Lincoln in writing, but he clearly held him in high regard, identifying him with other prophets and political leaders as "maladjusted" for having "the vision to see that this nation could not exist half slave and half free."[54] In explaining his decision to support Kennedy in the 1960 election he wrote that "No President except perhaps Lincoln had ever sufficiently given that degree of support to our struggle for freedom to justify our confidence."[55] He was aware of Lincoln's internal conflict over slavery, characterizing him as "tortured by doubts"[56] and "vexed" over the problem of slavery. But out of his tormented soul came the courageous decision to issue the Emancipation Proclamation, King declared.[57] Utilizing a favorite technique of metonymy and antithesis, King wrote that, "A civil war raged within Lincoln's own soul, a tension between the Dr. Jekyll of freedom and the Mr. Hyde of slavery, a struggle like that of Plato's charioteer with two headstrong horses each pulling in different directions. Morally Lincoln was for black emancipation, but emotionally, like most of his white contemporaries, he was for a long time unable to act in accordance with his conscience."[58]

Thus King did not seem to share the perspective of Hostadter and others which viewed Lincoln's anti-slavery convictions and actions as the insincere result of expediency or ambition.[59] However, King's simplistic psychological explanation of Lincoln's decision misses the provenance of Lincoln's agony, a misunderstanding that has larger than speculative repercussions. Tortured Lincoln undoubtedly was, but not for lack of nerve or conviction about the evil of slavery. On this point he was unshakable. But Lincoln's great genius, the key to his success, was the recognition that the necessary condition for the eventual abolition of slavery was the preservation of the same Union which tolerated and even protected it.[60] Perhaps one sees in King's explanation the source of later difficulties he faced in his feverish attempt at the end of his life to satisfy the final demands of his Dream.

As if to preempt any argument that Lincoln's presidency marked a revolutionary break with the past, King in the spirit of Lincoln turns to the Founding, to the Declaration of Independence and the Constitution. A more careful (and Lincolnian) argument would not have identified the Constitution as a promise, because the original Constitution tolerated slavery. Lincoln expressed the relationship between the Declaration and Constitution by way of allusion to a Scriptural figure (Prov. 25:11). According to him, "a word fitly spoken is like apples of gold in pictures of silver. The expression of that principle in our Declaration of Independence . . . was the word '*fitly spoken*' which has proved an 'apple of gold' to us. The *Union* and the *Constitution* are the *picture of silver*, subsequently framed around it. The picture was made, not to *conceal* or *destroy* the apple; but to *adorn* and *preserve* it. The *picture* was made *for* the apple—not the apple for the picture."[61] Still, King grasps the fundamental point, that the principles of the Declaration impose a duty on America to secure "the inalienable rights to life, liberty and the pursuit of happiness" for all of its citizens, regardless of race or color.

Whether King understood those rights in the same way that the founders or Lincoln did remains to be seen. Already in the exordium, however, there are hints of his understanding. In his first anaphoric display King reminds his audience that "one hundred years later" (he repeats the phrase three times) Negroes in America are not only subject to discrimination and segregation, they also live on "a lonely island of poverty in the midst of a vast ocean of material prosperity." It is also notable that King uses the image of a "promissory note" and a "check" to express the American promise, suggesting that the promise has some relation to economic status. Finally, his suggestion that the check will provide "the riches of freedom and the security of justice" indicates that he expects something more substantive than mere equality before the law.

Further evidence for King's expansive understanding of the demands of freedom can be found in his remarks on the Emancipation Proclamation. King called the Emancipation Proclamation "a great beacon of light and hope," one which thus far had done little to disperse the darkness of bondage.[62] "The pen of the Great Emancipator," he once wrote, "had moved the Negro into the sunlight of physical freedom, but actual conditions had left him behind in the shadow of political, psychological, social, economic and intellectual bondage. In the South, discrimination faced the Negro in its obvious and glaring forms. In the North, it confronted him in hidden and subtle disguise."[63] King is clearly using a metaphorical argument here which is of questionable validity, though it may accurately express the great expectations of the freedmen after emancipation.[64] The Emancipation Proclamation, a wartime emergency measure, certainly was not intended to provide "political, psychological, social, economic, and intellectual" freedom to the freedmen. Whether it represented a movement in that direction remains to be examined.[65]

In conclusion, the enthymeme of King's exordium is a powerful rhetorical display, meeting the formal requirements of validity and thereby serving to establish King's *ethos* as a reliable speaker. One finds in it most of the basic elements of the American jeremiad mentioned in the introduction to this study, with the exception of the transcendent grounding that gives the American jeremiad its politico-religious significance. King will supply this grounding abundantly in the peroration. But to say that the enthymeme meets the formal requirements of validity says nothing about its substantive content. In other words, if the Declaration of Independence establishes principles of justice toward which America has an obligation to strive, and if Lincoln's primary purpose was to re-affirm and realize those principles, then the most important question becomes, what precisely are those principles, and is King's purpose, like Lincoln's, to affirm those principles?

Militant Call for Action (6-8)

King's exordium is essentially moderate. This is necessary because he must win the attention and trust of his audience before he can make his more militant plea. Having established his *ethos*, King is now ready for confrontation. His words in this section are directed not toward his immediate audience, but toward his televised audience, and ultimately toward his political audience. He reminds his listeners of the "fierce urgency of now" and warns against the "tranquilizing drug of gradualism." In his second display of anaphora King repeats "now is the time" four times, concluding that "it would be fatal for the nation to overlook the urgency of the moment," and that "this sweltering summer of the Negro's discontent will not pass until there is an invigorating autumn of freedom and equality." One cannot help but notice the King's aggressive diction in this section. His use of terms like "fierce," "fatal," "urgency," "rude awakening," "whirlwinds of revolt," and "shake the foundations," all serve as a warning, and perhaps even a threat, that unless action is taken immediately "to make justice a reality for all God's children" America will be troubled by unrest.

In the immediate background of King's warning/threat are the Birmingham protests, which galvanized American support for civil rights through televised pictures of policemen attacking peaceful protesters with snarling police dogs, fire hoses, and cattle prods. But King may also have been alluding to the dangers of violence on other fronts. By this time Malcolm X had become increasingly vocal in his criticisms of King and nonviolence, and his popularity was growing in urban circles, perhaps presaging the cycle of violent urban ghetto riots that began in 1965. That this was in the back of King's mind is evidenced by the next phase of his argument.

Plea for Moderation (9-11)

Having warned America not to ignore the demands of justice, King now turns from his televised and political audience to his immediate audience, warning them against violence and racial bitterness. Echoing Gandhi, King reminded his listeners that "we must rise to the majestic heights of meeting physical force with soul force." "Soul force," an approximate translation of Gandhi's concept of "Satyagraha," literally meaning "truth" force, or "love" force, represented for King the ultimate reality of nonviolent protest, which for him was not merely a means to an end but a state of being and a way of life.[66] For King "soul force" represented the ultimate superiority of principle over expediency, love over hate, and good over evil. King also resists calls for black nationalism (represented again by Malcolm X and others) by reminding his audience that racial justice is the interest of all races, and not simply Afro-Americans. A similar argument was made by Lincoln with respect to slavery when he pointed out that any arguments one used to defend the enslavement of others (e.g., color of skin, intelligence, strength, etc.) could similarly be used against oneself.[67] Both King and Lincoln understood that justice demands consistency of first principles.

"When Will We Be Satisfied?" (12-14)

From his exhortation to moderation King turns again to a more militant posture, addressing a legitimate question that was often used for expedient purposes, "When will you be satisfied?" This question gets to the heart of the political problem in general, and it is significant that King concludes it with a climactic recitation of a Scriptural verse with eschatological meaning.

King's demands appear reasonable: no more police brutality, and no more racial discrimination in public accommodations, housing, and voting. But the climax of this section makes a surprising turn to a more comprehensive demand: "No, we are not satisfied, and we will not be satisfied until justice rolls down like waters and righteousness like a mighty stream." Here King merged his voice with the prophet Amos.[68] In his first book King referred to this same passage when he exhorted Christian ministers to become prophetic witnesses to justice.

> Any discussion of the role of the Christian minister today must ultimately emphasize the need for prophecy. Not every minister can be a prophet, but some must be prepared for the ideals of this high calling and be willing to suffer courageously for righteousness. May the problem of race in America soon make hearts burn so that prophets will raise up, saying, "Thus saith the Lord," and cry out as Amos did, " . . . let justice roll down like waters, and righteousness like an ever-flowing stream."[69]

In a college course on the religious teaching of the Old Testament King identified this passage as "the key passage of the entire book" because it revealed the true message of Christianity. "It reveals the deep ethical nature of God. God is a God that demands justice rather than sacrifice; righteousness rather than ritual. The most elaborate worship is but an insult to God when offered by those who have no mind to conform to his ethical demands. Certainly this is one of the most noble idea [sic.] ever uttered by the human mind." King called this ethical imperative of "justice between man and man . . . one of the divine foundations of society." "Such an ethical ideal is at the root of all true religion," he wrote. "This high ethical notion conceived by Amos must always a challenge to the Christian church [sic.]"[70]

Of all Old Testament prophets Amos is perhaps most explicit in his teaching that true piety is impossible without social and economic justice.[71] Writing in the eighth century B.C. at a time when Israel was experiencing great material prosperity, and also falling subject to moral and religious corruption, he was sent to warn Israel of her imminent destruction at the hands of a pagan nation, Assyria.[72] Amos showed concern for the poor and disadvantaged, sharply criticizing the injustice of his fellow Israelites: "You trample on the poor and force him to give you grain. Therefore, though you have built stone mansions you will not live in them; though you have planted lush vineyards you will not drink their wine. For I know how many are your offenses and how great your sins. You oppress the righteous and take bribes, you deprive the poor of justice in the courts. Therefore the prudent man keeps quiet in such times, for the times are evil." According to Amos, God disapproved of the hypocritical ceremonies and rituals of the Israelites which were not supported by obedience to God. They had forgotten that the ceremonies were meant to *serve and supplement* righteous obedience, and not to *replace* it. This theme is repeated by the other prophets.[73]

Thus "I Have a Dream" again alludes indirectly to the economic dimensions of King's vision of justice while at the same time bringing out its religious dimensions. The intention of his "prophetic" allusion seems to be twofold: First, public celebrations and festivals, like the Hebrew ceremonial rituals, are intended to be a communal commemoration of an event or person which represents the dedication of that community to its principles of justice. On the centennial celebration of the Emancipation Proclamation in 1963, King was using this powerful scriptural parallel to remind Americans not to forget the substance of their political religion, their devotion to justice. He was telling America: Do not make this an empty celebration. Do not forget the demands of the principles on which you were established. Do not betray the Declaration of Independence and the Emancipation Proclamation. Secondly, King was warning Americans not to be seduced by prosperity and wealth into neglecting the demands of justice.

But the passage also presents significant difficulties when applied in a literal way to the practice of politics, difficulties that are relevant to this study as a whole. A careful study of Plato's *Republic*, King's favorite book, reveals that the desire/demand for justice cannot be satisfied by political life without the assistance of chance and considerable violence to human nature. Instead, the desire for justice must be turned upward and inward, first to the "pattern in heaven" and next to "the city within" oneself.[74] In religious terms, this means that the ultimate satisfaction of justice comes in the contemplation of God in the afterlife. In other words, the desire for the satisfaction of justice is ultimately a religious/philosophical passion for ultimate significance. When that desire is directed exclusively toward politics then it becomes extremely dangerous, ultimately destroying the very thing it seeks.[75] Lincoln the contemplative politician seemed to understand this difficulty quite well, but did the preacher King?[76]

Peroration (15-27)

The peroration to "I Have a Dream" takes up nearly half of the speech. Its complex fusion of religious, geographic, and lyrical imagery makes it the most memorable, most remarkable, and most quoted portion of the speech, without which the speech as a whole would now be long forgotten. Nowhere else can sermonic discourse in politics be more clearly illustrated, and the message of the sermon can be summarized in three words: hope through faith.

King begins the peroration by acknowledging the suffering many activists had been subjected to. He urges them to "continue to work with the faith that unearned suffering is redemptive." There is not enough that can be said about the importance of such faith for King. It forms the very bedrock of successful nonviolent direct action, for if unearned suffering has no meaning, then it is something to be avoided and overcome. The alternative to redemptive suffering is retaliation, and ultimately violence. It is proper to refer to the belief in the redemptive quality of unearned suffering as faith, for it would seem to require a transcendent ground insofar as it defies the normal categories of human experience. King's theodicy has solid Christian roots, but its demands on human nature are very high and therefore it is uncertain whether it is a working formula for politics. When in the next paragraph he urges his audience to return to the states of the south and urban ghettos "knowing that somehow this situation can, and will be changed," his words ring somewhat hollow. How does one *know* this? Something is missing, and King fills it in with the "I Have a Dream" sequence.

Surprisingly, the namesake portion of the "I Have a Dream" speech was extemporaneous. David Garrow cites King's own words from an interview to describe King's spontaneous departure from his written text:

"I started out reading the speech," he recalled in a private interview three months later, and then, "just all of a sudden—the audience response was wonderful that day—and all of a sudden this thing came to me that I have used—I'd used it many times before, that thing about 'I have a dream'—and I just felt that I wanted to use it here. I don't know why, I hadn't thought about it before the speech." So he dispensed with the prepared text and went on extemporaneously.[77]

King's account makes sense stylistically, for one notices that the faith of paragraph sixteen is dropped during the Dream sequence and then taken up again in paragraph twenty-three. Presumably, then, when King says "this is our hope" and "this is the faith that I go back to the south with," he is referring primarily to his Dream, and not to the faith in the redemptive value of unearned suffering (although as will be seen later, the latter is essential for King's success).

Whether spontaneous or planned, nearly every allusion, reference, and metaphor (including the "Dream" image) had been used by King in previous speeches.[78] Of particular importance to this study is the Dream metaphor, which he had used in a commencement address delivered at Lincoln University in 1961. There he claimed that "America is essentially a dream, a dream as yet unfulfilled. It is a dream of a land where men of all races, of all nationalities, and of all creeds can live together as brothers."[79] As usual, he identified the American Dream with the principles of the Declaration of Independence:

> The substance of the dream is expressed in these sublime words, words lifted to cosmic proportions: "We hold these truths to be self-evident, that all men are created equal, that they are endowed by their Creator with certain unalienable rights, that among these are life, liberty, and the pursuit of happiness." This is the dream.[80]

The "profoundly eloquent and unequivocal language" of the Declaration contained the normative dimensions of the Dream, King claimed. Thus, "America is challenged to bring her noble dream into reality, and those who are working to implement the American dream are the true saviors of democracy." Referring to "the strange paradoxes" of slavery and segregation, he pointed out that "ever since the Founding Fathers of our nation dreamed this noble dream, America has been something of a schizophrenic personality, tragically divided against herself."[81]

But his Dream was not limited to racial concerns. In an earlier speech, delivered to the National Urban League in 1960, King first gave the dimensions of the American Dream. In another rhetorical foreshadowing, he claimed that America is a "dream of a land where men do not argue that the color of a man's skin determines the content of his character." But he moved beyond segregation and discrimination. According to him, America consists of a "dream of equality of opportunity, of privilege and property widely distributed." It is "a dream of a land where men will not take necessities from the many to give luxuries to the few," and "a place where all our gifts and resources are held not for ourselves alone but as instruments of service for the rest of humanity." Finally, it is "the dream of a country where every man will respect the dignity and worth of all human personality, and men will dare to live together as brothers."[82]

Most Americans would have been familiar with King's deployment of a classical American metaphor, the American Dream. In its traditional meaning the America Dream refers to the promise that any person in America with sufficient intelligence and hard work can achieve a successful life, or at least reach the limits of their individual ability. Critical to this promise is a democratic implication that success and power will not depend upon "arbitrary" traits like birth, religion, class, or race.

In King's rhetoric the image of the American Dream goes through two subtle but significant changes. First, the American Dream is given a normative political meaning. In the original understanding, as suggested above, the American Dream was primarily descriptive rather than normative, though the description had normative implications that the political system would eliminate arbitrary restraints on individual achievement and thus provide the conditions for substantive justice. King's Dream is a substantive idea of justice toward which America has an obligation to strive. Perhaps more significantly, in "I Have a Dream" King for the first time *personalizes* the Dream (*I* have a Dream). It is no longer the American Dream, but *King's Dream*, even if it is "deeply rooted in the American dream." For the first time King appears to be suggesting that he will depart from American principles, even as he is engaging in a most extraordinary celebration of them. It is especially notable, then, that King's Dream becomes the basis for the "hope" and "faith" that he returns to immediately after the sequence. Is there a radical shifting here, then, of the American faith?

From the elements King outlines in this speech, the nature of the Dream does not appear to have shifted significantly. In fact, King's most famous statement from the Dream sequence—"I have a dream that my four little children will one day live in a nation where they will not be judged by the color of their skin but by the content of their character"—can be taken as a near perfect expression of the normative principles of the American Dream. Conservatives have seized this passage and sought to capitalize on it in their efforts to resist the forces of affirmative action. Unfortunately, King himself supported affirmative action, making the conservative use of the passage questionable.

Like the conclusion of the previous section, the "I Have a Dream" sequence uses an anaphoric technique which climaxes in another eschatological allusion. This time King merges his voice with a passage from Isaiah chapter 40 which would be familiar to both Christians and Jews: "I have a dream that one day every valley shall be exalted, every hill and mountain shall be made low, the rough places shall be made plain, and the crooked places shall be made straight and the glory of the Lord shall be revealed and all flesh shall see it together."[83] The context of this passage is the restoration of Jerusalem from captivity. In Isaiah the words King recites are those of "a voice of one calling in the desert, 'Prepare the way for the Lord; make straight in the wilderness a highway for our God.'" In the Christian tradition this passage is regarded as a foreshadowing of John the Baptist preparing the way for Christ. Thus King assumes the prophetic role of Isaiah and John the Baptist, both of whom announce a new dispensation of God in the world.

This Isaiah passage was a favorite of King's, and he used it in several notable instances during the latter half of his career. In the conclusion of his last book he exhorted his readers to "go out into a sometimes hostile world declaring eternal opposition to poverty, racism and militarism." "With this powerful commitment," he wrote, "we shall boldly challenge the status quo and unjust mores and thereby speed up the day when 'every valley shall be exalted, and every mountain and hill shall be made low: and the crooked shall be made straight and the rough places plain.'"[84] He repeated this phrase line for line in his controversial "Riverside" speech.[85] For King, the Isaiah passage represented the consummation of justice and the concrete realization of his Dream.

Of course, in assimilating Old Testament imagery to American principles King was drawing on an old rhetorical tradition dating back to the Mayflower Compact and John Winthrop's "City on a Hill" speech, the "I Have a Dream" of the seventeenth century. In the Mayflower Compact the colonists aboard the Mayflower consented to form "a community" for action in the New World. What is notable about the compact is that its authors refer to their own action as a "covenant," not a compact. This fact has great significance, for a "covenant" is a term loaded with both legal and religious significance. While Roman and Anglo law provided a more limited legal meaning to the term covenant as a written agreement between two parties, its older and more dense meaning referred to both an *originating act* and *continuing relationship* between God and a politico-religious community, a relationship which, like a marriage, entailed indissolubility and monogamy (that is, devotion to God's high purposes). This latter understanding of covenant was especially present in the Puritans coming to America, for whom the archetypal covenant was that between God and Moses on Mount Sinai. Evidence of this significance finds its perfect expression in John Winthrop's sermon *A Modell of Christian Charity*, delivered aboard the Arabella in 1630.[86] As Winthrop himself was not a minister, his sermon can be regarded as the first (and exemplary) use of political sermonic discourse, delivered to, quite literally, the ship of state. This rich rhetorical legacy, rooted in the historical origins of American colonization, has been a source of America's greatest possibilities as well as her greatest difficulties.[87]

Having professed his faith and hope in his Dream, King continues his "ordering" of the community for action under that faith by representing the nation as a "symphony of brotherhood" which will not only work for freedom, but will sing in unity and with new meaning the patriotic hymn "My Country 'tis of Thee."[88] The song is continued into paragraph twenty-six, where it explodes into a celebratory litany of America's physical landscape. In this fourth and final use of anaphora King urges his audience to imagine a redemptive event which resonates in unison from the high places of America.[89] Is King subtly suggesting that the political high places also must sing the song of redemption before the event can be realized? In any case, the speech concludes with a very notable and unexpected change of song. It appears the patriotic hymn "My Country 'tis of Thee" is not the chorus after all, but merely a prelude to the real chorus, which consists of "the words of the old Negro spiritual, 'Free at last, free at last; thank God Almighty, we are free at last.'" In concluding this way, King is suggesting that Afro-Americans will have a special role to play in the final realization of his Dream, that it is they who will provide the unifying music that will bind the nation together. It is fitting, then, that these words mark the inscription on King's tomb.[90]

King's concluding remarks can be understood within the context of what has been called by Dean Howard-Pitney and others "the Afro-American jeremiad."[91] Numerous writers have interpreted the Afro-American jeremiad in racial terms, suggesting that the black race posesses certain values which are necessary for world liberation.[92] Lewis Baldwin, for example, writes that both King and Du Bois believed that "black America's role in humanizing the world would be fulfilled only if it maintained and cultivated those artistic, spiritual, and aesthetic qualities so endemic to its culture."[93] Thus Baldwin expresses disapproval of those blacks who abandon "the emotive, intuitive, and aesthetic values that link them to their slave forebears and to Africa" for "values undergirded by an abstract intellectualism, an excessive materialism, and a need to control the world through scientific, technological, and military advances."[94]

While Baldwin's thesis has some plausibility, it distorts the complete truth and ultimately does a disservice to the trans-racial dimensions of King's Dream. Du Bois, for instance, maintained that "Negro blood has a message for the world,"[95] but he also saw that truth and beauty transcend racial categories. "I sit with Shakespeare and he winces not . . . I summon Aristotle and Aurelius and what soul I will, and they come all graciously with no scorn or condescension. So, wed with Truth, I dwell above the veil."[96] King is credited with popularizing the slogan "black is beautiful,"[97] and from the beginning of his public ministry he speculated with Arnold Toynbee that "it may be the Negro who will give the new spiritual dynamic to Western civilization that it so desperately needs to survive,"[98] a speculation that increased in emphasis in the latter half of his career. But as suggested earlier, King never abandoned his ultimate goal of integration. As evidenced by his high regard for Plato's *Republic,* King also never abandoned his appreciation for the positive elements of Western civilization, elements which transcend race.

Far from a condescension to white prejudice, King remained deeply interested in the permanent questions of human existence until his death. For him, as for Du Bois, aesthetic, intellectual, and spiritual values transcend racial categories. Moreover, as demonstrated in the chapter on political economy, King admired the efforts of other minority groups in America to achieve equality, and he encouraged Afro-Americans to practice the "bourgeois" virtues which made that equality possible.

Conclusion

King's "I Have a Dream" speech is a magnificent rhetorical performance, and on those grounds alone it justly deserves renown. But precisely because of its power to move it is necessary to examine it further. King begins the speech with an enthymeme grounded in the Declaration of Independence and Lincoln which reminds Americans of their national commitment to the principles of justice. But apart from ending discrimination and segregation, it is not clear what those principles require, though there is some suggestion that elimination of poverty may be part of them. Alternating between militancy and moderation, King navigates carefully through his various audiences, only hinting at more radical demands and reserving his strongest verbal ammunition for his peroration. There King draws upon prophetic scripture, patriotic lyric, geographic attachment, and historic memory to organize Americans for action on behalf of justice. But in doing so, he makes a subtle but significant shift in which he incorporates the American Dream image into his personalized vision. The nature of King's personalized vision and its relation to the historic American vision is unclear. This fact, along with the eschatological nature of his prophetic scriptural allusions, raises additional questions about how to understand King's place in the American political tradition. Therefore, after looking at the primary elements of the "I Have a Dream" speech, it is now necessary to begin unraveling and examining the various parts of King's Dream.

Notes

1. See President Reagan's statement in *Weekly Compilation of Presidential Documents,* vol. 19, No. 44 (1983): No. 2. King had spoken before the Lincoln Memorial in Washington, D.C. once before, on 17 May 1957, at a March on Washington which had been organized by the same leaders as this March. The great success of the later March shows the progress of the nation in six years. For an account of the earlier march, see Lawrence Reddick's *Crusader Without Violence: A Biography of Martin Luther King, Jr.* (New York: Harper, 1959), 183-97.

2. 98th Cong., 1st sess., Congressional Record (2 August 1983), vol. 129, no. 112, H6239.

3. Garrow, *Bearing,* 287.

4. Garrow, *Bearing,* 284.

5. James Reston, "I Have a Dream . . . Peroration by Dr. King Sums Up a Day the Capital Will Remember," *New York Times,* 29 August 1963, 1.

6. Smith, "The Radicalization," 271.

7. Smith, "The Radicalization," 276.

8. In Washington, *Testament,* 240.

9. See Dyson, *I May Not,* 11-29.

10. In a 1957 speech King had already excoriated the triple evils of racism, poverty, and militarism: "I never intend to adjust myself to the evils of segregation and the crippling effects of discrimination. I never intend to adjust myself to the tragic inequalities of an economic system which takes necessities from the masses to give luxuries to the classes. I never intend to become adjusted to the madness of militarism and the self-defeating method of physical violence." Clayborne Carson, ed., *The Papers of Martin Luther King, Jr.* vol. 4 (Berkeley: University of California Press, 1994), 276.

11. Miller, *Voice,* 10.

12. This conclusion follows from Tocqueville's observation in numerous places that democratic peoples are suspicious of form and ritual as obstacles to their freedom and as potential sources of oppression.

13. Grammar, rhetoric, and logic comprised the trivium of the liberal arts.

14. Moses, *Black Messiahs,* 156.

15. King, *Stride,* 59-60.

16. Needless to say, an examination of King's first speech to the MIA shows his rhetorical principles being put into practice. See Clayborne Carson and Kris Shepard, eds., *A Call to Conscience: The Landmark Speeches of Dr. Martin Luther King, Jr.* (New York: Warner Books, 2001), 7-12.

17. "King's very tendencies toward compromise and caution, his willingness to negotiate and bargain with White House emissaries, and his hesitancy to risk the precipitation of mass violence upon demonstrators further endear him to whites. He appears to them a 'responsible' and 'moderate' man . . . His caution and compromise keep open the channels of communication between the activists and the majority of the white community. In brief: King makes the nonviolent direct action movement respectable." August Meier, "On the Role of Martin Luther King," in August Meier and Eliot Rudick, eds., *Along the Color Line: Explorations in the Black Experience* (Urbana, Ill.:

University of Illinois Press, 1976), 179.

18. Garrow, *Bearing*, 262.

19. King, *Stride*, 63.

20. Reddick, *Crusader*, 202-6.

21. Reddick, *Crusader*, 215-29.

22. Reddick, *Crusader*, 209-12.

23. Garrow, *Bearing*, 207. But King learned his lesson in Albany, and chose to disobey a similar order in Birmingham. It was this disobedience that led to his famous imprisonment and Letter from Birmingham Jail. See King, *Why*, 68-75.

24. Garrow, *Bearing*, 282.

25. Juan Williams, *Eyes on the Prize: America's Civil Rights Years 1954-1965* (New York: Penguin Books, 1988; Viking Penguin 1987), 197. For more on the March, see Williams' account in general, 197-205. Prior to this time there were other small actions by Congress and the Executive branch against discrimination, but nothing of major significance. See Hugh Graham, *The Civil Rights Era: Origins and Development of National Policy, 1960-1972* (New York: Oxford University Press, 1990), 10.

26. Garrow, *Bearing*, 281. This is a very important point for refuting arguments that King changed his thinking later in his career, or that "I Have a Dream" expresses an "Uncle Tom" King, as some have argued.

27. See, for example, James H. Cone, *Martin and Malcolm and America: A Dream or a Nightmare?* (New York: Orbis, 1991).

28. *New York Times*, 29 August 1963, 16.

29. "'The fact that he took that attitude rather than the attitude of almost everyone else in the Senate and Congress . . . made a difference to the character of the march,' remembers Burke Marshall, the assistant attorney general for the Justice Department's civil rights division, 'because if he had opposed it, it would have been more of a rebellious type of march.'" Quoted in Williams, *Eyes on the Prize*, 198.

30. Garrow, *Bearing*, 285.

31. This fact is one reason why politics and rhetoric are not identical: rational persuasion is only effective on men who are good, and persuasion alone cannot make men good, which is one function of education and coercive law. See Larry Arnhart, *Aristotle on Political Reasoning: A Commentary on the 'Rhetoric'* (De Kalb: Northern Illinois University Press, 1981), 6.

32. Aristotle *Rhetoric* 1356A.

33. See Arnhart, *Aristotle*, 35-39, 52-53. Arnhart demonstrates that it is not proper to identify enthymemes with logos, as most commentators on Aristotle do. Rather, the enthymeme involves all the components of rhetoric, with emphasis upon argument. Enthymemes, according to Aristotle, are the rhetorical counterpart to dialectic, which is for the sake of science or philosophy. Both enthymemes and dialectic consist of syllogisms, and both work from opinions about what is true and good, rather than from scientific first principles. Dialectic, however, is for the sake of knowledge or truth, while enthymemes are for the sake of persuasion and thus treat particular cases.

34. Quote is a paraphrase of Richard Lischer, *The Preacher King: Martin Luther King, Jr. and the Word That Moved America* (New York: Oxford University Press, 1995), 38-39.

35. This point has been emphasized in numerous works on King, including Baldwin, *There is a Balm in Gilead,* Miller, *Voice of Deliverance,* and Lischer, *The Preacher King.*

36. "Face to Face Television Interview," quoted in Washington, *Testament,* 408.

37. Calloway and Lucaites, *Martin Luther King, Jr.*, 3.

38. Calloway and Lucaites, *Martin Luther King, Jr.*, 3.

39. Calloway and Lucaites, *Martin Luther King, Jr.*, 3.

40. Abernathy, "Martin Luther King's Dream" in Lynda R. Obst, ed., *The Sixties* (New York: Random House/Rolling Stone Press, 1977), 94.

41. I am resisting the urge to integrate into this essay Bellah's useful understanding of the "dialectic between liberation and liberty, revolution and constitution, conversion and covenant." Bellah, *Broken Covenant,* 83.

42. See Reddick's comments on King's speaking ability in general: "King's voice is possibly his most magnetic power. It is a rich, natural baritone with a wide range . . . Mrs. Almena Lomax of the Los Angeles Tribune is more lyrical when she writes: 'His voice has great power, passion, great depths of tenderness and an overlay of gentleness to charm your heart out of your body.'" Reddick, *Crusader,* 8. Later Reddick writes: "[King's] great delight is in speaking and preaching. Essentially Martin Luther King is an orator. He himself admits that the eloquent statement of ideas is his greatest talent, strongest tradition, and most constant interest. It is his first love. King has been rated among the top public speakers of the nation." Reddick, *Crusader,* 11. See also Aristotle *Rhetoric* 1414A: "The epideictic style is most like writing: for its objective is to be read."

43. See Aristotle *Rhetoric* 1408B.

44. Thus King fulfills one of the four primary purposes of the epilogue: moving the hearer into emotional reactions. See Aristotle *Rhetoric* 1419B.

45. According to Aristotle delivery, while important to consider, is secondary to argument. "The subject of expression, however, has some small necessary place in all teaching: for to speak in one way rather than another does make some difference in regard to clarity, though not a great difference; but all these things are forms of outward show and intended to affect the audience. As a result nobody teaches geometry this way." See his comments in the *Rhetoric* 1403B-1404B.

46. To my knowledge, there does not exist a perfectly accurate written transcript of "I Have a Dream." See Haig Bosmajian, "The Inaccuracies in the Reprintings of Martin Luther King's 'I Have A Dream' Speech," *Communication Education* 31, (April 1982). I have chosen to use the transcript printed in Washington, *Testament,* 217-20, supplemented by an audio recording of the speech contained on Gordon Skene, Great American Speeches cassette, *Great American Speeches,* volume 3, *The Dreams, The Inspirations, The Accomplishments* (Santa Monica: Rhino Records, 1991). I have numbered the paragraphs of the text from one to twenty-seven, counting the "let freedom ring" sequence as one complete paragraph, and I have placed the paragraph numbers in parenthesis.

47. Reddick, *Crusader,* 11.

48. For a strong foreshadowing of many of the rhetorical terms of "I Have a Dream," including the Dream metaphor, see King, "Address at the Freedom Rally in

Cobo Hall," in Carson, *A Call,* 61-73.

49. Richard Hofstadter, *The American Political Tradition & the Men Who Made It* (New York: Vintage Books, 1974; Alfred A. Knopf, 1948), 169.

50. As he wrote in a letter to Horace Greeley in 1862: "My paramount objective in this struggle is to save the Union, and is not either to save or to destroy slavery. If I could save the Union without freeing any slave I would do it, and if I could save it by freeing all the slaves I would do it; and if I could save it by freeing some and leaving others alone I would also do that. What I do about slavery, and the colored race, I do because I believe it helps to save the Union; and what I forbear, I forbear because I do not believe it would help to save the Union." Letter to Horace Greely, 22 August, 1862, in Don E. Fehrenbacher, ed., *Abraham Lincoln: Speeches and Writings,* vol. 2 (New York: The Library of America, 1989), 357. Lincoln concludes this letter with the following words: "I have here stated my purpose according to my view of official duty; and I intend no modification of my oft-expressed personal wish that all men every where could be free." See also Lincoln's dialogue with the representatives of the Chicago Emancipation Memorial, 13 September, 1862, Fehrenbacher, *Abraham Lincoln,* 361-67. Here Lincoln acknowledges that "slavery is the root of the rebellion," but he questions whether an emancipation proclamation will be the most effective means to end it. Finally, he maintains that constitutional government is a noble enough cause for fighting the war. The memorial representatives respond: "The value of constitutional government is indeed a grand idea for which to contend; but the people know that nothing else has put constitutional government in danger but slavery; that the toleration of that aristocratic and despotic element among our free institutions was the inconsistency that had nearly wrought our ruin and caused free government to appear a failure before the world, and therefore the people demand emancipation to preserve and perpetuate constitutional government. Our idea would thus be found to go deeper than this, and to be armed with corresponding power. ('Yes,' interrupted Mr. Lincoln, 'that is the true ground of our difficulties.') That a proclamation of general emancipation, 'giving Liberty and Union' as the national watch-word, would rouse the people and rally them to his support beyond any thing yet witnessed—appealing alike to conscience, sentiment, and hope."

51. For arguments from the right, see George Cary and Willmoore Kendall, *The Basic Symbols of the American Political Tradition* (Baton Rouge: Louisiana State University Press, 1970), and M. E. Bradford, *A Better Guide than Reason: Studies in the American Revolution* (LeSalle, Ill.: Sugden & Co., 1979). For arguments from the left, see Hofstadter, *American.* For a vindication of Lincoln's position, see especially Herbert J. Storing, *Toward A More Perfect Union,* ed. Joseph M. Bessette (Washington, D.C.: AEI Press, 1995); Harry V. Jaffa, *Crisis of the House Divided: An Interpretation of the Issues of the Lincoln-Douglas Debates* (Chicago: University of Chicago Press, 1959, 1982) (and other writings generally), and Thomas G. West, *Vindicating the Founders: Race, Sex Class and Justice in the Origins of America* (Lanham, Md.: Rowman & Littlefield, 1997). For a different spin on the argument, see also Richard M. Weaver, *The Ethics of Rhetoric* (Davis, Calif.: Hermagoras Press, 1985).

52. See Herman Belz, *Emancipation and Equal Rights: Politics and Constitutionalism in the Civil War Era* (New York: W. W. Norton and Co., 1978), and especially

Abraham Lincoln, Constitutionalism, and Equal Rights in the Civil War Era (New York: Fordham University Press, 1998).

53. See James M. McPherson, *Abraham Lincoln and the Second American Revolution* (New York: Oxford University Press, 1991).

54. See, for example, "The Power of Nonviolence," in Washington, *Testament*, 14.

55. See Martin Luther King, Jr., *Why We Can't Wait* (New York: Harper & Row, 1964; New York: Mentor, 1964), 147.

56. "Bold Design for a New South," in Washington, *Testament*, 116.

57. See Martin Luther King, Jr., *Where Do We Go From Here: Chaos or Community* (Boston: Beacon Press, 1968), 77-78.

58. King, *Where*, 78.

59. For a good overview of various historiographical approaches in scholarship on Lincoln, see Belz, *Abraham Lincoln*. See also Frederick Douglass' opinion of Lincoln, "Oration at the Memorial of Abraham Lincoln," in *The Life and Writings of Frederick Douglass*, ed. Philip Foner, vol. 4 (New York: International Press, 1995), 309-20.

60. See footnote 50 above.

61. *Abraham Lincoln: His Speeches and Writings*, ed. Roy Basler, one volume edition (New York: World Publishing, 1946), 513.

62. See introduction to Robert Goldwin, ed, *100 Years of Emancipation* (Chicago: Rand McNally, 1964): "Can anyone claim to understand the staggering events of 1963, in Oxford and Birmingham and Washington and everywhere throughout our nation, who is ignorant of the events of 1863 and before? And is there hope that we as a nation can free ourselves from our present dark plight if we fail to grasp its true source in the long career of American slavery?"

63. King, *Why*, 23. See the words of President Johnson in a speech delivered in 1965: "But a century has passed—more than 100 years—since the Negro was freed. And he is not fully free tonight. It was more than 100 years ago that Abraham Lincoln signed the Emancipation Proclamation. But emancipation is a proclamation and not a fact. A century has passed—more than 100 years—since equality was promised, and yet the Negro is not equal. A century has passed since the day of promise, and the promise is unkept." "The Right to Vote: Equal Standards for All," *Vital Speeches of the Day*, 31:12, 1 April 1965, 355.

64. See Howard-Pitney, *Afro-American*, 44-46.

65. Elsewhere King describes the Emancipation Proclamation as a "start" which had been made on a "noble journey toward the goals reflected in the Preamble to the Constitution, the Constitution itself, the Bill of Rights and the Thirteenth, Fourteenth and Fifteenth Amendments." King, *Why*, 25.

66. See Ansbro, *Martin Luther King*, 3-7.

67. See Fehrenbacher, *Lincoln*, vol. 1, 303, "Fragment on Slavery."

68. The full passage from Amos reads as follows: "I hate, I despise your religious feasts; I cannot stand your assemblies. Even though you bring me burnt offerings and grain offerings, I will not accept them. Though you bring choice fellowship offerings, I will have no regard for them. Away with the noise of your songs! I will not listen to the music of your harps. But let justice roll on like a river, righteousness like an ever-

falling stream!" Amos 5: 21-24.

69. Martin Luther King, Jr., *Stride Toward Freedom* (New York: Harper & Row, 1958; San Francisco: HarperSanFransisco, 1986), 210. King also referred to this passage in his very first speech to the MIA, the speech which launched his civil rights activism. See Carson and Shepard, *A Call*, 10.

70. These statements were written on note cards, which may explain the grammatical errors. Carson, *The King Papers*, vol. 2, 165.

71. Amos was also one of the favorite prophets of Walter Rauschenbusch.

72. This background information is taken from the introduction to Amos in the NIV study bible.

73. For example, in Hosea 6:6 God says, "For I desire mercy, not sacrifice, and acknowledgment of God rather than burnt offerings." And Micah 6:6-8 writes: "With what should I come before the Lord and bow down before the exalted God? Shall I come before him with burnt offerings, with calves a year old? Will the Lord be pleased with thousands of rams, with ten thousand rivers of oil? Shall I offer my firstborn for my transgression, the fruit of my body for the sin of my soul? He has showed you, O man, what is good. And what does the Lord require of you? To act justly and to love mercy and to walk humbly with your God" [italics mine]. See also Isaiah 1:11-15.

74. See Allan Bloom, trans., *The Republic of Plato* (New York: Basic Books, 1968), 592B.

75. This, I believe, is the fundamental argument of Eric Voegelin, *The New Science of Politics* (Chicago: University of Chicago Press, 1952).

76. See Lincoln's "Address to the Washington Temperance Society of Springfield, Illinois" in Fehrenbacher, *Lincoln*, vol. 1, 81-90. See especially Jaffa's remarkable essay on this speech in Jaffa, *Crisis*.

77. Garrow, *Bearing*, 283. See also Branch, *Parting*, 875-76, 881-83, 886-87.

78. Richard Lischer suggests that King received the inspiration for the dream image from a young woman in Albany. Lischer, *The Preacher*, 93-94.

79. "The American Dream," The Negro History Bulletin 31 (May 1968): 10-15, in Washington, *Testament*, 208-16.

80. Washington, *Testament*, 208.

81. Washington, *Testament*, 209. King made a similar argument in the peroration to an earlier speech delivered to the National Urban League in 1960: "We must work assiduously and with determined boldness to remove from the body politic this cancerous disease of discrimination which is preventing our democratic and Christian health from being realized." He concluded that "Then and only then will we be able to bring into full realization the dream of our American democracy—a dream yet unfulfilled" Washington, *Testament*, 105.

82. Washington, *Testament*, 151. Compare to a later speech by King, "The American Dream," Washington, *Testament*, 208-16, delivered at the commencement of Lincoln University in 1961. In the later speech he hardly mentions the comprehensive understanding of justice contained in the earlier speech.

83. Washington, *Testament*, 219.

84. King, *Where*, 190.

85. Washington, *Testament*, 242.

86. See Bellah's comments on Winthrop's significance in *The Broken Covenant*, especially 13-16. He cites Perry Miller on this speech: "Winthrop stands at the beginning of our consciousness." Perry Miller, *Nature's Nation* (Cambridge: Belknap Press of Harvard University Press, 1967), 148-49, quoted in Bellah, *Broken Covenant*, 13.

87. See the next chapter for a more extended discussion of this problem.

88. The image of the nation as a chorus reminds one of the education in music proposed in book 3 of Plato's *Republic*.

89. It appears that King may have borrowed these words from Chicago preacher Archibald Carey. See Carson, *King Papers*, vol. 4, 13.

90. One already finds hints of King's black messianism in his first speech. See Carson and Shepard, *A Call*, 12: "Right here in Montgomery, when the history books are written in the future (Yes), somebody will have to say, 'There lived a race of people (Well), a black people (Yes sir), fleecy locks and black complexion (Yes), a people who had the moral courage to stand up for their rights. [Applause] And thereby they injected a new meaning into the veins of history and of civilization.'"

91. See Howard-Pitney, *Afro-American*.

92. For works that attempt to sort out distinct elements of Afro-American culture, see John Lovell, Jr.,: *Black Song: The Forge and the Flame. The Story of How the Afro-American Spiritual was Hammered Out* (New York: Macmillan, 1972), and Lawrence W. Levine, *Black Culture and Black Consciousness: American Folk Thought from Slavery to Freedom* (New York: Oxford University Press, 1977).

93. Baldwin, *There is a Balm*, 261.

94. Baldwin, *There is a Balm*, 271.

95. W. E. B. Du Bois, *The Souls of Black Folk* (New York: A Penguin Book, 1989), 5.

96. Du Bois, *Souls*, 90.

97. See Moses, *Black Messiahs*, 178.

98. King, *Stride*, 224.

Chapter Two

The Foundations of Liberalism in America and in King

Introduction

In a critique of communism King wrote: "The trouble with Communism is that it has neither a theology nor a Christology; therefore it emerges with a mixed-up anthropology. Confused about God, it is also confused about man."[1] King accepted what today has become questionable: Ideas, especially about the highest things, have consequences. For King ideas were not epiphenomenal manifestations of entrenched racial, sexual, or economic interests, they were originating principles of action. A critical examination of the substance of King's Dream, then, must begin with some general treatment of the theological /philosophical principles upon which it was based. While King's theological /philosophical principles have been comprehensively explained and developed in other places, as yet there has been no attempt to situate those principles within the political context of American theological/philosophical principles.[2] This is especially surprising when one considers that fact that again and again in his speeches and writings King attempted such a synthesis. This chapter will attempt to supply the defect in King scholarship by summarizing King's theological and philosophical understanding and then, following King himself, situating that understanding in the context of the American political tradition.

King's Principles

King declared that the "substance" of the American Dream was expressed in the "sublime words"[3] of the Declaration of Independence: "We hold these truths to be self-evident, that all men are created equal, that they are endowed by their Creator with certain unalienable rights, that among these are life, liberty and the pursuit of happiness." What did these words mean to King?

First, for King the ground of human dignity is God, and not the state. According to him, the words of the Declaration expressed this dignity of the human person, a dignity confirmed by his study of personalism. In his first book

King declared personalism to be his "basic philosophical position."[4] An examination of King's personalism as the foundation of his understanding of liberalism serves to position King within the context of competing conceptions of liberalism in America today. This is not an easy project. First of all, personalism, or the philosophical study of the person, is a broad, amorphous, and somewhat complicated field of inquiry with diverse and even contradictory branches. One finds, for example, theistic and nontheistic personalists, realist and idealist personalists, Catholic and Protestant personalists, individualist and communitarian personalists, and so on. While King derived much of his personalist thinking from a group of Protestant personalists who established what became known as the Boston School of Personalism, he never systematically developed his own understanding. This prevents one from exploring the full philosophical depths of that understanding, and has forced scholars to construct that understanding from King's statements on personalism and from his teachers with whom he expressed agreement.[5]

According to his autobiographical account, personalism strengthened two basic ideas for King: First it gave him a "metaphysical and philosophical grounding for the idea of a personal God," and second, it gave him "a metaphysical basis for the dignity and worth of all human personality."[6] Thus he was convinced that the sacredness of the human personality had a Divine source, and he cited both "the Biblical term *the image of God*" and also the Declaration of Independence as evidence. "Every human being has etched in his personality the indelible stamp of the Creator," he said. "This idea of the dignity and worth of human personality is expressed eloquently and unequivocably [sic] in the Declaration of Independence . . . Never has a sociopolitical document proclaimed more profoundly and eloquently the sacredness of human personality."[7]

Second, following these first principles, King declared that the power of the state was limited by certain rights. He repeatedly affirmed that "each individual has certain basic rights that are neither conferred by nor derived from the state." "To discover where they came from," King claimed, "it is necessary to move back behind the dim mist of eternity, for they are God-given."[8] Because "man is an end" and because "he is a child of God," King concluded that "Man is not made for the state; the state is made for man." King was not a secular humanist, and he strongly resisted efforts to "deify man" or to declare "that humanity is God."[9]

What was King's understanding of natural rights? At the very least rights provided a moral boundary against the monstrosity of slavery, as well as against its ugly stepchildren, state enforced segregation and discrimination. But for King the natural rights to life, liberty, and the pursuit of happiness articulated in the Declaration of Independence also require that individuals should have "three meals a day for their bodies, education and culture for their minds, and dignity, equality and freedom for their spirits."[10] While King's understanding of rights will be treated more comprehensively in subsequent chapters, it is fair to suggest now that King's efforts to assimilate the liberal and progressive rights traditions threatens the overall philosophical coherence of his Dream.

Third, despite the fact that he affirmed the sacredness of the human personality, he was critical of those, like Rousseau, who asserted that "human nature is essentially good," and that "evil is to be found only in institutions."[11] King observed that "a persistent civil war rages within all of our lives" and that "there is some good in the worst of us and some evil in the best of us." According to him, each man is "something of a schizophrenic personality, tragically divided against" himself. While he was optimistic about the possibilities of human beings, he did not abide in the liberal hope that human nature would eventually evolve into a state of goodness. According to him, sin is a permanent condition of human nature. Thus, the "tendency on the part of some liberal theologians to see sin as a mere 'lay of nature' which will be progressively eliminated as man climbs the evolutionary ladder seems . . . quite perilous."[12] King believed that "the word sin must come back into our vocabulary."[13] Progress, King argued, would only be the result of regular and concerted moral vigilance on the part of individuals.

Fourth, the dignity of the person for King did not mean the right to choose or create one's own ends, as it did for Kant and his American successors.[14] Few leaders of the twentieth century defended the natural law more eloquently than King. For King the same Creator who is the source of equality and human rights has woven laws into the universe. In one of his first and most famous sermons, King said,

> Our world hinges on moral foundations. God has made it so! God has made the universe to be based on a moral law. So long as man disobeys it he is revolting against God . . . This is a law-abiding universe. This is a moral universe. It hinges on moral foundations.[15]

Thus King was not an advocate of the liberalism which underlies what Michael Sandel has called "the procedural republic," as articulated by liberal scholars like Ronald Dworkin, Richard Rorty, John Rawls, Bruce Ackerman, and others, for whom American liberalism consists precisely in the *agreement* to disagree. According to this conception, liberalism requires that both citizens and government refrain from imposing their conception of the good on others.[16] The "central idea" of liberalism, communitarian Michael Sandel writes, "is that government should be neutral toward the moral and religious views its citizens espouse." "Instead," Sandel continues, "it should provide a framework of rights that respects persons as free and independent selves, capable of choosing their own values and ends." Sandel calls this framework "the procedural republic."[17] The understanding of liberty at the foundation of the procedural republic was affirmed recently by three justices of the Supreme Court in the famous "mystery passage." Writing for the majority in *Planned Parenthood of Southeastern Pennsylvania v. Casey*, they said: "At the heart of liberty is the right to define one's own concept of existence, of meaning, of the universe, and of the mystery of human life."[18]

This understanding of liberalism has resulted in enormous changes to America's social and political landscape, effecting everything from religion to pornography to property rights. The effect of these changes, generally speaking, has been a kind of moral libertarianism on the one hand, and a social collectivism on the other. Most scholars have suggested that these changes are the natural and logical conclusion of the principles upon which America was founded. Michael Sandel, for example, argues that liberalism in America was previously tempered by a now diminished republican tradition. And Robert Bork writes in *Slouching Towards Gommorah* that "liberalism does not vary." According to him, "What distinguishes apparently different stages of liberalism—classical liberalism from modern liberalism, for example—is not any difference in liberalisms but a difference in the admixture of other elements that modify or oppose it." Thus Bork is suspicious of the source of American liberalism, the Declaration of Independence, whose "ringing phrases are hardly useful, and indeed may be pernicious, if taken, as they commonly are, as a guide to action, governmental or private. Then the words press eventually towards extremes of liberty and the pursuit of happiness that court personal license and social disorder."[19]

Whether or not Bork is correct in this argument—and it shall be argued below that he is not—he rightly implies that any understanding of America must come to terms with the principles of liberalism contained in the Declaration of Independence. The declaration was "the fundamental act of the Union" of the states in their separation from Britain, and is legally recognized as the first organic document of America. Its language was imitated, almost verbatim, in most state constitutions written after the declaration, a fact which attests to broad acceptance of its principles. In designing a government curriculum for the University of Virginia, James Madison, generally regarded as the "father of the Constitution," agreed with Thomas Jefferson that the first "best guide" for "the true doctrines of liberty" was the Declaration of Independence, which he considered to be "rich in fundamental principles."[20] Such principles guided Lincoln through his political career. But perhaps most important for the present argument, if Bork is correct that the Declaration of Independence was not intended to be a guide for political action, then King's whole project is questionable, for King repeatedly claimed that the declaration was a critical source for understanding justice in America.

Against contemporary liberal thought, King constantly criticized "ethical relativism" and the "doctrine of self-expression," and he objected strongly to the "quasi-liberalism" which "is based on the principle of looking sympathetically at all sides." This liberalism is "so bent on seeing sides that it fails to become committed to either side. It is a liberalism that is so objectively analytical that it is not subjectively committed. It is a liberalism which is neither hot nor cold, but lukewarm."[21]

To complete the theological form, King declared that the same God who wove a law into the cosmos is also concerned with its proper execution. As he said in a sermon on the problem of evil, God "is at work in his universe, and as we struggle to defeat the forces of evil, the God of the universe struggles with us." Evil is defeated not only by man's "endless struggle" against it, but also "because of God's power to defeat it."[22] This executive power of God is not merely naturalistic; for King, God is the supreme and perfect person, and thus "Life as applied to God means that in God there is feeling and will, responsive to the deepest yearnings of the human heart; this God both evokes and answers prayer."[23] In short, God is Providence.[24]

King's theology and anthropology shaped his understanding of statesmanship. While acknowledging the role of law "in molding public sentiment,"[25] he maintained that the force of law was not a sufficient condition for perfect justice: "The law needs help," he said. "The courts can order desegregation of the public schools. But what can be done to mitigate fears, to disperse hatred, violence, and irrationality gathered around school integration, to take the initiative out of the hands of racial demagogues, to release respect for the law? In the end, for laws to be obeyed, men must believe they are right."[26] Thus King acknowledged that the "ultimate solution to the race problem lies in the willingness of men to obey the unenforceable."[27] But when or how will this happen? According to King, "We must depend on religion and education to alter the errors of the heart and mind."[28]

The foregoing statement reveals the strong role religion was to play in King's Dream. It also emphasizes the necessary point of departure for any adequate study of King: he was a preacher, not a politician. As he stated in an interview in 1967, "I was a clergyman before I was a civil rights leader, and when I was ordained to the Christian ministry, I accepted that as a commission to constantly and forever bring the ethical insights of our Judeo-Christian heritage to bear on the social ills of our day."[29] From the very beginning it was clear that King's movement would be inspired by Christian teaching, as suggested both by the name of his organization, *The Southern Christian Leadership Conference*, and by the sermonic form of his public addresses. According to Kenneth Smith and Ira Zepp, Jr., "Both his concern for social justice and his nonviolent strategy were rooted in Christian theology and ethics." "He was sustained throughout his career by a deeply personal religious faith, including a firm belief in a personal God." "His conception of hope," they continued, "was expressed in terms of the Christian doctrine of the Kingdom of God. He accepted the love ethic of Jesus as one of his basic principles, and his optimism was rooted in his belief that man's natural inclination to altruism could always be appealed to with positive results."[30] King's religious assimilation was magnificent, but as suggested below, it was not unproblematic.

Finally, for King personality implies community. Thus the liberal structure for King did not justify individualism. He defended the principles of the declaration while at the same time encouraging Americans to "rise above the narrow confines of [their] individualistic concerns to the broader concerns of humanity."[31] He stated that "the universe is so structured that things go awry if men are not diligent in their cultivation of the other-regarding dimension. 'I' cannot reach fulfillment without 'thou.' The self cannot be self without other selves."[32] He liked to repeat John Donne's phrase that "No man is an island, entire of itself" and in his "Letter from Birmingham Jail" he wrote that "we are caught in an inescapable network of mutuality, tied in a single garment of destiny. Whatever effects one directly affects all indirectly."

Principles of the American Founding

A study of the American founding, rooted in a careful reading of the Declaration of Independence, reveals close parallels to King's personalist political theology and anthropology, a theology and anthropology which are strongly affirmed by other speeches, writings, and legal institutions of the time. And while it would be an anachronism to call the framers personalists—the term was not the subject of a disciplined study until the twentieth century—one can find in their liberal principles many of the same elements articulated later in some schools of personalism, including King's.

Consider the four references to God in the declaration. These references are typically ignored or treated as a dispensable scaffolding which can (and indeed must) be removed once the "true" liberal structure is complete.[33] Such was not the conception of the founders. First God is a lawgiver ("the Laws of Nature and Nature's God") who has woven his laws into the nature he has created. By referring to the God of Nature, rather than the God of Divine Revelation, the declaration asserts that this is a God that can be known just as the Laws of Nature are known, by the light of natural reason. Second, God is a Creator and the ground of rights. Thus, attempts to ground American liberalism in more secular sources, such as competing interests or mutual desire for self-preservation, fundamentally misunderstand American liberalism. Third, the continental representatives appeal to "the Supreme Judge of the world for the rectitude" of their intentions. Thus God is not just a lawgiver; he is also a judge of that law. Finally, the representatives assert their "firm reliance on the protection of Divine Providence," thus rounding out a Creator-God who is the archetype for the three powers of government, legislative ("Law of Nature and Nature's God"), judicial ("Supreme Judge") and executive ("Divine Providence"). Far from the disinterested clock-worker of Deism, this is a God who is actively concerned with justice and with human affairs.³⁴

An objection to the foregoing thesis might point out Jefferson's famous dictum in his *Notes on the State of Virginia* (Query 17) that "it does me no injury for my neighbor to say there are twenty gods, or no god. It neither picks my pocket nor breaks my leg." Yet in the very next passage (Query 17) of the same work Jefferson says, "And can the liberties of a nation be thought secure when we have removed their only firm basis, a conviction in the minds of the people that these liberties are of the gift of God? That they are not to be violated but with his wrath?"³⁵ In this respect it is important to point out that the four references to God were not in Jefferson's original draft; the last two references were deliberately added by the Continental Congress, indicating that these references were not arbitrary.

This political theology provides the framework within which the rest of the liberal structure must be understood. Thus the purpose of government is to "secure" the trans-political, divinely grounded rights. Implied by this word security is an understanding of human beings who are good enough to be capable of liberty, but who are also capable of abusing that liberty. If human nature were thoroughly evil, as Thomas Hobbes well understood, then the only effective form of government would be an absolute monarchy. If men were angels, as James Madison argued in *Federalist* 51, no government would be necessary. Republican government (to use Madison again) presupposes the existence of "a certain degree of depravity in mankind which requires a certain degree of circumspection and distrust," as well as "other qualities in human nature which justify a certain portion of esteem and confidence." As pointed out above, King shared this anthropology.

These similarities between King and the declaration extend to their conceptions of statesmanship. According to the declaration, there are two requirements for just government: (1) Just government must secure the rights of the governed, and (2) government must derive its just powers from the consent of the governed. It has been pointed out by many others that these two requirements are not necessarily compatible, that a people might very well consent to deprive themselves or others of their rights. This tension between consent and protection of rights opens a window for wise statesmanship which seeks to bring them together in part through a proper arrangement of Constitutional devices, and in part by maintaining a regime of intelligent and virtuous citizens through responsible activity in speech and action.³⁶ The first element is the usual subject of courses in American politics: separation of powers, federalism, republicanism, etc. The second element, manifested in a long tradition of speeches, writings, songs, and public rituals which form the substance of what amounts to an American civil religion, is often ignored.[37] Because the writers of *The Federalist Papers* frankly acknowledged that "neither moral nor religious motives can be relied on" to ensure liberty, many thinkers have concluded that the founders believed that moral and religious motives are unnecessary, and perhaps even dangerous to liberty. They claim that the founders were attempting to meliorate the influence of moral and religious passions, which were viewed as the largest threat to liberty.[38] This reading of the founding, while plausible, avoids an abundance of evidence to the contrary. Although Madison concedes the limitations of religion and virtue to control moral behavior, he does not thereby argue that it is unnecessary. Indeed, he makes clear in *Federalist* 55 that republican government presupposes certain qualities in human nature "which justify a certain portion of esteem and confidence . . . in a higher degree than any other form." And several paragraphs later he argues that the first object of every political constitution is "to obtain for rulers men who possess most wisdom to discern, and most virtue to pursue, the common good of the society." Finally, he concedes that the final check on the abuse of government is "above all, the vigilant and manly spirit which actuates the people of America—a spirit which nourishes freedom, and in return is nourished by it."[39]

America is founded upon self-evident truths, yet those truths are not always self-evident. Observe that "self-evident truth" is an equivocal term, which designates on the one hand a truth that is immediately obvious in the sense of ordinary colloquial speech, and on the other hand a logically necessary conclusion whereby a predicate is contained within its subject.[40] In the words of Thomas Aquinas: "A thing is said to be self-evident in two ways: first, in itself; secondly, in relation to us. Any proposition is said to be self-evident in itself if its predicate is contained in the notion of the subject: although, to one who knows not the definition of the subject, it happens that such a proposition is not self-evident." [41] These two meanings do not necessarily correspond. For the declaration to be effective, then, there is the minimum requirement that people *believe* it is true, and agree to subject themselves to it. The founders were moderate realists, and thus were well aware that while man possesses the faculty of reason, he is not always a reasonable creature. For men to behave reasonably, then, requires the force of an orthodox opinion to counteract what Publius in *Federalist* 10 calls the subsisting connection between "reason and self-love."[42] One way this was achieved was through a civil religion based upon the political theology of the declaration, a religion which would fortify the passions and opinions of Americans in rational dedication to free government.

Because civil religion is a complex, ambiguous, and somewhat controversial term—especially when applied to the American context—some clarification of my meaning is in order. By civil religion I do not mean a formal institutional structure supported by the state, and to the exclusion of other religions. Nor am I referring to a completely conventional artifice for political ends with no transcendent ground. I mean simply the shared system of beliefs and opinions about justice (including beliefs about God and man) that bind a people together. In America, the ground for this civil religion is unique: it is not based upon any Gnostic claim to a secret knowledge, nor is it based on faith in particular claims of revealed truth. It is based upon the simple claim that reason is able to discern the fundamental truths revealed in nature. Belief in a God with certain attributes is not an expendable accretion to the self-evident truths of the declaration, it *is* one of the truths. But this ground historically extends into modest claims of Biblical revelation which are consistent with the ground and usually complement its spare formulation. It is this combination of natural and revealed religion in America's rhetorical and political tradition that provides it with both its greatest aspirations and largest difficulties.

That such a religion is still necessary is indicated by the very fact that America celebrates a King federal holiday, a feast day of the American political religion.[43] Another place is in the speeches and writings of George Washington, the only other American for whom America celebrates a federal holiday. True to the form above, virtually all of Washington's references to God are shorn of attributes which might encourage religious conflict. Thus God is "that Almighty Being who rules over the universe," and "the Great Author of every public and private good." But if his references to God are shorn of religious dogma, they are not shorn of moral dogma. Indeed, in his Farewell Address, Washington called religion and morality "indispensable supports" of political prosperity, and warned against those who would "indulge the supposition, that morality can be maintained without religion." Yet Washington was also an advocate of the right of religious liberty, and he welcomed persons of different religious persuasion, as can be seen in his numerous addresses to the various Hebrew, Quaker, and Roman Catholic communities. All of these themes from Washington's speeches are reinforced in those of King. And all of them find their theoretical foundations in the Declaration of Independence.

Even Benjamin Franklin, who was more liberal in his theology than most of the other founders, expressed his belief in these minimum conditions. In his *Autobiography*, which was unparalleled in popularity and influence, Franklin gives the basics of a creed which he believed contained "the essentials of every known Religion," without offending the "Professors of any Religion." The creed consists of the following: "That there is one God who made all things. That he governs the World by his Providence. That he ought to be worshipped by Adoration, Prayer and Thanksgiving. But that the most acceptable Service of God is doing Good to Man. That the soul is immortal. And that God will certainly reward virtue and punish Vice either here or hereafter." While this creed is missing certain elements (e.g., the affirmation of equality and natural rights) and adds certain others (e.g., immortality), the basic affirmations are the same: God created all things and governs them by his Providence.

[margin note: providence is also equivocal though]

The importance of this civil religion for liberty was powerfully expressed by Abraham Lincoln, who said in a debate with Stephen Douglas, "In this and like communities, public sentiment is everything. With public sentiment, nothing can fail; without it nothing can succeed." "Consequently," he said, "he who molds public sentiment, goes deeper than he who enacts statutes or pronounces decisions. He makes the statutes and decisions possible or impossible to be executed." Civil religion—a term used by Lincoln in his *Address to the Young Men's Lyceum* in 1838—was a critical part of Lincoln's extraordinary effort to mold public sentiment, an effort so magnificent and powerful that it remained unrivaled in American politics until King.

Lincoln's words should remind us of King's remarks above, "We must depend on religion and education to alter the errors of the heart and mind." Both Lincoln and King made powerful rhetorical use of religious imagery, Lincoln perhaps most famously in his "House-Divided" speech. Lincoln, however, in contrast to King, was decidedly agnostic about the will of God. While he affirmed God's goodness, and God's concern for justice, Lincoln declared in his Second Inaugural Address—and this was typical of his remarks on God—that "The Almighty has His own purposes," and he conditioned all of his statements about God's will with an "if." King on the other hand was much more aggressive about identifying his own understanding of justice with God's will. This began with his very first speech ("If we are wrong, God Almighty is wrong") and extended all the way to the end, when he asserted in his last speech that God had privileged him to "go up to the mountain" and see "the Promised Land."[44]

King never advocated anything like an establishment of religion. To the contrary, when asked for his opinion on a Supreme Court decision prohibiting public school systems from requiring school prayer King expressed support for the decision, stating that "in a pluralistic society such as ours, who is to determine what prayer is to be spoken, and by whom? Legally, constitutionally, or otherwise, the state certainly has no such right."[45] Yet did King make religious demands on the regime in a different way? How did his religious views affect his expectations for political life, and how is one to understand these expectations from the perspective of the American political tradition? King's religious perspective is so important for understanding the dimensions of his Dream that it merits a brief digression.

[margin note: The stuff on civil religion is too underdeveloped.]

King on Religion and Politics

The combination of biblical and civil religion in King's rhetoric was enormously effective, but it also risked confusing the essential differences between the two religions.[46] Put simply, the political ends of the American covenant after the Revolution were relatively limited. Not the perfect justice of holy purity, but the more limited justice of protection of rights under consent would be the primary end of government. This was a limited justice which allowed room for the "better angels" of human nature, but which also made concessions for the limitations and imperfections of fallen human nature.[47] Even the "realist" James Madison acknowledged in the *Federalist Papers* that "Justice is the end of government." But he also realized the dangers of its unlimited pursuit: "[Justice] ever has been and ever will be pursued until it be obtained, or until liberty be lost in the pursuit."[48] And here is the great danger, that the immoderate pursuit of justice, the demand for perfect justice, presents great dangers to liberty and to the regime as a whole. This may be especially true of demands for justice informed by biblical revelation and reinforced by religious enthusiasm. Did King seek "the immanentization of the Christian eschaton," to use the phrase of Eric Voegelin?[49] That is, did he seek the actualization of the millennium through nonviolent direct action? Smith and Zepp suggested this when they wrote, "King's conception of the Beloved Community was grounded, in the final analysis, not in the tradition of the enlightenment or secular democratic theory but in the millennial hope of Judeo-Christian religion."[50]

According to Richard Lischer, King played at least two different roles in America. In the first phase of his career King served a priestly function in which "he mediated a covenant with which white moderates and liberals were comfortable." This was a stage in which King largely identified with the "traditionally white consensus ideals of America."[51] But in his last three years "something turned in King," Lischer argues. "Those who arrest King's rhetorical development at the identification stage will always be comfortable with him," he wrote. "But if they read the sermons and speeches of his final three years, they will encounter a prophet who was past identifying with the oppressor's values and had gone on to confronting them." Consequently, "He reduced the number of authorities in his sermons to one: Almighty God. He began saying, 'Thus says the Lord.'"[52] "His rhetoric becomes more confrontational, more prophetic, in nature. The multiple 'authorities' upon which his earlier sermons rested have been reduced to One. In a variety of ways he says, in effect: This is God's will for America. You can take it or leave it."[53] King, Lischer argues, deliberately sought to demythologize American civil religion. For evidence he cited King's claim that "our nation was born in genocide when it embraced the doctrine that the original American, the Indian, was an inferior race . . . We are perhaps the only nation which has tried as a matter of national policy to wipe out its indigenous population."⁵⁴

Lischer's arguments have merit. King took his primary responsibility as a Christian preacher seriously, and on those rare occasions when he saw a conflict between the nation's ideals and what he regarded as a divine standard, he chose the latter. For example, in his "Riverside" speech against the Vietnam War King said the following about "the calling to be a son of the living God":

> This I believe to be the privilege and the burden of all of us who deem ourselves bound by allegiances and loyalties which are broader and deeper than nationalism and which go beyond our nation's self-defined goals and positions. We are called to speak for the weak, for the voiceless, for victims of our nation's self-defined goals and positions. We are called to speak for the weak, for the voiceless, for the victims of our nation and for those it calls enemy, for no document from human hands can make these humans any less our brothers.⁵⁵

It is difficult to know what objection King is responding to here. He certainly could have used the American creed to defend his position against the war, as he had used it numerous times to oppose segregation and discrimination. Why in this case he chose to depart from the American jeremiad is not clear. That he continued to rely on the American jeremiad in subsequent speeches suggests that this was more of a rhetorical gesture than a genuine loss of confidence in the American creed.

Lischer's thesis, however, has some weaknesses. First, King was prophetic from the very beginning of his career, and if he comforted Americans by reminding them of their noble creed, he also sharply criticized them for failing to live up to it. Thus some of Lischer's own evidence for King's change is taken from an earlier part of King's career.⁵⁶ Second, if King's voice becomes more shrill, desperate, and defiant in the last phase of his career, it is still a voice that affirms the goodness of the American creed. As he wrote in his last book, "The home that all too many Americans left was solidly structured idealistically. Its pillars were soundly grounded in the insights of our Judeo-Christian heritage."⁵⁷ There is no demythologizing of civil religion happening here, only a stronger confrontation of American complacency. Without American civil religion prophecy would be absolutely ineffective.

Nevertheless, Lischer does identify a difficulty in King's rhetoric, especially near the end of his career, when he increasingly relied upon God as the sole authority of judgment for American political life. He began to practice "the prophetic privilege of speaking univocally for the Lord."⁵⁸ Lischer doesn't seem to find a difficulty in this rhetorical transformation. Indeed, he concludes that "White American liberalism embraced the victim but rejected the prophet. It accepted its own guilt but not the radical changes necessary for its liberation."⁵⁹ This conclusion ignores the possibility that King's divine authority may have been the projection of King's ego, and not a divine mandate. Why should Americans unconditionally accept such an authority whose origin is so uncertain? If anything, King's retreat to the privileged status of "God's trombone" was an indication that his vision no longer had the power to persuade in the public square. Obedience to his voice on these terms might have meant the death of political democracy.

Did King encourage millenarian hopes for political ends? It was observed above that King recognized the intransigence of human sin and doubted the inevitability of progress.⁶⁰ He also taught belief in another world after death, and warned against those who would conflate the two. Finally, he understood that the greatest changes happen in the human soul through God's grace, and beyond the power of the law. King was not teaching the advent of the earthly kingdom of God, but he was teaching the duty of every Christian people to seek justice, and thus "prepare the way of the Lord." As the first John the Baptist helped prepare the way for the coming of Christ, so King was acting the part of a second John the Baptist, helping prepare the way for the return of Christ by calling the nation to repentance and justice. He was reminding America of her divine calling and dedication as "one nation under God" to the "proposition that all men are created equal." It was only under such conditions that God would have favor upon the nation, and thus reveal the glory of his justice.

In many respects King's understanding of religion was orthodox. He was a sharp critic of modernity, celebrating the great improvements in material conditions provided by modern science and technology, but also warning against their philosophical presuppositions and subsequent dangers. He upbraided Americans for failing to "keep your moral advances abreast of your scientific advances" and cleverly parodied the claims of modern science as the substitute for faith and religion.

> Witnessing the amazing advances of science, modern man exclaimed:
> Science is my shepherd; I shall not want.
> It maketh me to lie down in green pastures;
> It leadeth me beside the still waters.
> It restoreth my soul . . . .
> I will fear no evil: for science is with me;
> Its rod and it staff they comfort me.
> Man's aspirations no longer turned Godward and heavenward. Rather, man's thoughts were confined to man and earth. And man offered a strange parody on the Lord's Prayer: "Our brethren which art on earth, Hallowed by our name. Our kingdom come. Our will be done on earth, for there is no heaven." Those who formerly turned to God to find solutions for their problems turned to science and technology, convinced that they now possessed the instruments necessary to usher in the new society.⁶¹

In his sermon "Paul's Letter to the American Christians" he described Americans as allowing their "material means . . . to outdistance the spiritual ends" for which they were to live,[62] and accused them of being more "concerned about making a living than making a life."[63] This warning against the tyranny of technical rationality and immoderate acquisitiveness was a message Americans needed—and need—to hear, but this was not a new message for them. More than a century before Tocqueville had noted the American tendency toward materialism and warned of its dangers. Tocqueville also saw the antidote to materialism in America's religious tradition, which set limits to material acquisition and reminded human beings of their responsibility to their fellow human beings and to God.

King also recognized both the difference and the tension between transcendent truth and political truth, the "City of God" and the "City of Man." Consider statements he made on Walter Rauschenbusch, the social gospel theorist who he claimed had left "an indelible imprint" on his thinking.[64] According to King, "Rauschenbusch had done a great service for the Christian Church by insisting that the gospel deals with the whole man, not only his soul but his body; not only his spiritual well-being but his material well-being. It has been my conviction ever since reading Rauschenbusch that any religion which professes to be concerned about the souls of men and is not concerned about the social and economic conditions that scar the soul, is a spiritually moribund religion only waiting for the day to be buried. It well has been said: 'A religion that ends with the individual, ends.'" But he also expressed reservations about Rauschenbusch's reduction of the content of Christianity to ethical and social norms and his historical optimism. "I felt that he had fallen victim to the nineteenth century 'cult of inevitable progress,'" King wrote, "which led him to a superficial optimism concerning man's nature. Moreover, he came perilously close to identifying the Kingdom of God with a particular social and economic system—a tendency which should never befall the Church."[65]

One can discern at least two important things here about King's understanding of religion. First, he rejected an optimistic progressive liberalism which posited an evolution in human nature from evil to good.[66] In a college paper he expressed reservations about the principle of inevitable progress. He repeated his theme that technological progress does not necessarily translate into moral progress, and he warned against an "ethical religion" which was too optimistic about human nature. "We in the Anglo-Saxon world," he wrote, "securely relying upon our vast natural resources, our highly developed science and technology, and our fairly stable social institutions, have been thinking and talking far too glibly about the Kingdom of God as of something that we might hope to 'bring in' by our own human efforts. Half unconsciously, we have been confusing the ancient hope of the coming of God's Kingdom with the modern doctrine of progress. Have not we depended too much on man and too little on God?" He then warned against millennial expectations on the part of Christians. "Although . . . ethical religion is humane and its vision a lofty one," he continued, "it has obvious shortcomings. This particular sort of optimism has been discredited by the brutal logic of events. Instead of assured progress in wisdom and decency man faces the ever present possibility of swift relapse not merely into animalism but into such calculated cruelty as no other animal can practice."[67] "We must lift up our minds and eyes unto the hills from whence come our true help. Then and only then, will the advances of modern science be a blessing rather than a curse."[68]

King's orthodoxy left room for Divine intervention. Indeed, he claimed that nonviolent direct action "is based on the conviction that the universe is on the side of justice. Consequently, the believer in nonviolence has deep faith in the future."[69] But this belief in God's concern for justice in the universe should not be taken to mean that God's ways are manifested in some necessary progressive development in history which is accessible to human beings.

Secondly, King rejected the simple identification of Christianity with a particular social or economic system, and thus he also rejected Rauschenbusch's immanentist interpretation of Christianity, which would conflate the kingdoms of heaven and earth. Instead he maintained a more orthodox, Augustinian approach. Consider the following:

> The Church must remind its worshipers that man finds greater security in devoting his life to the eternal demands of the Almighty God than in giving his ultimate allegiance to the transitory demands of man. The Church must continually say to Christians, "Ye are a colony of heaven." True, man has a dual citizenry. He lives both in time and in eternity; both in heaven and on earth. But he owes his ultimate allegiance to God. It is this love for God and his devotion to His will that casteth out all fear.[70]

King wrote that "[God's] creative power is not exhausted by this earthly life, nor is his majestic love locked within the limited walls of time and space." In Kantian fashion, he made an ethical argument for immortality: "Would not this be a strangely irrational universe if God did not ultimately join virtue and fulfillment, and an absurdly meaningless universe if death were a blind alley leading the human race into a state of nothingness?"[71] But his formulation was also distinctly Christian: "God through Christ has taken the sting from death by freeing us from its dominion. Our earthly life is a prelude to a glorious new awakening, and death is an open door that leads us into life eternal."[72] Continuing the Kantian assimilation, King wrote that "The end of life is not to be happy nor to achieve pleasure and avoid pain, but to do the will of God, come what may."[73]

King sought to navigate the extremes of orthodoxy and liberal Christianity, retaining what he regarded as true from each and discarding what he thought was false. He maintained that "otherworldly concerns have a deep and significant place in all religions worthy of the name" and that "when religion overlooks this basic fact it is reduced to a mere ethical system in which eternity is absorbed in time and God is relegated to a sort of meaningless figment of human imagination."[74] At the same time, however, he warned that "a religion true to its nature must also be concerned about man's social conditions. Religion deals with both earth and heaven, both time and eternity . . . It seeks not only to integrate men with God but to integrate men with men and each man with himself."[75] Thus King envisioned a critical role for the church in bringing justice to the world.[76]

In sum, King's understanding of the relationship between religion and politics was complicated. Most of the time he served in a role as prophet of American civil religion. He tirelessly challenged Americans to live up to their creed and was willing to negotiate the compromises necessary for achieving justice. But in the last phase of his career King began to take on characteristics of a Biblical prophet, abandoning much of his earlier insight regarding the limitations of politics and demanding more radical implementations of justice. While unfortunate, it is also fitting that this last phase would lead almost inexorably to King's death, for in it lay a divine dissatisfaction with the imperfections of the world and a longing for transcendent justice, a longing that could only be satisfied by a perfection not possible in this world. But if King's message largely fell on deaf ears, his witness was not without value insofar as it reminded Americans of the limitations, and thus the guilt, of every temporal regime. It also warned Americans against the dangers of falling subject to the tyranny of technical rationalism and crass pragmatism. In so doing, he discouraged complacency and the pride that blinds nations to greater justice in the world. Moreover, the example of King's life and death also brought his vision closer to reality, for it was a life spent in service to the cause of justice. It was itself a high form of the *agape* love he constantly preached.

Liberal Communitarianism

Finally, like King's personalism, the political anthropology of the founding conceived human nature as essentially social, if not political. This fact is generally ignored by both communitarian and liberal critics of liberalism. According to the standard argument, because the protection of rights are the first object of government, and because rights are private (that is, prior to government), government exists only to facilitate private transaction and offers no independent conception of a public good. In other words, the principles of the declaration elevate selfish individualism over political liberty, resulting in the anomalous "private citizen" (to use the term of Bruce Ackerman) who has been the subject of the most trenchant critique of liberal democracy, especially in America. One finds a steady line of this criticism in literature on America, in both fiction and nonfiction, stretching from Tocqueville's *Democracy in America*, to its more vulgar twentieth century forms in David Riesman's *The Lonely Crowd* and Robert Bellah's *Habits of the Heart: Individualism and Commitment in American Life*.[77] It was a popular theme of the New Left, and continues to receive attention from communitarians like Michael Sandel, and New Democrats like Bill Clinton. As observed above, King did not hold this opinion of liberalism. Neither did the founders.

It is important to see that behind many of these criticisms is a misunderstanding and distortion of American liberalism brought to America in the early twentieth century, exemplified by the critique of liberalism outlined above. It consists of an odd compound of distortions of John Stuart Mill's utilitarianism and Kantian personalism, the first of which divorces liberalism from any objective conception of the good, and the second of which elevates the principle of radical autonomy to the center of political life. In either case, liberalism can offer no meaningful guidance for how one ought to live, and government in particular is prevented from offering any such guidance. Natural rights are severed from any connection to moral virtue or to a meaningful social and political life.

If the founders looked to establish a "commercial republic" in which the private pursuit of material gain was to be protected and even encouraged through the protection of private property, they did not thereby diminish the importance of virtue or the dignity of political life. They understood that even in a commercial republic certain virtues are required in order to succeed. The success of commerce requires, for example,

> honesty (because credit is indispensable in commercial transactions), sobriety (or the job will not be done well), frugality (to save in order to buy property or invest), civility (to please the boss and customers), self-restraint (to prevent one's capital from being squandered), and justice (to enable lawful satisfaction of one's needs through labor).[78]

Virtue is also necessary for the success of liberty. While the Declaration of Independence is relatively silent about the need for virtue (remember that it is not primarily a constitution), a number of the state constitutions of the Revolutionary era, which imitate the natural rights terminology of the declaration, are explicit about the political need for moral virtue. An examination of these constitutions reveals a striking difference between the liberalism of the founders and today's regnant liberalism. They affirm the liberal principles of just government found in the declaration (natural rights, equality, consent, limited government) while at the same time affirming the need for and exhorting citizens to virtue. The first section of the Pennsylvania Constitution of 1776, for example, states that "all men are born equally free and independent, and have certain natural, inherent and inalienable rights, amongst which are the enjoying and defending of life and liberty, acquiring, possessing and protecting property, and pursuing and obtaining happiness and safety," thus imitating both the argument and diction of the Declaration of Independence. Section 14 of the same constitution states that "a frequent recurrence to fundamental principles and a firm adherence to justice, moderation, temperance, industry and frugality, are absolutely necessary to preserve the blessings of liberty, and keep government free. The people ought therefore to pay particular attention to these points in the choice of officers and representatives, and have a right to exact a due and constant regard to them from their legislatures and magistrates, in the making and executing such laws as are necessary for the good government of the state." There is no problem here combining recognition of and security to natural rights with provisions for moral virtue. The very clause of the Virginia Declaration of Rights, which affirms the right to religious liberty, also declares "that it is the mutual duty of all to practise Christian forbearance, love, and charity, towards each other."[79] This same formula can be found in the Constitutions of Massachusetts (1780), New Hampshire (1784), and Vermont (1777).

It might be supposed that this combination of natural rights with political exhortations to religion and virtue was only an awkward compromise with Puritan prejudice, and would eventually be abolished as the true principles of natural rights came to fruition.[80] The evidence does not support this conjecture. The founders took their cue from John Locke, who argued in his *Second Treatise* that although man's natural state is one of liberty, it is not a "State of License," for it has a "Law of Nature to govern it."[81] This theme was repeated over and over in political sermons and writings. Thus, in a political sermon delivered in 1776 Samuel West, using Locke as an authority, said that "the highest state of liberty subjects us to the law of nature and the government of God. The most perfect freedom consists in obeying the dictates of right reason, and submitting to natural law." Moreover, said West, "The law of nature gives men no right to do anything that is immoral, or contrary to the will of God, and injurious to their fellow-creatures; for a state of nature is properly a state of law and government, even a government founded upon the unchangeable nature of the Deity, and a law resulting from the eternal fitness of things."[82]

If the above is true, then there is no tension between government and liberty. Rather, government is a provision for natural liberty. As Locke writes: "the Obligations of the Law of Nature cease not in Society, but only in many Cases are drawn closer . . . Thus the Law of Nature stands as an Eternal Rule to all Men, *Legislators* as well as others."[83] And Samuel West, following

Locke, says: "the end and design of civil government cannot be to deprive men of their liberty or take away their freedom; but, on the contrary, the true design of civil government is to protect men in the enjoyment of their liberty."[84] The understanding of liberty which situates it within the framework of "autonomy," inherited from Kant, was a late and clandestine arrival to America, and directly contradicts the founder's more classical view.

It follows from the founder's conception that man is not by nature exclusively the self-interested individual hypothesized by many liberal thinkers. In other words, while he may (and indeed often does) act out of base self-interest, such actions are *contrary* to his nature. Moreover, while the founders may have agreed that man is not a *political* animal by nature, they all would have agreed that he is a *social* animal by nature.[85] We might look again at Locke, whose social compact theory is often regarded as a source of liberal individualism. According to Locke, "God having made Man such a Creature, that, in his own Judgment, it was not good for him to be alone, put him under strong Obligations of Necessity, Convenience, and Inclination to drive him into society as well as fitted him with Understanding and Language to continue and enjoy it."[86] And Thomas Jefferson, for evidence that human nature has a "moral sense," argued that "the Creator would have been a bungling artist, had he intended man for a social animal, without planting in him social dispositions."[87] This theme is also repeated in the political sermons and writings of the founding era. In an election sermon delivered in 1768, Daniel Shute stated that men enter civil society "to secure to them those natural rights and privileges which are essential to their happiness. Life, Liberty and property are the gifts of the creator, on the unmolested enjoyment of which their happiness depends." At the same time, however, he argued that "the nature of the human species . . . being so adapted to society as that society will afford vastly more happiness to them, than solitary existence could do, indicates the will of their creator, and makes it morally fit that they should associate."[88] In the same sermon discussed above, Samuel West said that "The great Creator, having designed the human race for society, has made us dependent upon one another for happiness. He has so constituted us that it becomes both our duty and interest to seek the public good, and that we may be more firmly engaged to promote each other's welfare, the Deity has endowed us with tender and social affections."[89]

This communitarian conception of liberalism is not a contradiction when the principles of American liberalism are properly understood as primarily *ontological*, rather than historical. In other words, liberal principles provide a powerful, imaginative conception of human nature which affirms the essential teaching of Aristotle, Augustine, and St. Thomas Aquinas that man has a place in the chain of being between beast and God, and that in their place they share in the politically relevant characteristics of reason and free will, if not in equal degree. Augustine in book 19 of *The City of God* writes that "[God] did not wish the rational being, made in his own image, to have dominion over any but irrational creatures, not man over man, but man over the beasts."⁹⁰ And St. Thomas, referring to this same passage, argues that mastership would have existed before the fall, not in the sense of slavery or servitude, but in the sense of a master being "he who has the office of governing and directing free men."⁹¹

[margin note: Lockean, Thomistic, and Augustinian]

It is fair to say that both of these men, like the founders, annunciated an argument that human beings, made in the image and likeness of God, are equal in the political sense. Yet they also maintained that man was a political animal. In Aristotle the argument is more complicated, but a fair reading may justifiably conclude that Aristotle recognized the equality of human beings and opposed virtually all forms of slavery as a violation of nature. For Aristotle, what distinguishes man from beast is the faculty of speech, which "serves to reveal the advantageous and the harmful, and hence also the just and the unjust."⁹² Thus in his investigation whether "it is better or just for anyone to be a slave or not" Aristotle argues that "those who are as different [from other men] as the soul from the body or man from beast—and they are in this state if their work is the use of the body, and if this is the best that can come from them—are slaves by nature." Such a person is one who "participates in reason only to the extent of perceiving it, but does not have it."⁹³ One might find here the strongest critique of slavery as it existed in the ancient world.

In sum, the teaching on the state of nature, properly understood (as the founder's understood it), is fully compatible with an argument that man is by nature a political animal. The liberalism of the declaration can and should support a rich moral, social, and political life.⁹⁴ This should not be interpreted to mean that the founder's "liberalism" was really conservatism *a la* Russell Kirk, or in another version of a similar argument, that it was the expression of an ideal of classical republicanism *a la* J. G. A. Pocock.⁹⁵ There is some truth in both of these arguments, but they both miss the essentially "modern" features of American liberalism, among which are a more radical application of human equality (i.e., the abolition of an aristocracy and titles of honor, extension of suffrage, etc.), limited government, religious toleration, and an openness to commercial and industrial life based on the protection of private property.⁹⁶

Conclusion

King shared critical aspects of his theology and anthropology with the American founders. Indeed, the entire foundation of his political understanding, his Dream, was situated within the context of a robust conception of a provident

God to whom human beings are responsible—a conception hinted at in the Declaration of Independence and manifested in other speeches and writings. But unlike the founders and Lincoln, who merely located support for "Nature's God" in Revelation (thus leaving room for a separation between religion and politics), King risked making the God of Revelation his ultimate ground for the demands of political life, even as he opposed any kind of established church. He did so despite his own warnings in other places against conflating the respective cities of God and Man, making his entire project problematic.

King also shared with the founders a conception of human beings who are social by nature, inclined toward goodness and marred by evil. Like the founders King argued that natural rights are grounded in God and constitute a barrier against government action. Unlike the founders, however, King's conception of natural rights also imposed substantial obligations on government toward its citizens. Whether King was able to do this consistently will be considered in the next two chapters.

Finally, King's anthropology made the realization of his Dream ultimately dependent upon nongovernmental factors. Well into the last phase of his career he held that "the ultimate solution to the race problem lies in the willingness of men to obey the unenforceable." Such a state of affairs would only occur as human beings became "possessed by the invisible inner law which etches on their hearts the conviction that all men are brothers and that love is mankind's most potent weapon for personal and social transformation."[97] King was hearkening back to his first book, in which he wrote that "love must be our regulating ideal,"[98] and that "we must depend upon religion and education to alter the errors of the heart and mind."[99] King understood that true love by definition must be the result of a free choice, and thus cannot be coerced by government. But the distinction between the demands of love and justice in his thought are not clear (see chapter 5).

Despite the truths King's anthropology taught him about the limitations of human nature, King longed for a justice that will never be satisfied by any earthly order. The last words of the "I Have a Dream" speech form the basis for the epitaph inscribed upon his tombstone. They reveal a profound truth of the human condition, revealed in Christ, that true liberty is found in perfect self-gift, even unto death. Perhaps in his death King realized his Dream, and through that death drew America one step closer to realizing her own.

Notes

1. Martin Luther King, Jr., *Strength to Love* (Philadelphia, Christian Education Press, 1959), 100.

2. See especially Kenneth L. Smith and Ira G. Zepp, *Search for the Beloved Community: The Thinking of Martin Luther King, Jr.* (Valley Forge, Pa.: Judson Press, 1974) and John J. Ansbro, *Martin Luther King, Jr.: The Making of a Mind* (Maryknoll, New York: Orbis Books, 1982). Both of these excellent books make note of King's appeal to American principles, but neither one of them develops the argument.

3. Washington, *Testament*, 208.

4. Although he held a Ph.D. in Systematic Theology from Boston University, most recent treatments of King have called into question the putative provenance of his ideas in his education in western philosophy and theology. They point out that his plagiarism is both a sign of his insincerity, insecurity, and/or disinterest with respect to the material, and also his attachment to the sermonic habits of black folk religion. The most that is conceded to King is that he had a "singular ability to intertwine his words and ideas with those of others to express his beliefs persuasively and to construct a persona with broad transracial appeal." Clayborne Carson, Peter Holloran, Ralph E. Luker and Penny Russell, "Martin Luther King, Jr., as Scholar: A Reexamination of His Theological Writings," in *Journal of American History*, 78 (June 1991), 94. See also Miller, *Voice of Deliverance*; and Lewis Baldwin's companion volumes *There is a Balm in Gilead: The Cultural Roots of Martin Luther King, Jr.*, and *To Make the Wounded Whole: The Cultural Legacy of Martin Luther King, Jr.* I believe Eugene Genovese is more accurate when he writes "From his undergraduate days [King] displayed a deep thirst for a knowledge of God, making a constant effort to understand his nature and will. Plagiarized or no, his papers, from Morehouse to Crozer to Boston University, provide ample evidence that he was thinking hard and trying to find Christian ground on which to stand." See Eugene Genovese, *Southern Front: History and Politics in the Culture War* (Columbia, Mo.: University of Missouri Press, 1995). For a sharp and controversial critique of King's plagiarism, see Theodore Pappas, *Plagiarism and the Culture War: The Writings of Martin Luther King, Jr. and Other Prominent Americans* (New York: Hallberg Publishing, 1998).

5. This has been adequately done by Ansbro, *Martin Luther King, Jr.*

6. King, *Stride*, 100.

7. Washington, *Testament*, 119.

8. Washington, *Testament*, 208.

9. King, *Strength*, 73.

10. *Negro History Bulletin*, vol. 31, no. 5 (May, 1968), 17. Quoted in Smith and Zepp, *Search*, 127.

11. King, *Strength*, 73.

12. Carson, *King Papers*, vol. 2, 137.

13. King, *Strength*, 31.

14. See Ansbro, *Martin Luther King, Jr.*, 71-76.

15. "Rediscovering Lost Values," in Carson, *King Papers,* vol. 2, 252-53.

16. Thus renowned philosopher Ronald Dworkin writes that government "must not constrain liberty on the ground that one citizen's conception of the good life of one group is nobler or superior to another's." Ronald Dworkin, *Taking Rights Seriously* (Cambridge, Mass.: Harvard University Press, 1977), 273. Self-described liberal ironist Richard Rorty opines that the only "social glue" required by the "ideal liberal society" is that "everybody have a chance at self-creation to the best of his or her abilities." According to Rorty, "This conviction would not be based on a view about universally shared human ends, human rights, the nature of rationality, the Good for Man, nor anything else." Richard Rorty, *Achieving America: Leftist Thought in Twentieth Century America* (Cambridge, MA: Harvard University Press, 1998), 84. And John Rawls, defending his concept of "justice as fairness," argues that "there is no necessity to invoke theological or metaphysical doctrines to support its principles, nor to imagine another world that compensates for or corrects the inequalities which the two principles [of fairness] permit in this one." John Rawls, *A Theory of Justice.* (Cambridge, Mass.: The Belknap Press of Harvard University Press, 1971), 454, 214.

Finally, Yale law professor Bruce Ackerman argues that "rather than linking liberalism to ideas of natural right or imaginary contract, we must learn to think of liberalism as a way of talking about power, a form of political culture." Bruce Ackerman, *Social Justice and the Liberal State* (New Haven: Yale University Press, 1980), 6. The principle of neutrality which guides this liberal conversation prohibits "the power holder to assert . . . that his conception of the good is better than that asserted by any of his fellow citizens." Ackerman, *Social Justice,* 11. Ackerman's principles lead to some frightening eugenic conclusions, the shocking nature of which he appears unaware. See particularly his discussion entitled "Birthrights," 107-38.

17. Michael J. Sandel, *Democracy's Discontent: America in Search of a Public Philosophy* (Cambridge, Mass.: Belknap Press of Harvard University Press, 1996), 4.

18. *Planned Parenthood of Southeastern Pennsylvania v. Casey,* 112 S.Ct. 2807 (1992). These justices were Sandra Day O'Connor, Anthony Kennedy, and David Souter. On the foundations of American liberalism, see John Courtney Murray, *We Hold These Truths: Catholic Reflections on the American Proposition* (New York: Sheed & Ward, 1960), 80-96. Murray articulates concisely the foundations of American liberalism rooted in the declaration, but then he rejects it on the grounds that many Americans contest it. This causes Murray to conclude that "there is today a need for a new moral act of purpose and new act of intellectual affirmation, comparable to those which launched the American Constitutional commonwealth, that will put us in possession of the public philosophy, the basic consensus we need." Murray, *Reflections,* 87. I think Murray's method (and therefore conclusion) is flawed, for reasons I hope will become clear in the remainder of this chapter.

19. Robert H. Bork, *Slouching Towards Gomorrah: Modern Liberalism and American Decline* (New York: Regan Books, 1996), 57.

20. Marvin Meyers, ed., *The Mind of the Founder: Sources of the Political Thought of James Madison* (London: University Press of New England for Brandeis University Press, 1973; revised ed. 1981), 349.

21. Washington, *Testament,* 199.

22. King, *Strength*, 84.

23. Carson, *King Papers*, vol. 2, 512.

24. For an extensive discussion of King's views of God, see Ansbro, *Martin Luther King, Jr.*, 37-70.

25. King realized that "when the law regulates behavior it plays an indirect part in molding public sentiment," and that "the enforcement of the law is itself a form of peaceful persuasion." According to him, "The law itself is a form of education. The words of the Supreme Court, of Congress, and of the Constitution are eloquent instructors." King, *Stride*, 199. He warned against the temptation to downplay the educative function of law: "Let us never succumb to the temptation of believing that legislation and judicial decrees play only minor roles in solving [segregation and discrimination]. Morality cannot be legislated, but behavior can be regulated. Judicial decrees may not change the heart, but they can restrain the heartless. The law cannot make employer love an employee, but it can prevent him from refusing to hire me because of the color of my skin. The habits, if not the hearts, of people have been and are being altered every day by legislative acts, judicial decisions and executive orders," King, *Strength*, 37.

26. King, *Stride*, 216.

27. King, *Strength*, 37-38.

28. King, *Stride*, 198.

29. Washington, *Testament*, 408.

30. Smith and Zepp, *Search*, 11.

31. Washington, *Testament*, 138.

32. King, *Where*, 180.

33. I first discovered this careful reading of the declaration in the writings of George Anastaplo. See for example, "Abraham Lincoln and The Constitution of 1787" in *Abraham Lincoln: a Constitutional Biography* (Lanham, Md.: Rowman & Littlefield, 1999), 21-22.

34. How the God of the declaration is reconciled with the God of Christianity requires a much longer treatment than this study will permit. Like that of many of the founders, King's Christianity was far from orthodox. In brief, my judgment is that the civil theology of the declaration is informed by and fully compatible with Christian doctrine.

35. Harvey C. Mansfield, Jr., ed., *Thomas Jefferson: Selected Writings* (Wheeling, IL: Harlan Davidson, 1979), 48 and 51.

36. One can find such a design outlined in the *Federalist Papers*.

37. See the important article by Robert Bellah, "Civil Religion in America," *Deadalus* vol. 96 (Winter 1967):1-21. Also see Bellah's book *The Broken Covenant*. See also Thomas G. West, "Religious Liberty: The View from the Founding," in Daniel C. Palm, ed., *On Faith and Free Government*. (Lanham, MD: Rowman & Littlefield, 1997).

38. For an argument that this was the founder's position, see Kenneth R. Craycraft, *The American Myth of Religious Freedom* (Dallas: Spence Publishing, 1999).

39. On this argument (which involves a response to Diamond) see Charles Kesler, "Federalist 10 and American Republicanism," and "Natural Law and the Constitution: The Federalist's View," in Sarah Baumgartner Thurow, ed., *Constitutionalism in Perspective: The United States Constitution in Twentieth Century Politics*, vol. 3 (Dallas: University of Dallas Press, 1988), 155-81.

40. St. Thomas Aquinas, *Summa Theologica*, vol. 1-2, q94, a2, corpus.

41. For this observation I thank an insightful essay by Glen E. Thurow, "The Gettysburg Address and the Declaration of Independence," in Leo Paul de Alvarez, ed., *Abraham Lincoln, the Gettysburg Address, and American Constitutionalism* (Irving, Tex.: The University of Dallas Press, 1976), 55-76.

42. On this point one should also consult Publius' argument in *Federalist* 49.

43. Walter Berns contrasts the natural rights theory of the declaration with religious belief, implying throughout his discussion that the two are necessarily incompatible, and that the founders sought to diminish and subordinate the latter to the former. Walter Berns, "Religion and the Founding Principle," in Robert Horwitz, ed., *The Moral Foundations of the American Republic* (Charlottesville: University Press of Virginia, 1977), 157-82. This seems to me a confused way of viewing the matter, and quite contrary to the spirit in which it was presented and accepted.

44. King had used the "I've been to the mountain top" line as early as 1957. See Carson, *King Papers*, vol. 4, 114.

45. King, "Playboy Interview," in Washington, *Testament*, 373. The decision referred to is probably *Abington School District v. Schempp* and *Murray v. Curlett*, 374 U.S. 203, 83 S. Ct. 1560 (1963).

46. See McWilliams, "The Bible in the American Political Tradition," in Myron J. Aronoff, ed., *Political Anthropology, Volume 3: Religion and Politics* (New Brunswick and London: Transaction Books, 1984.)

47. See Richard Niebuhr's contast between the utopianism of the founders and the later, more progressive expressions. Richard Niebuhr, *The Kingdom of God in America* (New York: Harper 1959), especially 49.

48. *Federalist* 51.

49. Voegelin, *New Science*, 156.

50. Smith and Zepp, *Search*, 128.

51. Lischer, *Preacher*, 10.

52. Lischer, *Preacher*, 11.

53. Lischer, *Preacher*, 162.

54. Lischer, *Preacher*, 158. Also in King, *Why*, 120.

55. Washington, *Testament*, 234.

56. King's quote on genocide, cited above, was written in 1963, before the major civil rights victories were won.

57. King, *Where*, 84.

58. Lischer, *Preacher*, 181.

59. Lischer, *Preacher*, 193.

60. According to Tuveson, faith in progress is a central tenet of millennialism.

See Ernest Lee Tuveson, *Redeemer Nation: The Idea of America's Millenial Role* (Chicago: The University of Chicago Press, 1969; Midway Reprint, 1980), 39.

61. King, *Strength*, 74.

62. Carson and Holloran, *Knock*, 27.

63. Carson and Holloran, *Knock*, 28.

64. Walter Rauschenbusch, *Christianity and the Social Crisis* (Louisville, KY: Westminster/Knox Press, 1991; first published by The Macmillan Company, 1907).

65. King, *Stride*, 91. This theme is repeated over and over in King's speeches and writings.

66. Such an understanding of liberalism presumably would seek to do away with the institutional structure of the founding, which presumes a careful balance of both virtue and vice in human nature. As long as human nature has a proclivity for evil, perfect justice will be impossible, and its pursuit without institutional restraint is a prescription for tyranny. King, however, did not necessarily come to this conclusion.

Though King doubted the inevitability of progress, he maintained that it was still possible. Nevertheless, he tempered expectations that "the kingdom of God" would be established on earth through the action of men. See *Strength:* "Even though all progress is precarious, within limits real social progress can be made. Although man's moral pilgrimage may never reach a destination point on earth, his never-ceasing striving may bring him ever closer to the city of righteousness. And though the Kingdom of God may remain not yet as a universal reality in history, in the present it may exist in such isolated forms as in judgment, in personal devotion, and in some group life. 'The kingdom of God is in the midst of you'"(83-84). See also Smith and Zepp, *Search*, 138-40.

67. Carson, *The King Papers*, vol. 2, 136-37.

68. King, *Strength*, 74-75.

69. King, *Stride*, 106.

70. King, *Stride*, 207.

71. King, *Strength*, 96.

72. On King's orthodoxy in this regard, see *Strength*, 143.

73. King, *Strength*, 143.

74. King, *Stride*, 36.

75. King, *Stride*, 36.

76. See King, *Stride*, 205-11.

77. Although the political dangers of individualism first received serious attention in Tocqueville, I would argue that Tocqueville's conception of American liberalism, in its intrinsic elements, is far closer to that depicted in this paper than to that of contemporary liberalism. Indeed, part of the reason Tocqueville wrote *Democracy in America* is because he saw features in American liberalism that counteracted its more confused and dangerous continental form. Many of these features are identified in this paper. First, Tocqueville repeatedly stressed the critical role religion plays in preserving democratic liberty, and he favorably observed in America a largely unquestioned opinion that religion, operating primarily through nonpolitical channels, provides for and protects liberty. Similarly, he observed a shared opinion in America that liberty is to be

understood as obedience to the moral law. Finally he noted with approval a robust habit of public life expressed through political and civic associations.

78. West, *Vindicating,* 69.

79. For the Virginia Declaration of Rights of 1776, see Philip B. Kurland and Ralph Lerner, *The Founder's Constitution,* vol. 1 (Chicago: University of Chicago Press, 1987), 6-7.

80. Bellah sees a tension between these two traditions, which he identifies as the civil (Calvinist, classical) and utilitarian. *Broken Covenant,* 31. This was also the interpretation offered by Gordon S. Wood in *The Creation of the American Republic 1776-1789* (Chapel Hill: The University of North Carolina Press, 1969). While it is fair to distinguish between both elements in the minds of the founders, presenting them as dichotomous and contradictory is unfair. To the minds of the founders, both principles derived their origin from aspects of human nature, and thus both aspects needed to be provided for in a just regime.

81. John Locke, *Second Treatise,* chapter 2, par. 6. It is important to understand that whatever innovative (and even insidious) intentions the "esoteric" Locke may have had (and the evidence that he had such intentions is considerable), it was the "exoteric" Locke the founders used in defense of their liberty. On the esoteric Locke, see Leo Strauss, *Natural Right and History* (Chicago: The University of Chicago Press, 1953; paperback 1965), and Thomas Pangle, *The Spirit of Modern Republicanism: The Moral Vision of the American Founders and the Philosophy of Locke* (Chicago: The University of Chicago Press, 1988).

82. Samuel West, "On the Right to Rebel Against Governors," (1776) in Charles S. Hyneman and Donald Lutz, *American Political Writing During the Founding Era: 1760-1805,* vol. 1 (Indianapolis: Liberty Fund, 1983), 414-15.

83. John Locke, *The Second Treatise,* ch. 11, par. 135.

84. Hyneman and Lutz, *American Political Writing,* 416.

85. See Barry Allan Shain, *The Myth of American Individualism: The Protestant Origins of American Political Thought* (Princeton, N.J.: Princeton University Press, 1994). Shane, however, continues the tradition of contrasting a liberal and reformed protestant tradition in America. The argument in this chapter is that Americans assimilated both to one another, and saw no tension in that assimilation. See also Bellah, *Broken Covenant,* 16-35.

86. Locke, *The Second Treatise,* ch. 7, par. 77.

87. "Letter to Thomas Law" (13 June, 1814), in Mansfield, *Thomas Jefferson: Selected Writings,* 80.

88. Hyneman and Lutz, *American Political Writing,* 111-112.

89. Hyneman and Lutz, *American Political Writing,* 410.

90. Augustine, *The City of God,* trans. Henry Bettenson (London: Penguin Books 1984), 875.

91. See Aquinas, *Summa Theologica,* 1, q96, a4. Of course, there are significant differences between the political thought of Augustine and Aquinas on the one hand, and that of modern liberalism, even of the communitarian strain, on the other. But as Brian Tierney and others have persuasively demonstrated, medieval society already was

working out an understanding of natural rights in a way that was viewed as compatible with natural law, virtue, and the common good. See Brian Tierney, "Origins of Natural Rights Language: Texts and Contexts, 1150-1250," *History of Political Thought*, 10:4 (Winter 1989), 625-46. See also Richard Tuck, *Natural Rights Theories: Their Origin and Development* (Cambridge: Cambridge University Press, 1979). It is at least conceivable, if not likely, that the founders were as much influenced by this inherited medieval tradition as by the purported "possessive individualism" of Locke and Hobbes.

92. Aristotle, *The Politics*, trans. Carnes Lord (Chicago: The University of Chicago Press, 1984), 37 (125315-10).

93. Arstotle, *Politics*, trans. Carnes Lord, 41 (1245b15-25).

94. For a development of this argument see Harry V. Jaffa, *A New Birth of Freedom: Abraham Lincoln and the Coming of the Civil War* (Lanham, Md.: Rowman and Littlefield, 2000).

95. See Russell Kirk, *The Roots of American Order* (Washington, D.C.: Regnery Gateway, 1991), and J. G. A. Pocock, *The Machiavellian Moment: Florentine Political Thought and the Atlantic Republican Tradition* (Princeton, N.J.: Princeton University Press, 1975).

96. A fine study of the essentially modern features of American liberalism can be found in Pangle, *The Spirit of Modern Republicanism*. While Pangle ultimately gives a very "modern" reading of Locke, he concedes in his conclusion that this is not necessarily the founder's Locke. Unfortunately, he doesn't make clear the differences.

97. King, *Why*, 101.

98. King, *Where*, 62.

99. King, *Where*, 198.

Chapter Three

Racial Discrimination

Introduction

Although King's Dream was wide in scope, comprehending poverty and what he called "militarism," he is best remembered and celebrated for his efforts against racial discrimination. While the number of intricate moral, legal, constitutional, and historical issues involving racial discrimination in America is far too vast and complex for a comprehensive treatment in a single chapter, at least a general treatment is in order if we are to make sense of King's place in the context of the American principles to which he appealed. In treating this subject, it may be necessary to remind the reader that despite the nearly universal public approval the various Civil Rights Acts of the 1960s receive today, there existed considerable opposition to them at the time. And while much of that opposition was undoubtedly rooted in bigotry and racial prejudice, there were also valid Constitutional, political, and moral concerns about the nature and reach of civil rights legislation. To make matters even more difficult, King's position on discrimination is more complicated than is usually acknowledged in conservative circles. While aggressively opposing segregation and discrimination, King also supported preferential treatment under certain conditions. The purpose of this chapter is to summarize and then evaluate King's position on racial discrimination.

King's Ambiguous Position on Racial Discrimination

In 1962, King, "on behalf of the Negro citizenry of the United States of America in commemoration of the centennial of the Proclamation of Emancipation," submitted a striking letter to President Kennedy entitled "An Appeal to the President of the United States for National Rededication to the Principles of the Emancipation Proclamation."[1] In the appeal King attempted, unsuccessfully, to persuade President Kennedy to complete the work of emancipation by aggressive executive action. "We submit that the present state of the law with respect to state enforced segregation and discrimination based on race or color requires, at this juncture in history, catalytic enforcement of civil rights by a strong and morally committed Executive," he wrote. "The time has come, Mr. President, to let those dawn-like rays of freedom, first glimpsed in 1863, fill the heavens with the noonday sunlight of complete human dignity. Morality, and Man's dignity before Man and his God, demand this in this year Nineteen Hundred and Sixty-two."[2] According to King, "enforced segregation is but a new form of slavery—an enslavement of the human spirit and dignity rather than of the body." He also claimed that "the enacted legislation and judicially developed case law with respect to equal rights in America" requires "the fulfillment of the promise of emancipation." He admitted that this law was "subject to degrees of interpretation," but concluded that it was "in general weighted toward the elimination of any and all forms of state enforced segregation and discrimination."[3]

At least two points are notable about this "Appeal to the President." First, there is no mention of those forms of "private" discrimination that were eventually prohibited by Title 7 of the Civil Rights Act of 1964 (and *a fortiori*, no mention of the affirmative action which subsequently became part of the administrative enforcement mechanism of that act). The focus of the appeal is entirely upon state enforced segregation and discrimination in education, housing, and transportation. Second, the appeal is to the executive branch rather than the legislative branch. The implication is that segregation is already illegal or unconstitutional, and only requires vigorous enforcement. On a more pragmatic level, King was holding President Kennedy accountable for sweeping promises he had made during his campaign regarding civil rights, such as his promise to eliminate racial discrimination in federal housing programs "with a stroke of the pen." It is significant that both Kennedy and King would eventually turn to the legislative branch for redress.

Thus King argued that state enforced segregation and discrimination were already unconstitutional, and only required enforcement by the president. In support of this claim King relied on the Supremacy clause (Article 6) and the Equal Protection clause of the Fourteenth Amendment: "The requirements of the equal protection clause are simple and unequivocal. The Supreme Law of the Land forbids any state to enact separation of the races." According to him, "the simplicity of this Constitutional command pierces through the complexities and legalisms surrounding human rights. Direct and open state actions to compel segregation are forbidden. What a state cannot do directly it cannot do indirectly. There is no device, no legal technique, which is permissible to a state if the underlying reality is that the state by its action is recognizing, encouraging, or perpetuating segregation."[4] It is worth pointing out the broad ambiguity in these last terms "recognizing, encouraging, or perpetuating segregation." Perhaps King intended to include in this broad formulation forms of "private" discrimination that required state enforcement, though he is far from explicit on this point in the appeal.[5]

To support his interpretation of the Constitution, King relied on an impressive number of twentieth, century court decisions in education, housing, and transportation. He claimed that based on these decisions "*there is a plethora of law* entitling Negroes to protection against discriminatory treatment because of their race or color."[6]

After presenting evidence on the unconstitutionality of segregation, King concluded that the Constitution was not being enforced. Indeed, he went even further and cited specific examples of politicians like Governor Ross Barnett of Mississippi and Governor John Patterson of Louisiana who publicly flouted the law, declaring that they would not enforce anti-segregation rulings in their states. Thus King, himself accused of undermining respect for the law through civil disobedience, shrewdly made the counter charge that it was not *he* but the *segregationists* who were disobeying the law and thus undermining legitimacy. "All the judicial and legislative declarations of the rights of Negroes have not discouraged or prevented the nullification and frustration of the patiently won guarantees of human decency and fair play by many of the states of these United States. Public officials in the Southern States of our country have willfully disregarded, disobeyed, and flaunted the Constitution and statutes of the United States and the decisions of our highest court." Such blatant disregard for the law, according to King, posed a danger to democracy. "One of the basic premises on which our Government was organized and on which it continues to exist is a respect for and a belief in the rule of law. A truly democratic society does not close its eyes when a large number of states are consciously and deliberately pursuing a policy of defiance of its national laws."[7]

As an inducement to executive action, King quoted to Kennedy the 1960 platform of the Democratic Party: "It is the duty of the President to see that these rights are respected and the Constitution and laws as interpreted by the Supreme Court are faithfully executed."[8] He followed this quotation with numerous statements from Kennedy himself on the responsibility of the executive Office to lead the fight on behalf of Civil Rights and reminded him of his oath to "preserve, protect, and defend the Constitution of the United States." He cited statements by both Theodore Roosevelt and Woodrow Wilson on the expansive nature of Executive power, as well as federal statutes providing Executive enforcement power in civil rights.[9]

King's impressive display of astute Constitutional and legal analysis and his clever utilization of publicly pronounced commitments on civil rights by President Kennedy and the Democratic Party must have made President Kennedy at least a bit uncomfortable. But King's argument was not flawless. In particular, in his argument against segregation and discrimination he relied almost exclusively upon Supreme Court rulings—rather than legislative or executive action—for his interpretation of the Constitution. Moreover, the earliest case he cited was from 1917, and most of his evidence was based upon the

1954 *Brown* decision.¹⁰ The fact that the Court with few exceptions had consistently ruled in favor of segregation since 1883, most notoriously in *Plessy v. Ferguson,* raised serious questions about the legitimacy of *Brown*, especially after that decision was applied, *per curiam* to a host of segregation cases that fell far outside the scope of the Court's argument in *Brown*. As King himself noted in the "Appeal to the President," "The constitutional principles developed in the school segregation cases have been extended to other public facilities and institutions."¹¹ In his footnote, he cited court decisions ending segregation on public beaches,¹² public golf courses,¹³ and public parks.¹⁴

The *Brown* decision marked a significant victory over segregation forces, but at a considerable cost to Constitutional legitimacy. In large part this cost was the result, not of the Court's actual decision, but of the court's Constitutional argument in defense of that decision. In brief, Chief Justice Warren declared that evidence as to the original meaning of the fourteenth amendment was "at best . . . inconclusive." Instead of grappling directly with the court's constitutional argument in *Plessy v. Ferguson*, the court relied upon spurious studies in social science suggesting that segregated conditions cause a sense of inferiority in black children which affects their ability to learn.¹⁵ In *Plessy* Justice Brown had rejected this argument, declaring that any sense of inferiority caused by segregation was an artificial construction put on segregation by the segregated party, and not the result of anything in segregation itself. But the core of Justice Brown's argument in *Plessy* was that the equal protection clause of the Fourteenth Amendment was not intended to prohibit state enforced racial discrimination, that it allowed for racially segregated conditions under the police powers of the state, so long as those conditions are equal. Rather than challenge this argument directly, Chief Justice Warren—following NAACP legal strategy¹⁶—chose to exploit the "equality" requirement, with the result that the essential holding of *Plessy* that segregation is compatible with the equal protection clause has never been overturned. The way was then left open for forms of racial discrimination which do not "stigmatize" the party who is the object of discrimination—e.g., discrimination against whites in favor of racial minorities or other historically excluded groups.¹⁷ The story of the transformation in civil rights policy from a nondiscrimination model to racial preference model has been thoroughly documented.¹⁸ Less often observed is the way that Justice Warren's argument in *Brown* paved the way for the transformation. So did King.

Conservatives are most fond of quoting King's famous lines from "I Have a Dream": "I have a dream that my four little children will one day live in a nation where they will not be judged by the color of their skin but by the content of their character."¹⁹ Echoing this same principle in another place, he wrote that "Any program that elects all black candidates simply because they are black and rejects all white candidates simply because they are white is politically unsound and morally unjustifiable . . . The basic thing in determining the best candidate is not his color but his integrity."[20]

Each of King's remarks above might be regarded as a terse articulation of classical liberal principles in America. But conservatives should know that King was an advocate of preferential treatment.[21] Surprisingly, his most forthright statements supporting preferential treatment are found in *Why We Can't Wait*, which was published in 1964, the same year the Civil Rights Act was passed. There he argued that the nation "must incorporate in its planning some compensatory consideration for the handicaps [the Negro] has inherited from the past. It is impossible to create a formula for the future which does not take into account that our society has been doing something special *against* the Negro for hundreds of years."[22] Using words similar to Lyndon B. Johnson—words that have become common in the affirmative action debate—King called it "obvious that if a man is entered at the starting line in a race three hundred years after another man, the first would have to perform some impossible feat in order to catch up with his fellow runner."[23] He also cited India as an example of a nation making amends for historical discrimination by preferential treatment.[24]

King believed preferential treatment was a special case justified by the demand to eliminate poverty and by the legacy of slavery. "America must seek its own ways of atoning for the injustices she has inflicted upon her Negro citizens," he wrote. "I do not suggest atonement for atonement's sake or because there is need for self-punishment. I suggest atonement as the moral and practical way to bring the Negro's standards up to a realistic level." He viewed preferential treatment as a way to actualize equality for blacks in America. "In facing the new American dilemma, the relevant question is not: 'What more does the Negro want?' but rather: 'How can we make freedom real and substantial for our colored citizens? What just course will ensure the greatest speed and completeness? And how do we combat opposition and overcome obstacles arising from the defaults of the past?'"[25]

Thus preferential treatment was viewed by King as a *means* to realize the end of integration. For him the end would come when the proportion of racial representation in the work force was equal to the racial makeup of the community. Writing on "Operation Breadbasket," a boycott program designed to force businesses to hire minorities, King stated that "if a city has a 30 percent Negro population, then it is logical to assume that Negroes should have at least 30 percent of the jobs in any particular company, and jobs in all categories rather than only in menial areas, as the case almost always happens to be."[26] This argument is highly suggestive of the disparate impact theory of discrimination used to justify preferential treatment after 1964.[27]

King did not abandon color blindness as the desirable end in favor of permanent pluralist politics. And while he advocated racial solidarity he vehemently opposed "black power" for its emphasis on "power" at the expense of justice and love, its racially exclusive connotations, and ultimately for its despair in America.[28] He regularly repeated that the destiny of the Negro in America depended upon association and cooperation with white Americans. "In the final analysis the weakness of Black Power is its failure to see that the black man needs the white man and the white man needs the black man," he wrote. "However much we may try to romanticize the slogan, there is no separate black path to power that does not intersect white paths, and there is no separate white path to power and fulfillment, short of social disaster, that does not share that power with black aspirations for freedom and human dignity." He emphasized that cultural differences were not as significant as cultural similarities. "We are bound together in a single garment of destiny. The language, the cultural patterns, the material prosperity and even the food of America are an amalgam of black and white."[29] He reminded blacks of their American heritage.

> We are Americans . . . In spite of the psychological appeals of identification with Africa, the Negro must face the fact that America is now his home, a home that he helped to build through "blood, sweat and tears." Since we are Americans the solution to our problems will not come through seeking to build a separate black nation within a nation, but by finding that creative minority of the concerned from the oftentimes apathetic majority, and together moving toward that colorless power that we all need for security and justice.[30]

It is difficult to see how King was able to reconcile both of his positions on racial discrimination. On the one hand he maintained that the law prohibits "*the elimination of any and all forms of state enforced segregation or discrimination*" (emphasis mine).[31] He cited the Declaration of Independence and called for "all our citizens to rededicate themselves to those early precepts and principles of equality before the law."[32] On the other hand, he supported the kinds of preferential treatment outlined above, which constitute at the very least a "form" of discrimination. One way out of the difficulty might be to focus on the operative words "state enforced." Perhaps King was willing to allow for the continuation of "private" discrimination, and opposed affirmative action by the public sector? This conclusion, while it would resolve the difficulty, is not likely King's. All the evidence suggests that King supported Title 7 of the Civil Rights Act of 1964 (prohibiting racial discrimination in private employment) and that the preferential treatment plans he had in mind applied to the government as well as to the private sector. Another solution might be that King viewed preferential treatment as only a temporary measure to secure equality of result, after which the nondiscrimination model would be strictly enforced. But there is reason to believe that even temporary preferential treatment undermines the very changes needed to make the move to antidiscrimination by initiating an environment in which entitlement is based exclusively upon victim status determined by race group, thereby creating disincentives for achieving merit in the very group that most needs them to succeed.

King's ambiguity on racial discrimination raises a significant question: In what respects was King's position on racial discrimination a reflection of the declaration and Constitution, as he often claimed it was?

Racial Discrimination and American Principles

Before this question can be adequately treated, some comment must be made on the cycle of historiography on the Constitution and reconstruction. The first and thus most influential historians to chronicle reconstruction were progressive historians sympathetic to the southern interpretation on reconstruction. According to these historians, reconstruction, and especially the Civil War amendments, was a tragic conspiracy by northern Republicans to maintain indefinite control over southern states, in part by placing freedmen in positions of political power. In the progressive view, not only were the freedmen completely unfit for this responsibility, but the means used to secure them in power were wholly unconstitutional. Beginning in the 1930s a new school of revisionist historiography emerged which sharply challenged the progressive interpretation. The revisionist school pointed out both the commendable efforts of freedmen to secure their own economic, social, and political liberty, and the moderate but well intentioned efforts of the Civil War amendments to secure freedmen's rights.[33] The basic argument of this revisionist school was that "Reconstruction extended and completed the original Constitution by applying the principles of liberty and equality of the Declaration of Independence to the entire nation."[34] Finally, beginning in the 1960s a third school of Constitutional interpretation emerged, what Herman Belz has called the "neo-abolitionist" school.[35] According to this view, the original Constitution recognized and protected slavery without reservation, and was based upon a flawed view of human liberty based upon "possessive individualism." The Civil War amendments, in this interpretation, established a new Constitution on new principles of freedom and equality.[36]

In 1953 the Supreme Court delayed making a decision on the *Brown* case and instead requested reargument on the intent of the framers of the Civil War amendments. This further encouraged study of Reconstruction and raised expectations that the court's decision would be based upon some argument of original intent. The court's conclusion that discerning the intent of the framers of the Civil War amendments was "inconclusive at best" disappointed historians who believed they had discovered a strong original intent case for an antisegregation ruling. Jacobus ten Broek, one of the primary revisionist historians on the Civil War amendments remarked that it was "little short of remarkable that the Chief Justice [in *Brown*] should have cut himself off from these historical origins and purposes casually announcing . . . that 'at best they are inconclusive.'"[37]

As stated above, Chief Justice Warren's argument in *Brown* secured a laudable end by questionable means. Because the end received so much public support, at least in the north, there was little objection to the argument used to support it in this case. But beginning with *Brown* the Warren court embarked on a new era of judicial activism, handing down decisions affecting school prayer, pornography, criminal law, abortion, and a host of other issues that had far less popular support. These subsequent decisions challenged traditional conceptions of the separation of powers and raised significant questions about judicial legitimacy, especially among conservatives, that continue to this day.[38] The association of *Brown* with the era of judicial activism has forced a wedge into the conservative movement, forcing conservatives to either oppose the *Brown* decision and face appearing pro-segregation or racist, or support the *Brown* decision and thus appear supportive of judicial activism.

This conservative dilemma is not necessary, however. The revisionist school of historiography, if inconclusive, provides the most accurate interpretation of the events of reconstruction, establishing the basic continuity between the principles of the American founding and reconstruction, and lending Constitutional support for the initial demands of the Civil Rights era. In other words, a strong case can be made that racial segregation is a violation of the Fourteenth Amendment and of the principles of the declaration. Had the will of Congress to prohibit racial discrimination in civil rights, voting and segregation prevailed, the Civil Rights Revolution might never have been necessary.

The evidence for this argument is strong. According to Michael McConnell, "almost every Southern state passed laws during reconstruction guaranteeing equal access to transportation and public accommodations, and none mandated segregation by state law."[39] In fact, legal segregation, as C. Vann Woodward has shown, far from "an old and time-honored tradition," as its southern defenders claimed, developed well after reconstruction was over, probably in the late 1880s.[40] Congress also took action against the infamous "black codes" and against segregation in public transportation in the 1860s,[41] and banned segregation in public accommodations in the Civil Rights Act of 1875.[42] As Laurent B. Frantz has written, "for the first seven years after the fourteenth amendment was ratified, Congress believed it possessed, and actually exercised a power to protect the newly freed Negro from private aggression, as well as from 'state action' . . . The three implementing statutes [two Ku Klux Acts and Civil Rights Act of 1875] were sponsored and enacted by the same group in Congress, and to a large extent by the same individuals, as the amendment itself. They therefore amount to an almost contemporaneous construction of the amendment by its authors."[43]

As for public education, which was deliberately excluded from the Civil Rights Act of 1875, Michael McConnell has argued persuasively that "it is clear beyond peradventure that a very substantial portion of the Congress, including leading framers of the Amendment, subscribed to the view that school segregation violates the Fourteenth Amendment. At a minimum, therefore, the scholarly consensus must be corrected to admit that this interpretation is within the limited range of interpretations of the Amendment on originalist grounds."[44] Indeed, after extensive analysis of voting patterns subsequent to the passage of the Fourteenth Amendment, he asserts that it was the *preponderant* opinion of Congress during reconstruction that segregated schools were forbidden by the Fourteenth Amendment.[45] The argument against public school segregation became even stronger when public education, once reserved for a limited number of citizens, became a universal requirement. Chief Justice Warren relied upon this same observation in *Brown*. His error was his refusal to find an antidiscrimination intent in the equal protection clause of the Fourteenth Amendment.

According to McConnell, the Fourteenth Amendment "stood for the proposition that all citizens are entitled to the same civil rights, regardless of their race, color, nationality, social standing, or previous condition of servitude."[46] Public services were first an issue of common law, which required classifications to be reasonable. Courts differed on whether race could ever be a reasonable basis for classification, but there was considerable support for the argument that racial classification was invidious.[47] McConnell quotes a prominent railroad treatise written in 1857 that summarizes the law regarding "reasonable" discrimination. According to that treatise, while the company may refuse conveyance when means are full, or when persons persist in improper behavior, "it cannot make unreasonable discriminations between persons soliciting its means of conveyance, as by refusing them on account of personal dislike, their occupation, condition in life, complexion, race, nativity, political or ecclesiastical relations."[48]

After the Fourteenth Amendment these restrictions by public services "could be seen as discriminatory state action, thus transforming a question of common law into a constitutional issue."[49] In order to make this interpretation of the Fourteenth Amendment explicit it was codified in the Civil Rights Act of 1875. According to McConnell, the Civil Rights Act of 1866 protected the common law rights of contract, property, and security of the person. The Civil Rights Act of 1875 protected the common law rights of access to public inns and accommodations, amusements, common carriers, and the like. To its supporters, the constitutional basis for the two Acts was the same."[50]

Members of Congress defended the prohibition of racial segregation on several grounds: First, it was argued that the Fourteenth Amendment stands for "the proposition that all citizens are entitled to the same civil rights, regardless of race, color, nationality, social standing, or previous condition of servitude."[51] Second, it was pointed out that the common law provides "a peremptory rule opening the doors of inns to all travelers, without distinction, to the extent of authorizing not only an action but an indictment for the refusal to receive a traveler." Thus the civil rights bill "is only declaratory of existing law giving it the sanction of Congress." Third, to the objection that the Fourteenth Amendment only applies to "state action," proponents offered the "state failure" doctrine, replying that "If a state omits or neglects to secure the enforcement of equal rights it 'denies' the equal protection of the laws within the meaning of the fourteenth amendment."[52] Because state remedies were so ineffective, due to a variety of causes, federal remedies were necessary. Fourth, to the "separate but equal" argument, proponents of the bill offered a number of arguments around the same theme: segregation is unequal because it is an indignity. For example: the notion that "color and race are reasons for distinctions among citizens is a slave doctrine." Compelled by law, "segregation is an unjust and odious proscription." It is "an enactment of personal degradation" and a form of "legalized disability or inferiority," effectively a denial of citizenship and a return to slavery.[53] Fifth, to the distinction between the civil rights and social rights argument, defenders of the bill distinguished between the private sphere, such as one's home or friendships, and the civil sphere, such as public facilities in which "one has no option but to accept the company of others not of his own choosing."[54] Sixth, only such a bill, forbidding racial discrimination, would solve the many problems attendant upon a "separate but equal doctrine." The bill would provide a smoother transition into a post-slavery regime.[55] Finally, and perhaps most importantly, there was the argument that the Fourteenth Amendment represents the completion of the principles of the Declaration of Independence: "If it be asked what is the objection to classification by race . . . I reply . . . the objection to such a law on our part is that it would be legislation in violation of the fundamental principles of our nation."[56] As Rep. Alexander Stevens stated when the Fourteenth Amendment was introduced to the House: "It cannot be denied that this terrible struggle sprang from the vicious principles incorporated into the institutions of our country. Our fathers had been compelled to postpone the principles of their great Declaration, and wait for their full establishment for a more propitious time. That time ought to be present now."[57] Stevens then proceeded to introduce section 1 of the Amendment, which merits quoting at length:

> I can hardly believe that any person can be found who will not admit that every one of these provisions is just. They are all asserted, in some form or other, in our DECLARATION or organic law. But the Constitution limits only the action of Congress, and is not a limitation on the States. This

amendment supplies that defect, and allows Congress to correct the unjust legislation of the States, so far that the law which operates on one man shall operate *equally* upon all. Whatever law punishes a white man for a crime shall punish the black man precisely in the same way and to the same degree. Whatever law protects the white man shall afford "equal" protection to the black man . . . These are great advantages over their present codes . . . I need not enumerate these partial and oppressive laws. Unless the Constitution should restrain them those States will all, I fear, keep up this discrimination, and crush to death the hated freedmen.[58]

As suggested in his last line, Representative Stephens understood that "equal protection" means "no discrimination."

The courts also supported this reading of the equal protection, at least initially. In the first Supreme Court decision ever on segregation, *Railroad Co. v. Brown*,[59] decided on the eve of the Civil Rights Act of 1875, the court struck down the policy of segregation by a commuter railway and ordered it to desegregate. Although the court's decision did not reach the equal protection clause of the Fourteenth Amendment, it relied upon a similar clause attached to an authorization for the Alexandria and Washington Railroad Company to extend its line into Washington D.C., which stated "that no person shall be excluded from the cars on account of color."[60] According to the court, the "separate but equal" argument of the railroad company was "an ingenious attempt to evade compliance with the obvious meaning of the statute."[61]

Michael McConnell points out the significance of this case, in which the court found the antisegregation intent of the statute "obvious" and the counterargument "ingenious." It used the term "discrimination" three times as embracing segregation. The court specifically recalled "the temper of Congress at the time" and described it as "manifest" that Congress would not have allowed the railroad to extend its line if it were going to segregate cars. "This was the only time during reconstruction that the Supreme Court would address the issue of segregation, and the opinion in *Brown* reinforces the conclusion of the 1875 Act debates: that, contrary to the conventional wisdom, during the brief period between the end of the Civil War and the end of Reconstruction segregation was widely considered discriminatory and unjust."[62]

And in *Strauder v. West Virginia* (1880), holding that state exclusion of blacks on jury violated rights guaranteed by the Fourteenth Amendment, Justice William Strong stated that "the spirit and meaning of the [fourteenth] amendment . . . is to be construed liberally, to carry out the purposes of its framers . . . What is [the fourteenth amendment] but declaring that the law in the States shall be the same for the black as for the white; that all persons, whether colored or white, shall stand equal before the laws of the States, and, in regard to the colored race, for whose protection the amendment was primarily designed, *that no discrimination shall be made against them by law because of their color?"* "The words of the amendment, it is true, are prohibitory," he continued, "but they contain a necessary implication of positive immunity or right, most valuable to the colored race—*the right to exemption from unfriendly legislation against them distinctly as colored,* exemption from legal discriminations, implying inferiority in civil society, lessening the security of their enjoyment of the rights which others enjoy, and discriminations which are steps towards reducing them to the condition of a subject race."[63]

This argument was also supported by numerous state court decisions of the time. In *Board of Education v. Tinnon* (1881) Judge N. T. Stephens of the Franklin County District Court struck down the action of an Ottawa school board requiring segregated schools, holding that it was "a rule plainly discriminating against the relator on account of his race or color, pointing out himself and others of his class, by reason of their color, as not being eligible to school privileges with white children." He rejected the argument that segregation laws "equally" restricted the liberty of white and black children, calling it "evident . . . to every mind" in the purpose of the rule and Supreme Court's construction of that rule that "State of Kansas had no power to confer authority upon the School Board of the city of Ottawa to make the order complained of. The rule itself is a violation of the rights conferred by the Fourteenth Amendment, and is inoperative and void."[64] The Kansas Supreme Court upheld the ruling. While refusing to rule on the Constitutional question, Judge Valentine held that the intention of the Kansas statutes was "to abolish all distinctions on account of race, or color, or previous condition of servitude, and to make all persons absolutely equal before the law."[65] Michael McConnell further notes that "with the exception of a New York case in 1883,[66] no court in any other Northern state upheld school segregation after 1874." He follows this statement with a host of evidence that segregated schools were considered, *ipso facto,* to be in violation of equality.[67]

If it is true that the Fourteenth Amendment contained such large implications for antidiscrimination/segregation, then *a fortiori* the same must be true for the Fifteenth Amendment where the prohibition against discrimination is written plainly into the text.[68] This fact alone stands as a testimony against sometimes brutal southern obstruction through Jim Crow laws and intense psychological and even physical coercion.[69] King had little difficulty exposing the hypocrisy of these discriminatory practices. "It is surely ironical," he said, "that the states which have labored so diligently to keep the Negro masses ignorant through inferior segregated education now require 'literacy' as a prerequisite for voting. You hardly need much formal training to know who as sheriff will treat you like a human being and who will crack your skull!"[70]

Thus, it can be said again with respect to voting rights that if the law had been adequately implemented the "Mississippi Summer," the Civil Rights Acts of 1957 and 1965 and Selma might not have been necessary. But by 1965 only

26,000 of 450,000 eligible Negro voters in Mississippi had been permitted to register, and conditions were not much better in other states in the south.[71] King was always a strong advocate of voting rights for Negroes. One of the first things he did as pastor at Dexter Avenue Baptist Church, before the Montgomery boycott, was to establish a "Social and Political Action Committee," which was charged with the responsibility of "keeping the congregation intelligently informed concerning the social, political and economic situation" as well as keeping before them "the necessity of being registered voters." He further stipulated that "Every member of Dexter must be a registered voter." During elections the committee was required to "sponsor forums and mass meetings to discuss the relative merits of candidates and the major issues involved."[72] He called the right to vote "the foundation stone for political action." It would give Negroes the power "to vote out of office public officials who bar the doorway to decent housing, public safety, jobs and decent integrated education." "It is now obvious," he said, "that the basic elements so vital to Negro advancement can only be achieved by seeking redress from government at local, state, and federal levels. To do this the vote is essential."[73]

So how did so much good intention go awry? Certainly a large part of the explanation rests in the understandable intransigence of many in the South to implement the new legislation which required such a radical change from their previous way of life. But one can also look to the Supreme Court. In the *Civil Rights Cases* (1883) Justice Joseph Bradley ruled for the court that the Civil Rights Act of 1875 was unconstitutional because it was too broadly worded. The Fourteenth Amendment, according to Bradley, only provides for remedial or "corrective" legislation, not "primary and direct" legislation. (He conceded that the Thirteenth Amendment was broad enough for "primary and direct" legislation, but he denied that racial discrimination in public services had any relation to slavery or involuntary servitude.) He thus limited the application of the amendment: "It is state action of a particular character that is prohibited. Individual invasion of individual rights is not the subject matter of the amendment." Thus, the Fourteenth Amendment only allowed "appropriate legislation for correcting the effects of such prohibited state law and state acts, and thus to render them effectually null, void, and innocuous. This is the legislative power conferred on Congress, and this is the whole of it."[74] He expressed legitimate concern that the power exercised under the act would serve to completely undermine state authority. "If this legislation is appropriate for enforcing the prohibitions of the amendment," he wrote, "it is difficult to see where it is to stop. Why may not congress, with equal show of authority, enact a code of laws for the enforcement and vindication of all rights of life, liberty, and property?"

But Bradley's argument contained notable weaknesses. First, the Civil Rights Act of 1875, like the Act of 1866, did not propose to legislate on all matters under traditional state authority. It only proposed to legislate on matters now included under federal authority: racial discrimination in civil rights. Bradley wrote: "Positive rights and privileges are undoubtedly secured by the fourteenth amendment; but they are secured by way of prohibition against state laws and state proceedings affecting those rights and privileges." *Thus, according to Bradley's argument even the Civil Rights Act of 1866 would be unconstitutional.* But virtually every scholar on Constitutional law agrees that the Civil Rights Act of 1866 was intended to be part of the Fourteenth Amendment, and that *the Civil Rights Act of 1866 was not a restriction on state action, but was a provision of protection for civil rights.*

Second, Bradley's argument does not necessarily follow from the language of the Amendment: "No State shall . . . deny to any person within its jurisdiction the equal protection of the laws." Isn't state *inaction* against violations of civil rights equal to a "denial" of equal protection? The legislative history seems to bear out this interpretation. As McConnell writes, "The Equal Protection Clause deals with 'sins of omission as well as commission,' in the words of Representative Lawrence."[75] Even more, precedent strongly suggested that state failure to act was a form of state action subject to Congressional remedy.[76]

The indefatigable Justice John Harlan of *Plessy* fame wrote a biting dissent in the *Civil Rights Cases*. Harlan relied primarily on the Thirteenth Amendment for justification of the Civil Rights Act. According to him the prohibition of slavery included "burdens and disabilities which constitute badges of slavery and servitude." Such was the justification for the Civil Rights Act of 1866, and such was the case at hand. Harlan also responded to the argument that this gave Congress unlimited power: "Congress has not, in these matters, entered the domain of state control and supervision," he wrote. "It does not assume to prescribe the general conditions and limitations under which inns, public conveyances, and places of public amusement shall be conducted or managed. It simply declares in effect that since the nation has established universal freedom in this country for all time, there shall be no discrimination, based merely race or color, in respect of the legal rights in the accommodations and advantages of public conveyances, inns, and places of public amusement."[77]

Harlan also considered the act under the Fourteenth Amendment. Here he argued that the amendment required at the very least "exemption from race discrimination in respect of any civil right belonging to citizens of the white race in any state." Harlan pointed out that if the Fifteenth Amendment went so far as to prohibit all racial discrimination in a political right like suffrage, then surely the Fourteenth Amendment would cover such discrimination in civil rights. "It can hardly be claimed that exemption from race discrimination, in respect of civil rights, against those to whom state citizenship was granted by the nation, is any less for the colored race a new constitutional right, derived from and secured by the national constitution, than is exemption from such discrimination in the exercise of the elective franchise." "It cannot be that the latter is an attribute of national citizenship," he continued, "while the other is not essential in national citizenship, or fundamental in state citizenship."

Justice Harlan concluded that "Citizenship in this country necessarily imports equality of civil rights among citizens of every race in the same state. It is fundamental in American citizenship that, in respect of such rights, there shall be no discrimination by the state, or its officers, or by individuals, or corporations exercising public functions or authority, against any citizen because of his race or previous condition of servitude."[78]

Hardly a better case can be made for the Civil War amendments as a completion and realization of the principles of the founding. Indeed, the degree to which the regime strayed from its earlier commitment to civil rights was exemplified in *Plessy v. Ferguson (1896)*,[79] which decided not only that non-state discrimination was beyond federal remedy but also that *even state required racial discrimination was constitutional*. Despite the contradictions in the argument, the position would have been unthinkable to those who framed the Fourteenth Amendment.[80] As McConnell writes, "At issue in the 1875 Act debates was whether federal law could *forbid* private railroads and other common carriers to segregate their passengers by race. By the time of *Plessy v. Ferguson* in 1896, the issue was whether state law could *compel* segregation."[81] "The *Plessy* Court's position was more extreme even than that taken by the leading opponents of desegregation in 1875. In fact Plessy could have used the words of the *opponents* of the 1875 Act to support his attack on Jim Crow laws."[82]

From Reconstruction to the Civil Rights Revolution, and Beyond

Thus a strong case can be made that the primary demands of early civil rights activists, as exemplified in King's "Appeal to the President," were grounded in the text and intention of the Civil War amendments, and to the principles as expressed in the Declaration of Independence. In this respect they constituted a revolution in the literal sense, that is, a return to first principles. But perhaps the civil rights revolution also went beyond the demands and expectations of the Reconstruction Congress and the Founding in two ways: First, by prohibiting racial discrimination in private employment, and second—and more significantly—in the subsequent move from equal opportunity to equal result in the implementation of antidiscrimination law. Especially in this last respect the civil rights revolution constituted revolution in the more colloquial sense of a radical transformation in original principles.

So-called private discrimination raises difficult questions for liberal democracies by setting competing liberal values against one another. On the one hand is the value of individual rights, which implies that discrimination among individuals should be based upon qualities intrinsically related to the object (such as merit) rather than upon arbitrary characteristics like race or ethnicity.[83] On the other hand are the values of private property and freedom of association, which allow individuals to determine their friendships and other personal and professional associations for themselves based upon their own determinations of value, so long as these determinations do not prohibit others from forming similar associations.

This conflict might be resolved by recalling from the last chapter that freedom, including the freedom of association, must be understood within the context of the natural law, and it is quite clear from the natural law that considerations of race in most decisions constitutes a violation of justice, because justice requires that discrimination among persons be properly suited to a reasonable object or cause. St. Thomas Aquinas only summarized Christian teaching when he argued that "respect of persons" (by which he meant granting a particular favor or privilege to someone regardless of merit) is the opposite of respect for cause, is a violation of natural distributive justice and therefore a sin. "For the equality of distributive justice consists in allotting various things to various persons in proportion to their personal dignity. Accordingly, if one considers that personal property [i.e., related attribute of the person] by reason of which the thing allotted to a particular person is due him, this is respect not of the person but of the cause." He used Scripture to support his case. "Hence a gloss on Eph. vi. 9, *There is no respect of persons with God* (Vulg.,—Him), says that *a just judge regards causes, not persons*." And then he used an illustration to make his point. "For instance if you promote a man to a professorship on account of his having sufficient knowledge, you consider the due cause, not the person; but if, in conferring something on someone, you consider in him not the fact that what you give him is proportionate or due him, but the fact that he is this particular man (e.g., Peter or Martin), then there is respect of the person, since you give him something not for some cause that renders him worthy of it, but simply because he is this person.[84]

A reasonable inference from these principles is that racial discrimination is wrong. Indeed, using language that sounds decidedly modern, Aquinas suggests that discrimination not based upon cause violates personal dignity. Thus Senator Frelinghuysen, using a term that was common in the debates on the Civil Rights Act of 1875, called segregation by law "an enactment of personal degradation."[85] King, a student of personalist philosophy, also described segregation in these terms. As he wrote in his famous "Letter from Birmingham Jail," "Any law that uplifts human personality is just. Any law that degrades human personality is unjust. All segregation statutes are unjust because segregation distorts the soul and damages the personality."[86]

But the natural law must also be properly understood within the context of the common good, and the common good does not require the suppression of all vices. Citing St. Isidore, Thomas argues that human laws should be "possible both according to nature, and according to the customs of the country." Because the majority are not perfect in virtue, human laws forbid "only the more grievous vices, from which it is possible for the majority to abstain; and chiefly those that hurt others, without the prohibition of which human society could not be maintained."[87] A strong case can be made that racial discrimination is such a vice, harming both individuals and the community, especially as it was practiced prior to 1964. Before then, employers—especially in the south—were heavily pressured by custom and threats of violence to discriminate based on race. This was contrary to their economic interest, which would recommend employing the most capable or most cost-effective candidates irrespective of race. Federal force was necessary to break the back of this force and to free employers to make reasonable decisions based upon merit. But enforcement against racial discrimination is difficult because intent to discriminate can be very difficult to prove, with the result that enforcement agencies, the courts, and the executive branch all became complicit in rejecting the original statutory intention of the Civil Rights Act of 1964, which envisioned the prosecution of individual acts of overt intentional discrimination, in favor of a "systematic discrimination" approach which based evidence of discrimination on statistical racial disparities and which sought remedies in the form of preferential treatment. Thus present enforcement of laws against racial discrimination place an immense burden on the public and private system in the form of "transaction costs, information costs, agency costs, moral hazard costs, and political costs."[88] But even if racial discrimination were pursued on a case by case basis, based on the individual/intentional discrimination model, the costs would be considerable. Nevertheless, America cannot escape its long history of racial discrimination, and this fact must factored into laws against discrimination. Our nation has made the judgment that racial discrimination is so offensive that even discrimination by private businesses, despite difficulty of enforcement and unwieldy administrative and efficiency costs, ought not be tolerated; and this judgment is not forcefully contested, suggesting people's natural sense that it is just.

But if a strong moral and practical argument can be made for prohibiting racial discrimination by employers, the Constitutional argument is weak. Prior to 1964 many states had already prohibited employment discrimination and established FEPC-like commissions to enforce the laws.[89] But where does Congress have the power to pass such a law? Clearly it is not included in either the text or intention of the Fourteenth Amendment, and the expansive reading of the commerce clause which was used to justify Title 7—a reading largely inherited from the New Deal Supreme Court—obliterates the Constitutional distinction between federal and state powers and threatens the distinction between public and private space.[90] Nevertheless, by 1964 opposition to this expansive reading of the commerce clause was a lost cause, especially in the sensitive area of race relations in the 1960s. The preferable approach would have been a Constitutional amendment, or the expansion of state enforcement to those states where it did not yet exist, but these solutions were too slow for the increasingly aggressive demands of the civil rights establishment for results. These same demands, however, eventually led to a more radical transformation of civil rights policy in the form of preferential treatment.

According to Andrew Kull, in "the 1840's to the 1960's, the most profound claim of those who fought the institution of racial segregation was that the government had no business sorting people by the color of their skin, regardless of the quality with which they were treated. By some point in the mid-1960's—the enactment of the Civil Rights Act of 1964 makes a convenient benchmark—this once-radical idea had become part of the government liberal consensus of American political life." Then a change occurred in the argument and demands of civil rights advocates: "But the achievement at long last of 'equality before the law' revealed a harsh truth that the long struggle for civil rights had tended to obscure: the fact that guarantees of legal equality would be inadequate to redress the inequality of condition afflicting black Americans as a group. Almost at once, the field of the debate shifted; and the older civil-rights ideal has since stood as the most widely voiced objection to the race-conscious methods by which, in the post-civil rights era, a fuller measure of equality has generally been sought."[91]

Hugh Graham's lengthy study on the civil rights era largely supports Kull's argument. According to Graham, as late as 1960 arguments on behalf of preferential treatment were inconceivable. "Classic nondiscrimination was itself a radical proposition in 1961, especially in the segregated South," he wrote.[92] "The most strident demands of the Americans for Democratic Action, the NAACP, the National Urban League, the Congress of Racial Equality, the Political Action Committee of the AFL-CIO—indeed the entire spectrum captured under the umbrella of the Leadership Conference for Civil Rights—called consistently for racially neutral anti-discrimination."[93] But by 1963, "a minority of frustrated liberal reformers" was beginning to question the classic nondiscrimination model based on invidious and injurious acts of racial prejudice. Instead they advocated a "newly evolving view of institutional racism" for which "individual intent was at best a secondary consideration." Under the institutional racism model, "employment discrimination should be defined and attacked statistically as a differential . . . act of prejudice," and its measure should be "simply the gap between the white and minority employment rates." This result-oriented approach, Graham wrote, "begged the important and complicated questions of employability and motivation and fairness" that the traditional model was intended to address. According to him,

> This presumptive new definition in turn rested on an implicit normative theory of proportional representation in the work force, absent discrimination that institutional racism had brought into the employment structure. The chief political weakness of this theory was that it violated the American creed that rights inhered in individuals rather than in groups, and that immutable factors like race and ethnicity should be irrelevant as employment criteria. Its chief political strength lay in its practical utility as an implicit and self-justifying formula for equity.[94]

Graham pointed out four transformations that were necessary for implementation of the group rights model. First, the definition of discrimination would have to be transferred from an *intent* standard to an *effects* standard. Second, "an evolving effects standard would have to be based on a statistical distribution of jobs and rewards," which would require "a comprehensive, national data base to demonstrate such distributions." Third, "such a statistical demonstration would then require an appropriate model of fair distribution against which to compare actual discriminations for rendering judgments." Finally, authority would have to be given "to require specific measures of hiring and promotion sufficient to rectify discrepancies with the model." According to Graham, the Civil Rights Act of 1964 deliberately excluded *each* of these steps.[95] His work chronicles the ways in which the enforcement arm of the federal bureaucracy and the courts conspired to circumvent the text and intention of that act.

As pointed above, King himself supported the move to preferential treatment, even as he supported the classic antidiscrimination principles in the Civil Rights Act of 1964. Numerous individuals have attempted to defend preferential treatment on historical, constitutional, and theoretical grounds. James E. Jones, Jr., for example, has combined all of these arguments.[96] Building on the research of Eric Schnapper, he concludes that the framers of the Fourteenth Amendment could not have intended to prohibit affirmative action. Schnapper pointed to reconstruction laws providing exclusive privileges and protections to blacks and passed simultaneously with the Fourteenth Amendment as evidence that the framers of that amendment did not intend to prohibit affirmative action.[97] One can question Schnapper's account on a number of points, however. First, the Fourteenth Amendment is a limitation on states, while the freedmen's bills were national. Second, most examples he uses provide for "freedmen," not blacks. While freedmen were necessarily black, the primary object of the legislation was to help newly freed slaves, not blacks simply. Most of the legislation he cites provides for "refugees" (i.e., whites) also. Third, the "affirmative action" provisions were quite different from today's regime of affirmative action. Freedmen themselves had been subject to enormous burdens under slavery, and the war had wreaked havoc on the economy. Thus assistance to the freedmen was justified on grounds of restitution and emergency power. This can hardly be the case for today's affirmative action policies, which have no immediate relation to slavery and fail to assist those who are most in need.[98] Finally, Schnapper wants to use his model to apply to a number of court cases on affirmative action; but the proper authority for those decisions should be statutory law, not the constitution, and it is clear the statutes in question were meant to prohibit all race based classifications, including affirmative action.[99]

Jones distinguishes between two justifications for preferential treatment. First, it can be part of prospective relief in an adjudication process against a defendant found guilty of discrimination. Second, it can be part of an executive or legislative program to address a perceived problem. But Jones' arguments fail to persuade. In the first instance, Jones neglects the long established principle of law that prospective relief may not be required at the expense of innocent third parties. In remedial affirmative action plans otherwise qualified individuals are being harmed (by being denied employment, benefits, etc., due to their race) for the sake of individuals who have never proven that they have been harmed. This presents enormous problems for the principle of "equal protection of the law." Moreover, by pointing to executive and legislative programs of preferential treatment he is only begging the question. What Jones completely fails to discuss, or even mention, are the explicit statutory provisions in the Civil Rights Act of 1964 which first, prohibit racial discrimination,[100] second, prohibit "preferential treatment to any individual or group because of race . . . on account of an imbalance which may exist" in the workforce,[101] and finally, define the prohibited discrimination as "intentional."[102] Still, Jones accurately points out that even the Republican administrations of Nixon, Reagan, and Bush, especially the latter two who offered token lip service against affirmative action, continued the affirmative action policies of their predecessors.[103] But in pointing this out, Jones only proves the complicity of politicians in continuing to thwart the demands of the Fourteenth Amendment, the Civil Rights Act of 1964, and popular opinion. Finally, Jones makes a weak attempt to prove that preferential treatment is required to meet demographic changes in the workforce. Because future jobs will be high-tech, he argues, and because the larger proportion of the workforce will increasingly be dominated by minorities, it is necessary to prepare minorities for jobs through preferential treatment. Again, Jones begs the question. Perhaps preferential treatment is the very thing that will prevent minorities from securing the skills, education, and training necessary to compete in the modern workforce? But perhaps the most revealing and most troubling aspect of Jones' argument is his denial that there now exists or ever existed in America a principle of nondiscrimination. Moreover, he bases this opinion on Justice Taney's opinion in *Dred Scot!* Jones' treatment is disingenuous, and illustrates the kind of logical gymnastics required to justify preferential treatment to most Americans.

There can be little question that preferential treatment as it is practiced today sharply contradicts traditional American liberal principles. If America ever formally embraces the logical premises of preferential treatment that equal protection requires proportional representation of racial or ethnic classes, this will mark a radical shift from the individual rights principles on which America is based to a group-rights model. Such a move will constitute a retreat from natural rights liberalism, not progress, resulting in a balkanization of politics and a return to an order in which jobs, benefits, etc., are politically determined by arbitrary characteristics like race or birth rather than by individual ability and initiative.[104] But despite this departure from the letter and intent of the Civil Rights Act, nondiscrimination continues to be the nation's professed principle, as manifested in the Supreme Court's ambivalence over racial "quotas" and its multitiered standard of judgment. Since the New Deal the "rational basis" test has been applied to economic legislation, while a "strict scrutiny" test has been applied to issues of racial discrimination. According to the principle of strict scrutiny racial distinctions must be "narrowly tailored" (that is, necessary to accomplish its purpose) to achieve a "compelling" government interest. While this higher standard implies that the Constitution is not technically "colorblind"—there may be certain circumstances (e.g., law enforcement) in which considerations of race are legitimate—such circumstances are presumably rare.[105] The difficulty has been determining what factors constitute a "compelling" government interest and "narrowly tailored," but it is reasonable to believe that preferential treatment should be excluded.

Conclusion

In 1963, undoubtedly due to Kennedy's own hesitancy to act under a presumptive executive enforcement power, King turned from the executive to the legislative branch for recourse to the problems of segregation and discrimination which plagued the nation. This turn explains the March on Washington. Recall the first demand of the march: "A comprehensive civil rights bill guaranteeing access to public accommodations, adequate and integrated education, protection of the right to vote," and "better housing." The last demand was for an act "barring discrimination in all employment." Due in part to King's heroic leadership, these demands were eventually recognized in Title 2 and Title 7 of the Civil Rights Act of 1964, the Voting Rights Act of 1965, and the Fair Housing Act of 1968. These acts, along with the *Brown* decision, constitute the core achievements of the Civil Rights Revolution of the 1960s. Each of them represented an effort to eliminate racial discrimination from America and thus to realize further the principles of the declaration. With the possible exception of Title 7, most of these acts were long overdue, supported as they were by strong moral and Constitutional precedent.

But while King articulated a quintessential declaration of the traditional American creed when he expressed hope that his children would be judged by the content of their character, and not the color of their skin, he failed to apply its demanding requirements to his own policy recommendations. While he continued to emphasize the importance of character in achieving equality and refused to subsume it under permanent racial categories (like the black power movement), his advocacy of preferential treatment left a legacy of confusion over race relations in America that remains to this day. It is difficult to see how King could consistently both oppose racial discrimination and support it in the form of racial preferences. If racial discrimination "in all forms" is wrong, as he often stated, then it must always be wrong, and not just wrong when applied against blacks or other minorities, or as a temporary measure. As he often repeated, "the end represents the means in process and the ideal in the making. In other words, we cannot believe, or cannot go with the idea that the end justifies the means because the end is pre-existent in the means."[106] The history of affirmative action tends to bear out King's argument, as the "temporary" accommodation to racial discrimination in the form of preferential treatment moves toward becoming a permanent system of proportional representation.[107] In his zeal to realize his Dream more quickly, King may have approved of a means which ultimately threatens the Dream's full realization. It was this same zeal which caused King to push for the elimination of poverty. Whether he made the same mistake will be the subject of the next chapter.

Notes

1. Martin Luther King, Jr., *A Martin Luther King Treasury* (Yonkers, New York: Education Heritage, 1964), 290-348. It's not likely that King composed this letter by himself. For the legal analysis he was surely assisted by some of his aids. Nevertheless, there are elements of the letter that reflect King's distinctive style.

2. *Treasury*, 294.

3. *Treasury*, 296.

4. *Treasury*, 297.

5. See *Shelly v. Kraemer*, 334 U.S. 1, 68 S. Ct. 836 (1948) (prohibiting state enforcement of restrictive covenants) and *Burton v. Willimington Parking Authority*, 365 U.S. 715 (1961) (prohibiting a privately owned restaurant in a publicly owned parking garage from discriminating against blacks) in which the court used the "state action" doctrine of the Fourteenth Amendment to prohibit "private" forms of discrimination.

Prior to the Civil Rights Act of 1964, however, the court never extended these rulings to segregated lunch counters and restaurants.

6. *Treasury*, 304.

7. *Treasury*, 305.

8. *Congressional Quarterly*, Weekly Report, 22 July 1960 Supp., 1301; quoted in King, *Treasury*, 308. Executive power is provided when any "insurrection, domestic violence, unlawful combination, or conspiracy" (1) So hinders the execution of the laws of that state, and of the United States within the state, that any part or class of its people is deprived of a right, privilege, immunity, or protection named in the Constitution and secured by law, and the constituted authorities of that state are unable, fail, or refuse to protect that right, privilege, or immunity, or to give that protection. (2) Opposes or obstructs the execution of the law of the United States or impedes the course of justice under those laws.

9. Title 10, sections 332 and 333; quoted in King, *Treasury*, 314.

10. In *Buchanan v. Warley* the court struck down a racially restrictive zoning ordinance as a violation of the Fourteenth Amendment. 245 U.S. 60 (1917).

11. King, "An Appeal to the President of the United States for National Rededication to the Principles of the Emancipation Proclamation," in *Treasury*, 300.

12. *Mayor and City Council of Baltimore City v. Dawson*, 350 U.S. 877 (1955).

13. *Holmes v. City of Atlanta, Ga.*, 350 U.S. 879 (1956).

14. *Detiege v. New Orleans City Park Improvement Association*, 358 U.S. 54 (1958). Surprisingly, he did not mention in this place the court's decision ending transportation which came out of the Montgomery bus boycott and which explicitly cited *Brown* as evidence in its favor. 352 U.S. 903 (1956). He does mention the *Browder* decision later. *Treasury*, 304.

15. 347 U.S. 483 (1954), *Treasury*, 489.

16. The NAACP strategy for overturning *Plessy* relied upon the argument that separate cannot be equal. This argument succeeded a number of important court decisions prior to *Brown*, including *Missouri ex rel. Gaines v. Canada*, 305 U.S. 337 (1938); *Sweatt v. Painter*, 339 U.S. 629 (1950); and *McLaurin v. Oklahoma State Regents*, 339 U.S. 637 (1950).

17. See Edward J. Erler, "Sowing the Wind: Judicial Oligarchy and the Legacy of Brown v. Board of Education," *Harvard Journal of Law and Public Policy* 8:3 (Summer 1985), 400-413.

18. See, for example, Graham, *Civil Rights*; Herman Belz, *Equality Transformed: A Quarter-Century of Affirmative Action* (New Brunswick: Transaction Publishers, 1991); and Andrew Kull, *The Color-Blind Constitution* (Cambridge, Mass.: Harvard University Press, 1992). Preferential treatment continues to be widely encouraged by the federal government through the Department of Education's Office of Civil Rights (grant money); the Small Business Administration (contracts); the EEOC (contract compliance); the Department of Labour's Office of Federal Contract Compliance; highway construction set-asides; race-exclusive and sex-exclusive grant programs; federal government hiring; and litigation through the Justice Department's Civil Rights Division..

19. See, for example, Dinesh D'Souza's chapter "A Dream Deferred: Who Be-

trayed Martin Luther King, Jr.?" in *The End of Racism*, 163-200.
20. D'Souza, *The End of Racism*, 49.
21. See Dyson, *I May Not Get There with You*, 22-29.
22. King, *Why*, 134.
23. King, *Why*, 134. See Johnson, Commencement Address at Howard University: "To Fulfill These Rights," 4 June 1965: "You do not take a person who, for years, has been hobbled by chains and liberate him, bring him to the starting line of a race and then say, 'you are free to compete with all the others,'" and still justly believe that you have been completely fair." See also Whitney Young, *To Be Equal* (New York: McGraw Hill, 1964), 22-23.
24. King, *Why*, 134-35.
25. King, *Why*, 135.
26. King, *Where*, 144.
27. The most comprehensive history and criticism of this theory is Belz, *Equality*.
28. "Beneath all the satisfaction of a gratifying slogan, Black Power is a nihilistic philosophy born out of the conviction that the Negro can't win. It is, at bottom, the view that American society is so hopelessly corrupt and enmeshed in evil that there is no possibility of salvation from within." King, *Where*, 44.
29. King, *Where*, 53.
30. King, *Where*, 58.
31. King, "Appeal," in *Treasury*, 296.
32. King, "Appeal," in *Treasury*, 292.
33. The locus classicus of progressive historiography on reconstruction is William A. Dunning, *Reconstruction, Political and Economic, 1865-1877* (New York: Harper & Row, 1907). Dunning argued that Reconstruction was in effect a conspiracy by white Republicans to maintain indefinite control over southern states, in part by placing freedmen in positions of political power. For a good summary of the cycles of reconstruction scholarship see the introduction to Eric Foner, *A Short History of Reconstruction* (New York: Harper & Row Publishers, 1990). See also Belz, *Abraham Lincoln*, 187-216.
34. Belz, *Abraham Lincoln*, 209. In the field of Constitutional law, the foundations for the revisionist interpretation were laid before the Brown decision. See for example Howard J Graham, "The Early Antislavery Backgrounds of the Fourteenth Amendment," *Wisconsin Law Review* 610 (1950). See also John P. Frank and Robert F. Munro. "The Original Understanding of 'Equal Protection of the Laws,'" *Columbia Law Review* 50:2 (February 1950): 131-69.
35. Belz, *Abraham Lincoln*, 209.
36. For a concise statement of this view, see for example the remarks of Justice Thurgood Marshall, "Reflections on the Bicentennial of the United States," *Harvard L. Rev.* 101:1 (November 1987): 1-5. See also his dissenting opinion in the *Bakke* decision. 438 U.S. 265 (1978), 369-97.
37. ten Broek, "Equal," 25, quoted in Belz, "Civil War," 122.
38. See Mitch Muncy, ed., *The End of Democracy?: A Celebrated First Things Debate, With Arguments Pro and Con* (Dallas, TX: Spence, 1997).

39. McConnell, *Originalism*, 983.

40. See C. Van Woodward, *The Strange Career of Jim Crow* (London: Oxford University Press, 1966; second revised edition). See also McConnell, *Originalism*, 980-84.

41. Kull, *Color-Blind*, 22-39.

42. The relevant passage of the Civil Rights Act of 1875 read as follows: "That all persons within the jurisdiction of the United States shall be entitled to the full and equal enjoyment of the accommodations, advantages, facilities, and privileges of inns, public conveyances on land and water, theatres, and other places of public amusement; subject only to the conditions and limitations established by law, and applicable alike to citizens of every race and color, regardless of any previous condition of servitude." Compare with Title 2 of the Civil Rights Act of 1964. "All persons shall be entitled to the full and equal enjoyment of the goods, services and accommodations of any place of public accommodation . . . without discrimination or segregation on the ground of race, color, religion, or national origin." Title 2 of the Civil Rights Act of 1964 defined the covered places as those "affecting interstate commerce or supported in their activities by State action as places of public accommodation." The reference to commerce presumably was the result of questions over the constitutionality of the act.

43. Laurent B. Frantz, "Congressional Power to Enforce the Fourteenth Amendment Against Private Acts." *Yale Law Journal* 73:1357.

44. Frantz, "Congressional Power," 1093.

45. See Frantz, "Congressional Power," 1092-117. "This is what we know: (1) on ten recorded votes in the Senate and eight recorded votes in the House between 1871 and 1875, a majority (but always less than two thirds) voted for legislation premised on the unconstitutionality of school segregation; (2) efforts to approve separate-but-equal requirements for education were invariably defeated; and (3) there was a high correlation between votes on the Fourteenth Amendment and votes in favor of school desegregation," Frantz, "Congressional Power," 1093.

46. McConnell, *Originalism*, 992.

47. McConnell, *Originalism*, 980-84. Richard Epstein, *Forbidden Grounds: The Case Against Employment Discrimination Laws* (Cambridge, Mass.: Harvard University Press, 1992), 83-86. Earl M. Malz, "'Separate But Equal' and the Law of Common Carriers in the Era of the Fourteenth Amendment," 17 *Rutgers Law Journal* (1986).

48. Edward L. Pierce, "A Treatise on American Railroad Law," (New York: Voorhies, 1857), quoted in McConnell, *Originalism*, 981.

49. McConnell, *Originalism*, 982.

50. McConnell, *Originalism*, 994-95.

51. Of course, the decision of Justice Miller in Slaughterhouse, which "emasculated" the meaning of the privileges or immunities clause by making a sharp distinction between federal and state citizenship, forced proponents of the legislation to rely upon the "equal protection" clause, which applies to "persons" and thus is not limited to federal citizenship. The question then became, Does equal protection forbid racial segregation? See McConnell, *Originalism*, 997-1005. According to McConnell, the result of this shift has been "a loss of the distinction between rights pertinent to citizens, and

rights pertinent to noncitizens, which was significant to the framers of the Fourteenth Amendment" McConnell, *Originalism*, 1004.

52. McConnell, *Originalism*, 1003, 1034. This statement was made by Rep. William Lawrence, a former judge and supporter of the Fourteenth Amendment in the Thirty-ninth Congress.

53. Cong. Globe, 42nd Cong., 2nd sess. 3260 (8 May 1872) (statement of Sen. Edmunds); 3 Cong. Rec. 945 (3 Feb. 1875) (statement of Rep. Lynch); 2 Cong. Rec. 3452 (29 Apr. 1874). All of these are quoted in McConnell, *Originalism*, 1011-12.

54. McConnell, *Originalism*, 1021.

55. See the words of Senator Frelinghuysen on the Civil Rights Bill of 1975: "It is the friction created by discrimination among citizens in the administration of law that disturbs the harmony of government. Let us take away the foreign substance. We know we have proven that equality is the true principle on which to run society; give it full play with no obstruction, and the machine will run noiselessly and without a jar. On the contrary, keep four millions impressed with the conviction that they are denied the full and perfect enjoyment of that equality which all others have guaranteed to them, and that by a nation they are taxed to support, and to defend which they fought, and they will be dissatisfied, asserting, and obtrusive; and their obtrusions will engender prejudice and augment evil." Cong. Rec. (20 April 1874), 3451.

56. Cong. Rec. (29 April 1874) 3452.

57. Cong. Globe, 1st sess., 39th Cong., 8 May 1866, 2459.

58. Cong. Globe, 1st sess., 39th Cong., 8 May 1866, 2459.

59. 84 U.S. (17 Wall.), 445 (1873).

60. 84 U.S. (17 Wall.), 446 (1873).

61. 84 U.S. (17 Wall.), 442 (1873).

62. McConnell, *Originalism*, 1119. But see also Kull, *Color-Blind*, 91-93.

63. 100 U.S. at 307-8, quoted in Kull, *Color-Blind*, 93-94.

64. *Tinnon v. Wheeler*, *Daily Republican* (Ottawa, Kan.), 19 Jan. 1881, at 2, col. 1 (Dist. Ct. Franklin Co. 18 Jan. 1881). The opinion was reprinted in the paper's weekly edition the following day. Quoted in Kull, *Color-Blind*, 104.

65. *Board of Education of the City of Ottawa v. Tinnon*, 26 Kan. 16-18. Quoted in Kull, *Color-Blind*, 105.

66. The case referred to is *People ex rel. King v. Gallagher*, 93 New York, 438 (1883).

67. McConnell, *Originalism*, 975.

68. For more on the nation's response to the Fifteenth Amendment, see Foner, *A Brief History*, 191-93.

69. See Louis H. Pollak, "Emancipation and Law: A Century of Progress," in Goldwin, *100 Years*.

70. Washington, *Testament*, 186.

71. Washington, *Testament*, 182. According to Louis Pollak, three decades ago, in 1932, Negroes in the twelve Southern states "were so effectively disfranchised, regardless of the 14th and 15th amendments to the Constitution, that considerably fewer

that a hundred thousand were able to vote in general elections, and virtually none was permitted to vote in primary elections." In Goldwin, *100 Years*, 173. Pollak is quoting the U.S. Department of Justice.

72. *King Papers*, vol. 2, 290.

73. Washington, *Testament*, 183. See King's whole essay "Civil Right No. 1: The Right to Vote," in Washington, *Testament*, 182-88.

74. The criterion the Court provided was the following: "And so in the present case, until some state law has been passed, or some state action through its officers or agents has been taken, adverse to the rights of citizens sought to be protected by the fourteenth amendment, no legislation of the United States under said amendment, nor any proceeding under such legislation, can be called into activity, for the prohibitions of the amendment are against state laws and acts done under state authority." 109 U.S. 3, 3 S. Ct. 18 (1883), quoted in David O'Brien, *Constitutional Law and Politics, Volume Two: Civil Rights and Liberties,* 2d edition (New York: W. W. Norton, 1995), 1301.

75. "If a state omits or neglects to secure the enforcement of equal rights," he said, "it 'denies' the equal protection of the laws within the meaning of the fourteenth amendment." Federal remedies were needed, proponents maintained, because state remedies were so frequently inadequate—whether because they were too expensive, because state processes of enforcement were infected with racial prejudice, because common law rights and remedies were not specific enough, or because they had been abrogated by law or custom in the case of black citizens. Even if there were no "positive statutes" abrogating common law rights, federal intervention was deemed justified if state remedies were not effective. McConnell, *Originalism*, 1034. It should be remembered that this debate only concerned those service obligations already covered by common law. It did not include "private business." See also McConnell, *Originalism*, 1033: "The proponents argument was that once the law had intervened to guarantee white citizens the legally enforceable right of access to common carriers and public accommodations without arbitrary or unreasonable distinctions, the principle of the Fourteenth Amendment required that the same right be extended to black citizens." John P. Frank and Robert Munro agree with McConnell on this point. See "The Original Understanding," 163-66. They write: "It is clear beyond reasonable doubt that the Fourteenth Amendment was meant to enable Congress to legislate affirmatively in behalf of a racial group which a state might, because it was a racial group, choose not to protect from action of private persons. The major discussion of Congressional power under all of the new Amendments came in 1870 and 1871 with the enactment of the First and Second Enforcement Acts, and the Third Enforcement Act, usually known as the Ku Klux Act," Frank and Munro, "Original," 163.

76. See Laurent B. Frantz, "Congressional Power to Enforce the Fourteenth Amendment Against Private Acts." This includes Bradley's own precedent in *Cruikshank.*

77. Of course, concerns of federalism are very important, and often overlooked in earnest attempts to vindicate civil rights. For strong arguments defending both federalism and the protection of civil rights (and thus the continuity between the original Constitution and the reconstruction constitution, see Michael P. Zuckert, "Completing the

Constitution: The Fourteenth Amendment and Constitutional Rights," *Publius* (Spring 1992): 69-91, Michael McConnell, "The Forgotten Constitutional Moment," *Const. Comm.* 11:1 (Winter 1994): 115-44, and Belz, *Emmancipation* and *Abraham Lincoln*.

78. *The Civil Rights Cases*, 109 U.S. 3, 3 S. Ct. 18 (1883); quoted in O'Brien, *Constitutional Law*, 1299-309.

79. 163 U.S. 537, 3 S.Ct. 18 (1896).

80. See McConnell, *Originalism*, 1120-31.

81. McConnell, *Originalism*, 1120.

82. McConnell, *Originalism*, 1128-29.

83. Consider for example Thomas Jefferson's diatribes against the injustice of the aristocracy of the old world, based upon conventions, as well as his statements on the need for "a natural aristocracy among men" the grounds of which "are virtue and talents." Mansfield, *Thomas*, 75.

84. Thomas Aquinas, *Summa Theologica*, 2-2, q.63, a.1.

85. "The notion that 'color and race are reasons for distinctions among citizens,' they said, is a 'slave doctrine.' When compelled by law, the segregation of races is 'an unjust and odious prescription.' Segregation is tantamount to 'caste.' Senator Frelinghuysen called segregation by law 'an enactment of personal degradation' and a from of 'legalized disability or inferiority,' effectively a denial of citizenship and a return to slavery." McConnell, *Originalism*, 1011.

86. King, *Why*, 82. Of course this was one of the arguments of Justice Warren in *Brown:* "To separate [Negroes] from others of a similar age and qualifications solely because of their race generates a feeling of inferiority as to their status in the community that may affect their hearts and minds in a way unlikely ever to be undone." Quoted in O'Brien, *Constitutional Law*, 1331. The statement is probably true. But as I have argued above, to establish this psychological damage with empirical studies, and use that damage as the primary evidence for a wrong, is most tenuous. Why didn't Warren simply rely on the principle?

King made several other arguments against segregation in the appeal: 1) It "ends up relegating persons to the status of things." See also Thomas Aquinas: "Persons are of more importance than things, since things are for the benefit of persons and not conversely." *Summa Theologica*, 2-2, q. 63, a. 1. 2) As Paul Tillich says, "sin is separation," and what is segregation but separation? Both of these arguments, especially the latter, are a bit shaky, but perhaps they provide rhetorical force. See also Washington, *Testament*, 118-19.

87. Aquinas, *Summa Theologica*, 1-2, q96, a2.

88. Epstein, *Forbidden*, 7.

89. See Graham, *Civil Rights*.

90. See Richard A. Epstein, "The Proper Scope of the Commerce Clause." *Virginia Law Review* 73: 1443-455, and *Forbidden*, 135-40. The New Deal decisions which most notably expanded the commerce power were *National Labor Relations Board v. Jones & Laughlin Steel Corp.* 301 U.S. 1 (1937) and *Wickard v. Filburn* 317 U.S. 111 (1942).

91. Kull, *Color-Blind*, 1-2. Kull is ambiguous on whether this development is

good or bad. He seems to suggest that sometimes racial classifications may be rational and just. However, "A scrupulous nondiscrimination may yet prove, because of the limitations of human justice, to be the most effective contribution that law (as distinct from political action) can make to the achievement or racial equality in this country. No one will contend however, that a strict legal equality can of itself settle the score between the United States of America and the descendants of her slaves. Where race-specific measures direct benefits to persons whose ancestors were brought to this country in slavery, the sense that this discrimination works rough justice—unjust, but less unjust than doing nothing—cannot easily be dismissed," Kull, *Color-Blind*, 222-23. For a comprehensive treatment of this question see Herman Belz, *Equality*.

92. Graham, *Civil Rights*, 42.
93. Graham, *Civil Rights*, 34-35.
94. Graham, *Civil Rights*, 119-20.
95. Graham, *Civil Rights*, 191-92.
96. See Jones, "The Rise and Fall of Affirmative Action," in Herbert Hill and James E. Jones, eds., *Race in America: The Struggle for Equality* (Madison: The University of Wisconsin Press, 1993), 345-69.
97. Eric Schnapper, "Affirmative Action and the Legislative History of the Fourteenth Amendment." *Virginia Law Review.* 71:5 (1985): 753-98. See also Hill and Jones, "The Rise and Fall of Affirmative Action," in *Race in America*, 345-69.
98. William Julius Wilson (who continues to support affirmative action) points out that nearly all of the assistance provided by preferential treatment goes to those who are already advantaged by class, education, and other factors.
99. For a critique of Schnapper's arguments, see Paul Moreno, "Racial Class and Reconstruction Legislation," *The Journal of Southern History* vol. 61, no. 2 (May 1995). I disagree, however, with Moreno's narrow reading of the Fourteenth Amendment.
100. Title 7, Sec. 703.
101. Title 7, 703 (j).
102. Title 7, 706 (g).
103. Several people who initially helped enforce preferential treatment in federal contract compliance later expressed regret for their decision. See especially Lawrence Silberman, "The Road to Racial Quotas." *The Wall Street Journal.* 11 August 1977.
104. The psychological motivation for and effects of preferential treatment have been powerfully chronicled in the works of Shelby Steele.
105. According to Randall Kennedy, racial profiling "is a sensible, statistically based tool that enables [law enforcement officials] to focus their energies efficiently for the purpose of providing protection against crime to law-abiding folk." Kennedy, "Suspect Policy," 31. Yet Kennedy still opposes the practice on the grounds that "the making of racial distinctions has proven to be more destructive and more popularly distasteful than other lines of social stratification," Randall Kennedy, *Race, Crime and the Law* (New York: Vintage Books, 1997), 147. For a detailed development of his arguments, see Randall Kennedy, "Suspect Policy." *New Republic* 13 Sept. 1999, 30-36, and Kennedy, *Race*, chapter 4.

106. Washington, *Testament*, 45.
107. See Hermann Belz, "Comments on 'Equality as a Constitutional Concept.'" *Maryland Law Review* 47:1 (Fall 1987), 28-37.

Chapter Four

Political Economy

King on the Nature and Causes of Poverty

In "I Have a Dream" King compared the declaration and Constitution to a "promissory note." According to him, America had defaulted on this promissory note "in so far as her citizens of color are concerned." America had given them a "bad check; a check which has been marked 'insufficient funds.'" Nevertheless, speaking now on behalf of these citizens, King said, "We refuse to believe that there are insufficient funds in the great vaults of opportunity of this nation." The coffers of America are plentiful, and therefore, it is time to cash the check "that will give us upon demand the riches of freedom and the security of justice." For King, this was more than a metaphor.

David L. Lewis divided King's career into two parts, the first of which he sought traditional civil rights goals, and in the second "increasingly radical goals for the larger society."[1] King's "career change," however, was really a change in emphasis. From the beginning King was concerned with both poverty and discrimination. In his first book he wrote: "I . . . learned that the inseparable twin of racial injustice was economic injustice."[2] As he said in "I Have a Dream," the Negro "lives on a lonely island of poverty in the midst of a vast ocean of material prosperity." King used this same phrase another time to express his belief in the close connection between segregation and poverty: "The Negro also had to recognize that one hundred years after emancipation he lived on a lonely island of economic insecurity in the midst of a vast ocean of material prosperity." Observing that "Negroes are still at the bottom of the economic ladder," he declared that "They live within two concentric circles of segregation. One imprisons them on the basis of color, while the other confines them within a separate culture of poverty." "The average Negro is born into want and deprivation," King continued. "His struggle to escape his circumstances is hindered by color discrimination. He is deprived of normal education and normal social and economic opportunities."[3] And in reference to the "self-help" philosophy of Booker T. Washington he wrote, "When [the Negro] seeks opportunity, he is told, in effect, to lift himself up by his own bootstraps, advice which does not take into account the fact that he is barefoot."[4]

89

He criticized others who applied this metaphor to American blacks: "They never stop to realize that no other ethnic group has been a slave on American soil."[5]

King also maintained that poverty is "a structural part of the economic system in the United States."[6] Moreover, he considered it to be the root of many other social ills. Thus King believed that poverty was a *cause* rather than *caused*.[7]

> We are likely to find that the problems of housing and education, instead of preceding the elimination of poverty, will themselves be affected if poverty is first abolished. The poor, transformed into purchasers will do a great deal on their own to alter housing decay.[8]

He believed that the principle behind the War on Poverty, that poverty is caused rather than a cause, was the primary reason for its failure.[9] This belief led him to propose such things as a "Bill of Rights for the Disadvantaged," which would offer to the poor the same benefits as the GI Bill, guaranteed jobs and on-the-job training, a federal housing plan, and finally, King's primary objective, a "guaranteed income" which would directly abolish poverty and thus meliorate other social conditions.[10] King found precedent for his program in the GI Bill and the Marshall Plan. He cited a statement by the National Urban League which exposed the hypocrisy of providing technical assistance to "handicapped peoples around the world" while neglecting "our own handicapped multitudes."[11] Surprisingly, he did not cite the Freedman's Bureau, which has become an important subject of post–civil rights scholarship because of its apparent precedent for affirmative action, and for its failure to implement social democracy through confiscation and redistribution of property.[12]

By framing his proposals in the language of rights, King presaged the Supreme Court's decision in *Goldberg v. Kelly* (1970) that welfare benefits are property rights rather than privileges and thus cannot be removed without due process.[13] Discussing the guaranteed income on television King said: "If one has a right to life, liberty, and the pursuit of happiness, then he has a right to have an income."[14] Moreover, such persons have the right to "three meals a day for their bodies, education and culture for their minds and dignity, equality and freedom for their spirit."[15] This transformation of welfare benefits from special privileges to entitlements to rights represents a considerable shift from the principles of justice contained in the declaration, marking an abandonment of nature as a standard of justice.[16]

According to King, the meliorative effect of these programs would result in enhanced dignity and power in the hands of those subject to extreme poverty. "A host of positive psychological changes inevitably will result from widespread economic security," he wrote. "The dignity of the individual will flourish when the decisions concerning his life are in his own hands, when he has the assurance that his income is stable and certain, and when he knows that he has the means to seek self-improvement. Personal conflicts between husband, wife and children will diminish when the unjust measurement of human worth on the scale of dollars is eliminated."[17]

King on the Family, Traditional Virtues, and Personal Responsibility

Unlike many of his contemporaries King accepted the fundamental arguments of the famous Moynihan Report, which saw the greatest threat to equality in the breakdown of the black family.[18] For him, one of the greatest dangers of poverty was the damage it inflicted on the traditional family, the "fundamental social unit" which nurtures, educates, and prepares children for independence and success. According to him, "nothing is so much needed as a secure family life for a people seeking to rise out of poverty and backwardness."[19] "Economic insecurity strangles the physical and cultural growth of its victims," he wrote. "Not only are millions deprived of formal education and proper health facilities but our most fundamental social unit—the family—is tortured, corrupted, and weakened by economic insufficiency." He was particularly disturbed with the way the free market forced down wages, and thus forced mothers into the workforce. "When a Negro man is inadequately paid, his wife must work to provide the simple necessities for the children. When a mother has to work she does violence to motherhood by depriving her children of her loving guidance and protection; often they are poorly cared for by others or by none—left to roam the streets unsupervised."[20]

In advocating a "living wage" and emphasizing the centrality of the family, King sounded surprisingly distributivist, and differed significantly from those who connected welfare reform to other liberationist causes.[21] This fact is recognized by Cornel West who in his book *Race Matters* laments "King's sexism and homophobia and the relatively undemocratic character of his organization."[22] But at least West pays King the respect of acknowledging his position. The acclaimed animated film for children *My Friend Martin* explicitly ties King's accomplishments to the liberation of women. In the film the young black hero is conspicuously missing a father, although his mother reminds him that King made possible her professional career. Also, the children's liberated school teacher is present at the March on Washington in full hippie regalia, signifying the connection between the two movements. Needless to say, King did not approve of the moral and cultural nihilism of the '60s revolution. The fact that the film was produced by King's son makes the deception more questionable.

Unlike defensive reactionaries who attempted to justify ghetto culture in the wake of the Moynihan Report, King continued to encourage traditional bourgeois virtues of discipline, self-reliance, education, and hard work. For example, in his last book (and thus, presumably in his "radical phase") he took exception to the common myth that Jews succeeded in America merely because they were wealthy. Rather, their success was due to their moral, intellectual, and cultural resources. "Jews progressed because they possessed a tradition of education combined with social and political action. The Jewish family enthroned education and sacrificed to get it. The result was far more than abstract learning." Moreover, Jews became political active. "Uniting social action with educational competence, Jews became enormously effective in political life . . . Nor was it only the rich who were involved in social and political action. Millions of Jews for half a century remained relatively poor, but they were far from passive in social and political areas. . . . Very few Jews sank into despair and escapism even when discrimination assailed the spirit and corroded initiative. Their life raft in the sea of discouragement was social action."[23]

Applying what he learned from the Jewish experience—and using the very metaphor he maligned on other occasions—he wrote: "[The Negro] must develop habits of thrift and techniques of wise investment. He must not wait for the end of segregation that lies at the basis of his economic deprivation; he must act now to lift himself up by his own bootstraps."[24] This is accomplished by "making full and constructive use of the freedom" which is already possessed. "We must not wait until the full day of emancipation before we set out to make our individual and collective contributions to the life of our nation."[25] This applies to community and political action as well. In Tocquevillian fashion, King encourages Negro communities to become concerned and active on their own behalf:

> We must utilize the community action groups and training centers now proliferating in some slum areas to create not merely an electorate, but a conscious, alert and informed people who know their direction and whose collective wisdom and vitality commands respect. The slave heritage can be cast into the dim past by our consciousness of our strengths and a resolute determination to use them in our daily experiences. Power is not the white man's birthright; it will not be legislated for us and delivered in neat government packages. It is a social force any group can utilize by accumulating its elements in a planned, deliberate campaign to organize it under its own control.[26]

Thus, in the spirit of Booker T. Washington, King encouraged Negroes to make the best for themselves. "In the final analysis if first-class citizenship is to become a reality for the Negro he must assume the primary responsibility for making it so. The Negro must not be victimized into the delusion of thinking that others should be more concerned than himself about his citizenship rights."²⁷ And again, "The Negro must make a vigorous effort to improve his personal standards."²⁸ "Yet we cannot ignore the fact that our standards do often fall short," he wrote. "One of the sure signs of maturity is the ability to rise to the point of self-criticism. . . . So many have used their oppression as an excuse for mediocrity." He then gave special advice for dealing with the young.

> We must make clear to our young people that this is an age in which they will be forced to compete with people of all races and nationalities. We cannot aim merely to be good Negro teachers, good Negro doctors, or good Negro skilled laborers. We must set out to do a good job irrespective of race. We must seek to do our life's work so well that nobody could do it better. The Negro who seeks merely to be a good Negro, whatever he is, has already flunked his matriculation examination for entrance into the university of integration.²⁹

He even suggested at one point that the psychological changes required for Negro improvement could not be created by government action. "The Negro will only be truly free when he reaches down to the inner depths of his own being and sings with the pen and ink of assertive selfhood his own emancipation proclamation. With a spirit straining toward true self-esteem, the Negro must boldly throw off the manacles of self-abnegation and say to himself and the world: 'I am somebody. I am a person. I am a man with dignity and honor. I have a rich and noble history, however painful and exploitive that history has been. I am black *and* comely.'"³⁰

These statements are often ignored because they buck against liberal dogma. But they reveal that his views on poverty were more complex than many contemporary liberals like to think. In encouraging virtue as a means of overcoming poverty King would have found agreement from Thomas Sowell, Shelby Steele and others who have argued persuasively that it is not so much race as *culture* that determines success. Black West Indians, for example, who are physically indistinguishable from black Americans, have achieved tremendous economic success in America, as have other races who have been subject to historic discrimination (Chinese, Japanese, etc.). And when statistics are controlled by factors of home and family life, incomes between black and white families are virtually indistinguishable.³¹ As Booker T. Washington tirelessly repeated, in a free-market economy, virtues like intelligence, talent, discipline, industriousness, and hard work, regardless of race, are a premium which the racist employer ignores at his own cost.³² Washington's message was nearly identical to that of Benjamin Franklin nearly a century before, and it resonated strongly with the American experience. The repeated story of economic success in America was the same: Those who best exhibited these virtues achieved the greatest success.³³ While slavery was quite unique to blacks—a fact that is not negligible—it is undeniable that nearly every race in America has faced similar problems: disadvantage, poverty, and racism. Irish, Jews, Italians, Chinese, Japanese, and Indians have all overcome great odds to achieve economic success.

Yet despite his exhortations to self-reliance, discipline, and hard work, and despite abundant examples of racial and ethnic minorities overcoming poverty without government assistance, King maintained that poverty is caused by the political-economic system and not by individuals. He was aware of the argument against his idea, but rejected it: "Earlier this century this proposal [i.e., the guaranteed income] would have been greeted with ridicule and denunciation as destructive of initiative and responsibility. At that time economic status was considered the measure of the individual's abilities and talents. In the simplistic thinking of that day the absence of worldly goods indicated a want of industrious habits and moral fiber." Things changed, however. "We have come a long way in our understanding of human motivation and of the blind operation of our economic system. Now we realize that dislocations in the market operation of our economy and the prevalence of discrimination thrust people into idleness and bind them in constant or frequent unemployment against their will." "The poor are less often dismissed from our conscience today by being branded as inferior and incompetent," King said. "We also know that no matter how dynamically the economy develops and expands it does not eliminate all poverty."[34] Thus he argued that "if society changes its concepts by placing the responsibility [for poverty] on the system, not on the individual, and guarantees secure employment or a minimum income, dignity will come within the reach of all."[35]

The Second Phase of King's Movement

Thus King did not stop at equality of opportunity. He believed that after Selma and the Voting Rights Act of 1965 one segment of the movement (i.e., legal equality) had been completed, and that it was time for another (i.e., social equality) to begin.[36] The success of the first phase of the movement created its own problems, as the realization set in that freedom does not necessarily mean prosperity. The first phase had provided "decency." The second phase, according to King, would "realize" equality. "With Selma and the Voting Rights Act one phase of development in the civil rights movement came to an end. A new phase opened, but few observers realized it or were prepared for its implications. For the vast majority of white Americans, the past decade—the first phase—had been a struggle to treat the Negro with a degree of decency, not of equality." He was critical of those who would resist this second phase. His statements are worth quoting at length:

> White America was ready to demand that the Negro should be spared the lash of brutality and coarse degradation, but it had never been truly committed to helping him out of poverty, exploitation or all forms of discrimination. The outraged white citizen had been sincere when he snatched the whips from the Southern sheriffs and forbade them more cruelties. But when this was to a degree accomplished, the emotions that had momentarily inflamed him melted away. White Americans left the Negro on the ground and in devastating numbers walked off with the aggressor. It appeared that the white segregationist and the ordinary white citizen had more in common with one another than either had with the Negro.
>
> When Negroes looked for the second phase, *the realization of equality*, they found that many of their white allies had quietly disappeared. The Negroes of America had taken the President, the press and the pulpit at their word when they spoke in broad terms of freedom and justice. But the absence of brutality and unregenerate evil is not the presence of justice. To stay murder is not the same thing as to ordain brotherhood.[37]

By the realization of equality, King meant, among other things, economic equality: "From issues of personal dignity they [i.e., Negroes] are now advancing to programs that impinge upon the basic system of social and economic control. At this level Negro programs go beyond race and deal with economic inequality, wherever it exists."[38]

King stated that rather than seeking to abolish the system the Negro is simply seeking to "get in." "We want a share in the American economy, the housing market, the educational system and the social opportunities."[39] But he also frankly acknowledged that much of this second phase went beyond what the Constitution called for. "So far," he said, "we have had constitutional backing for most of our demands for change, and this has made our work easier, since we could be sure of legal support from the federal courts. Now we are approaching areas where the voice of the Constitution is not clear. We have left the realm of constitutional rights and we are entering the area of human rights."[40] He claimed that the nation required a "new mode of thinking," and it was "wasting and degrading human life by clinging to an archaic way of thinking."[41] "Let us . . . not think of our movement as one that seeks to integrate the Negro into all the existing values of American society. Let us be those creative dissenters who will call our beloved nation to a higher destiny, to a new plateau of compassion, to a more noble expression of humanness. We must have a passion for peace born out of the wretchedness and misery of war. Giving our ultimate allegiance to the empire of justice, we must be that colony of dissenters seeking to imbue our nation with the ideals of a higher and nobler order."[42]

The change King envisioned was a shift to a "person-oriented society."

The following paragraph offers a concise articulation of King's goals:

> The stability of the world house which is ours will involve a revolution of values to accompany the scientific and freedom revolutions engulfing the earth. We must rapidly begin the shift from a "thing"-oriented society to a "person"-oriented society. When machines and computers, profit motives and property rights are considered more important than people, the giant triplets of racism, materialism and militarism are incapable of being conquered. A civilization can flounder as readily in the face of moral and spiritual bankruptcy as it can through financial bankruptcy.[43]

He was aware that his ideas were unconventional, if not radical in scope. "In the days ahead we must not consider it unpatriotic to raise certain basic questions about our national character. We must begin to ask, Why are there forty million poor people in a nation overflowing with such unbelievable affluence? Why has our nation placed itself in the position of being God's military agent on earth, and intervened recklessly in Vietnam and the Dominican Republic? Why have we substituted the arrogant undertaking of policing the whole world for the high task of putting our own house in order?" He called for "a radical restructuring of the architecture of American society," declaring that "For its very survival's sake, America must re-examine old presuppositions and release itself from many things that for centuries have been held sacred. For the evils of racism, poverty, and militarism to die, a new set of values must be born. Our economy must be more person-centered than property-and-profit-centered. Our government must depend more on its moral power than on its military power."[44]

King rightly predicted that mainstream America would resist his recommended changes out of selfishness or fear of losing their economic privileges: "As Negroes move forward toward a more fundamental alteration of their lives, some bitter white opposition is bound to grow, even within groups that were hospitable to earlier superficial amelioration." He admitted the difficulties: "Conflicts are unavoidable because a stage has been reached in which the reality of equality will require extensive adjustments in the way of life of some of the white majority. Many of our former supporters will fall by the wayside as the movement presses against financial privilege. Others will withdraw as long-established cultural privileges are threatened. During this period we will have to depend on that creative minority of true believers."[45]

But even though he was leaving behind the old system of values—"The Constitution assured the right to vote, but there is no such assurance of the right to adequate housing, or the right to earn an adequate income"—he still maintained that his demands were just: "And yet, in a nation which has a gross national product of $750 billion a year, it is morally right to insist that every person have a decent house, an adequate education and enough money to provide basic necessities for one's family."[46] According to him, "the time has come for us to civilize ourselves by the total, direct and immediate abolition of poverty."[47]

Close advisor Stanley Levison (who, ironically, was suspected and repeatedly accused of being a communist) warned King that by moving his protest into the economic domain he risked fracturing the tenuous unity of the civil rights movement, and its great national appeal. In a letter to King he wrote that "The coalition of Selma and Montgomery, with its supporting millions is not a coalition with an unrestricted program. It is a coalition around a fairly narrow objective . . . It is basically a coalition for moderate change, for gradual improvements which are to be attained without excessive upheavals as it gently alters old patterns. *It is militant only against shocking violence and gross injustice*. It is not for deep radical change." "America today is not ready for a radical restructuring of its economy and social order," he continued. "Not even the appeal of equality will weld all into one fighting unit around a program that disturbs their essentially moderate tendencies." The challenge, according to Levison, was to achieve "great changes" that "may be possible within the limits of the basic system we now have." Though King's past actions had seemed radical in the south, in the north they had been accepted as essential parts of reform. Levison believed that King had achieved a rare place as "*one of the most powerful figures in the country—a leader not merely of Negroes, but of millions of whites*." He had achieved this status with an amazingly broad appeal. According to Levison, the civil rights movement was "one of the rare *independent* movements" America had seen, and King was "one of the exceptional figures who attained the heights of popular confidence and trust without having obligations to any political party or other dominant interests. Seldom has anyone in American history come by this path, fully retaining his independence and freedom of action." Levison advised King to take advantage of this rare and powerful position by appealing for more modest reforms:

> It is certainly poor tactics to present to the nation a prospect of choosing between equality and freedom for Negroes with the revolutionary alteration of our society, or to maintain the status quo with discrimination. The American people are not inclined to change their society in order to free the Negro. They are ready to undertake some, and perhaps major, reforms, but not to make a revolution.[48]

King did not heed his friend's advice.[49] The argument can be, and indeed is made that King was forced into a more radical position by the rise of new young radicals like Stokely Carmichal and Malcolm X, whose violent and separatist rhetoric was more suited to those subject to the social and economic problems of the urban ghetto.[50] King undoubtedly faced great obstacles in this regard. It is almost painful to see his descent in rhetorical influence and civil rights leadership in "the second phase" of the movement.⁵¹ The loss of his more moderate influence is perhaps one of the great tragedies of the movement, but like all great tragedies perhaps it could not have been avoided. Nevertheless, King's turn to a more radical position was not mere expediency, but was in fact continuous with his thinking from the start.

King's concern with poverty, along with "militarism," its counterpart, marks the second half of King's career. It was in the action of this cause that he was eventually killed in Memphis, where he had joined a strike of garbage workers. During this time he was also planning a massive second march on Washington, a march of the "poor and disinherited," which, unlike the previous march, would seek to shut down the city through civil disobedience until specific economic reforms were enacted.

Although he advocated a "radical restructuring" of the economy, it is fairly certain that King was not a communist.⁵² In a sermon entitled "How a Christian Should View Communism" he criticized capitalism for three things: First, it "has often left a gulf between superfluous wealth and abject poverty." Second, it "has created conditions permitting necessities to be taken from the many to give luxuries to the few." And third, it has "encouraged small-hearted men to become cold and conscienceless." On the other hand, Communism fails to recognize man's inalienable rights and the God from whom these rights derive. In typical fashion King then suggested that true justice rests in a synthesis between collective and individual enterprise. He acknowledged that "through social reform American capitalism is doing much to reduce" the bad tendencies of capitalism, but he also claimed that "there is much yet to be accomplished."⁵³

King never advocated anything so radical as abolishing the free market or economic competition (though it is not certain what he did mean to advocate when he referred to a "person-centered" economy), nor did he advocate state or popular ownership of the means of production. As he said in a sermon on the parable of the rich man, "Jesus never made a sweeping indictment against wealth. Rather, he condemned the misuse of wealth. Money, like any other force such as electricity, is amoral and can be used for either good or evil."

Writing on the story of the rich man who sadly refuses to sell all his possessions and give his money to the poor, King said: "It is true that Jesus commanded the rich young ruler to 'sell all,' but in this instance, as Dr. George A. Buttrick has said, Jesus was prescribing individual surgery, not making a universal diagnosis. Nothing in wealth is inherently vicious, and nothing in poverty is inherently virtuous."⁵⁴ King often said that rather than seeking to abolish the system the Negro is simply seeking to "get in." "We want a share in the American economy, the housing market, the educational system and the social opportunities."⁵⁵ Still, King's occasional phrasing of his demands in traditionalist language masked the more radical nature of the program suggested by his remarks above.

The Progressive Roots of King's Critique

Earlier it was suggested that King established his credibility (*ethos*) by appealing to American principles embodied in the declaration and Constitution. Now it appears that the principles themselves may be defective, or at least incomplete. King called for a "radical restructuring of the architecture of American society" which would require America to "re-examine old presuppositions and release itself from many things that for centuries have been held sacred." He stated that "Our economy must be more person-centered than property-and-profit centered," and he demanded the "realization of equality." From such statements one finds considerable evidence supporting statements like those from the House Committee on Post Office and Civil Service ("Martin Luther King, Jr. gave to this country a new understanding of equality and justice for all") and Senator Kennedy (King was "the second father of our country"). As Cornel West wrote, "King did not say 'my dream is America's,' but rather 'My dream is rooted in this tradition, but I'm going beyond it. My dream belongs to those despised people who have been locked out.'" One also finds basis for the criticism that King was seeking to radically alter American principles and institutions. What does it mean to say that King's Dream is "rooted" in the American tradition, and yet seeks to go beyond it? Is there an ambivalence in King's own position on America?

King did not invent most of his economic agenda. His demand for a "Bill of Rights for the Disadvantaged" echoed the efforts of Franklin Roosevelt decades earlier to win passage of a "second Bill of Rights," which would include, among other things, a "right to a useful and remunerative job," a "right of every family to a decent home," and a "right to earn enough to provide adequate food and clothing and recreation."[56] Roosevelt declared that the first Bill of Rights had secured "our rights to life and liberty." But "necessitous men are not free men," Roosevelt declared, and therefore certain "*economic* truths have become accepted as self-evident" (emphasis mine).[57] As for the Declaration of Independence, Roosevelt declared that the same freedom was at stake as in 1776: "In 1776 we sought freedom from the tyranny of a political autocracy. . . . Today we stand committed to the proposition that freedom is no half-and-half affair. If the average citizen is guaranteed equal opportunity in the polling place, he must have equal opportunity in the market place."[58] But Roosevelt's demands were never actualized. Instead an unemployment insurance program was implemented (social security) along with a modest assistance program based upon a means test (AFDC, etc.). While the program marked a shift in welfare concerns from the states to the federal government, test indicated that the system would continue to be viewed as an emergency system with emphasis on individual self-sufficiency.

Many constitutional scholars contend that the New Deal marked a critical turning point in American politics in which property rights would no longer be held sacrosanct.[59] Many of them note the change with approval, contending that the natural right to property (along with the whole regime of natural rights) is philosophically and ethically unsound, an antiquated concept of a bygone era.[60] The problem was how to maintain some semblance of limited government while removing protection for private property. Their solution has been to posit other terms like "autonomy," "privacy," and "deliberative democracy" as a barrier between individuals and government which would allow for programs of government regulation and income redistribution without totalitarianism. With the departure of private property as a privileged right of protection, the continuation of the free market becomes precarious. Thus, Bruce Ackerman asserts with confidence that "the Progressive battle against capitalism has been won. Fifty years after the New Deal, even conservative Americans have learned to live in an activist welfare state."[61]

But to understand Roosevelt and the New Deal one must go back even further to the Progressive era, in which, despite its many different and often contradictory voices, the first deliberate and systematic critique of the American political and economic tradition was launched. If one is to understand King's place in the American political tradition properly, it is necessary to understand both the substantive and rhetorical elements of this critique, which King largely shared. In particular, consideration must be given to how the Progressives accomplished the difficult task of combining a severe critique of the American political economy with an apparent deference to American principles.[62] The concern here is more with analogy than influence, though indirect influence is unquestionable (in King's case, through liberal theology and social gospel theory). For the sake of brevity, two progressives will be considered, Herbert Croly and Woodrow Wilson. While Croly and Wilson differed considerably on particular policy proposals (as did many of the progressives) one finds striking similarities in their critique, a critique that continues to be a vital force in America.

Herbert Croly was the author of the progressive manifesto *The Promise of American Life*,[63] published in 1909. There Croly sought to redefine America according to the "idea of democracy." Besides the fact that King often contrasted the idea of democracy and existing American institutions,[64] the term "promise" of American life is highly suggestive of King's Dream, helping to illuminate King's own project.

Croly began by suggesting that America is informed by an ideal national promise consisting of the "imaginative projection of a better future."[65] But what are the grounds for this promise he asked? In the past, Americans have been subject to a mixture of "optimism, fatalism, and conservatism," by which they believed that the promise would *automatically* take care of itself as long as they were faithful to their political and economic inheritance. "Our democratic institutions became in a sense the guarantee that prosperity would continue to be abundant and accessible."[66] To Croly, this traditional triumverate was incapable of sustaining the promise, and therefore what was required was a new national outlook which would give the promise *moral* significance by becoming collective *purpose*, a national *responsibility*. Thus, the future, "just in so far as it is better, will have to be planned and constructed rather than fulfilled by its own momentum."[67] This collective purpose would consist of a fundamental restructuring of the American economic system, a centralization of the national government, and a comprehensive redistribution of wealth. "The inference which follows may be disagreeable," he continued, "but it cannot be escaped. In becoming responsible for the subordination of the individual to the demand of the dominant and constructive national purpose, the American state will in effect be making itself responsible for a morally and socially desirable distribution of wealth."[68]

Croly was frank in admitting that his proposals required a fundamental departure from the American tradition. "In abandoning the older conception of an automatic fulfillment of our national destiny, [more enlightened reformers] have abandoned more of the traditional point of view than they are aware," he wrote. Sounding much like King, he continued: "The traditional American optimistic fatalism was not of accidental origin, and it cannot be abandoned without involving in its fall some other important ingredients in the accepted American tradition. Not only was it dependent on economic conditions which prevailed until comparatively recent times, but it has been associated with certain erroneous but highly cherished political theories. It has been wrought into the fabric of our popular economic and political ideas to such an extent that its overthrow necessitates a partial revision of some of the most important articles in the traditional American creed."[69] He did not hesitate to call his proposals "revolutionary," and to proudly name those assigned to implement them "heretics."[70] Yet he still maintained that only by these changes "can the American democratic ideal be made good."[71]

Thus there is confusion in Croly's account. On the one hand he criticized the traditional American political creed, which "was that of a rampant individualism, checked only by a system of legally constituted rights." "The test of American national success was the comfort and prosperity of the individual," he wrote, "and the means to that end—a system of unrestricted individual aggrandizement and collective irresponsibility."[72] In his view, the Declaration was fundamentally wrong and served only to divide America into selfish "particles" rather than combine them as patriotic brothers. The democracy identified with "a system of natural rights" is "perverted and dangerous," he wrote.⁷³ Such a system led to American individualism, characterized by the belief that "manifold benefits [are] to be obtained by liberating the enlightened self-interest of the American people." He denied that this equation was valid. "No preestablished harmony can . . . exist between the free and abundant satisfaction of private needs and the accomplishment of a morally and socially desirable result," he wrote. "The Promise of American life is to be fulfilled—not merely by a maximum amount of economic freedom, but by a certain measure of discipline; not merely by abundant satisfaction of individual desires, but by a large measure of individual subordination and self-denial."⁷⁴ To combat this individualism he proposed a massive collective and individual education which would teach Americans to work toward "collective responsibility" through "disinterested motives." It is the "collective purpose" according to Croly, in which the individual finds his genuine self-expression,⁷⁵ and it is "the economic individualism of our existing national system which inflicts the most serious damage on American individuality."⁷⁶

Here is where King and Croly diverge. Because Croly considered natural rights to be pernicious to his statist project, he agreed with many southerners that "the Negroes were a race possessed of moral and intellectual qualities inferior to those of the white men" and that "the Abolitionists were applying a narrow and perverted political theory to a complicated and delicate set of economic and social inequalities."⁷⁷ Thus he regarded the Civil War not as a conflict between the principles of the Declaration of Independence and the Constitutional compromise with slavery, but between "a common national idea—the idea of democracy—and the Constitution."⁷⁸ In other words, while Croly correctly pointed out that the Constitution was not the sufficient document to guide American politics, he sought to complement it with his own "idea of democracy" rather than with the Declaration of Independence, which would have been far truer to the actual history of the war and to the American founding.

Thus to his characterization—and perhaps caricature—of the American tradition Croly contrasted an ideal of democracy divorced from the natural rights tradition. For him democracy meant human improvement, and he was clear that the success of his project depended upon a belief that human nature can be improved. "Democracy must stand or fall on a platform of possible human perfectibility. If human nature cannot be improved by institutions, democracy is at best a more than usually safe form of political organization; and the only interesting inquiry about its future would be: How long will it continue to work? But if it is to work better as well as merely longer, it must have some leavening effect upon human nature; and the sincere democrat is obliged to assume the power of the leaven. For him the practical questions are: How can the improvement best be brought about? and, How much may it amount to?"⁷⁹ He hoped this improvement would eventually lead to its "consummate expression in the religion of human brotherhood."[80] This theological interpretation became the basis for the "social gospel" theorists, the foremost of whom was Walter Rauschenbusch, who had a significant influence upon King.

Another leading progressive, Woodrow Wilson, was more guarded about abandoning the Declaration, perhaps because he understood its central place in the American political tradition. But Wilson, like Roosevelt after him, retained the Declaration at the cost of honesty, by reinterpreting its understanding of liberty to include economic equality and comparing the Revolutionary War to the war against industrialism. "Some citizens of this country have never got beyond the Declaration of Independence, signed in Philadelphia, 4 July 1776. Their bosoms swell against George III, but they have no consciousness of the war for freedom that is going on today."[81] Wilson must have known the deception he was attempting. In an earlier essay he had compared socialism and democracy, approving of their shared principle that the state power is unlimited. He wrote that "The germinal conceptions of democracy are as free from all thought of a limitation of the public authority as are the corresponding conceptions of socialism: the individual rights which the democracy of our own century has actually observed, were suggested to it by a political philosophy radically individualistic, but not necessarily democratic." "Democracy is bound by no principle of its own nature to say itself nay as to the exercise of any power," he wrote. "Here, then, lies the point. The difference between democracy and socialism is not an essential difference but only a practical difference."[82]

Clearly this is not the teaching of the Declaration, but in Wilson's hands the Declaration took on a new meaning. It was "translated" into the new questions of the day. The Declaration, he wrote, "is of no consequence to us unless we can translate its general terms into examples of the present day and substitute them in some vital way for the examples it itself gives, so concretely, so intimately involved in the circumstances of the day in which it was conceived and written. It is an eminently practical document, meant for the use of practical men; not a thesis for philosophers, but a whip for tyrants; not a theory of government, but a program for action. Unless we can translate it into the questions of our own day, we are not worthy of it, we are not the sons of the sires who acted in response to its challenge."[83] There are many problems with Wilson's position, not the least of which is its historical inaccuracy. But more important are its consequences for statesmanship. If the principles of the Declaration are historically bound, then it can offer no guidance for political life. It simply merits honor as a historical artifact. But Wilson surprisingly draws the opposite conclusion: since the principles are time bound, we must substitute new principles *into the original document* as a guide for political action. Wilson's Declaration becomes an empty cup into which any statesman may pour in his or her favorite "historical" exigency. Wilson set a precedent that would be followed by subsequent American statesmen, resulting in much confusion about the national creed.

It would seem that King also "translated" the Declaration, though in a somewhat different way than Wilson and the progressives. One of the continuing themes of this study has been that King repeatedly affirmed the central premises of the American conception of justice. His argument was that Americans in practice had failed to live up to those premises. Even up to his last book, King wrote that "The home that all too many Americans left was solidly structured idealistically. Its pillars were soundly grounded in the insights of our Judeo Christian heritage[84]: all men are made in the image of God; all men are brothers; all men are created equal; every man is heir to a legacy of dignity and worth; *every man has rights that are neither conferred nor derived by the state, they are God-given* [italics mine]."[85]

But King objected to the free market anticipated by the principles of the Declaration. Thus, while he was able to make use of these same principles to gain popular support for traditional civil rights, they frustrated his quest for social and economic equality. Previous advocates of economic equality like Herbert Croly blamed the regime of natural rights for causing the problem, an alternative King did not recognize or endorse. According to Croly and Wilson, emphasis on natural rights, and in particular, the right to property, leads not just to economic oppression, but to selfish individualism. But these writers were not concerned with civil rights, and indeed were often quite sympathetic to the South.[86] King did not have this luxury. Rather than blame the natural rights regime, he indirectly infused it with a personalist philosophy. King thus provided the natural rights regime with a more comprehensive system of moral and political responsibility from which to critique it.[87]

The progressive critique continued into King's own day. Lyndon Johnson's War on Poverty took Roosevelt's original proposals farther than any president before or since. He declared that "The Great Society rests on abundance and liberty for all. It demands an end to poverty and racial injustice."[88] Like King, Johnson declared that America had reached "the next and more profound stage of the battle for civil rights. We seek not just freedom but opportunity. We seek not just legal equity but human ability, not just equality as a right and a theory but *equality as a fact and equality as a result*" (emphasis mine).[89] (The name of this speech, significantly, was "To Fulfill These Rights"). Johnson pushed through Congress an ambitious program to fight poverty, including Medicare and Medicaid, which provide medical assistance to the poor and elderly. With the War on Poverty America began to see a more radical departure from traditional welfare policy, but the essential "safety-net" principle continued to dominate.

Johnson's arguments were echoed by others in the civil rights movement. Close King advisor Bayard Rustin, for example, argued in a now famous article that the civil rights movement "was compelled to expand its vision beyond race relations to economic relations,"[90] and that it would now be concerned with "achieving the fact of equality."[91] Rustin conceded that "at issue, after all, is not *civil rights*, strictly speaking, but social and economic conditions."[92] He also conceded that the "Negro's struggle for equality in America is essentially revolutionary." "While most Negroes—in their hearts—unquestionably seek only to enjoy the fruits of American society as it now exists," he wrote, "their quest cannot *objectively* be satisfied within the framework of existing political and economic relations."[93] "Adding up the cost of such programs, we can only conclude that we are talking about a refashioning of our political economy."[94]

One finds these same arguments continued in more recent thinkers like William Julius Wilson, who argues that the massive failure of the War on Poverty can be explained by its failure to radically challenge traditional American beliefs about the causes of poverty. He contrasts the American welfare system with its emphasis upon individual rights and responsibility to the European system with its focus on "social rights" of all citizens, and he advocates a comprehensive social benefit system (based on the European model) which would provide child allowances, child care, housing subsidies, generous unemployment insurance, a revised "Works Progress Administration," and a program of balanced economic growth while sustaining a tight-labor market.[95] There are notable weaknesses in Wilson's argument, however. First, he doesn't address the counterargument that plenty of low-skill jobs continue to exist in urban areas, jobs that can serve as a first step up the economic ladder. This fact partially explains the tensions between Afro-Americans and immigrants in ghetto areas. Second, there is an underlying Marxist premise in Wilson's argument which asserts that culture is a phenomena of economics. Thus a simple economic change will effect cultural change. While one can concede that the economic structure and culture mutually interact and affect one another, it seems clear that culture is shaped by many more factors than economics, and indeed that culture alone can determine the success or failure of an economic system.[96] Third, he does not seem to be aware that the failure to implement a "a program of balanced economic growth while sustaining a tight labor market" is more the result of technical feasibility than failure of will. After all, who would resist such an economic arrangement were it feasible? Finally, he hardly considers how his proposals square with the principles of justice at the heart of the American political tradition, giving no attention to the Declaration or Constitution.

A proper treatment of King's proposals, then, must be viewed within the context of a long and complicated national economic history that continues to be disputed by competing parties. King's critique might be summarized as follows: First, the free market system, and not individuals or culture, is responsible for poverty. Second, the free market results in an unjust distribution of goods, resulting in an unjust distribution of power, thus perpetuating poverty. Third, the free market is based upon and encourages selfish individualism, which is immoral and un-Christian. Fourth, poverty, like a technical math problem, can be solved if political elites exercise their will to change the system. Finally, the free market is inextricably linked to racism and discrimination.[97] This critique merits closer examination if King's position in the American political tradition is to be properly understood.[98]

Critique of King's Understanding: Property

One already finds an anticipation of the progressive critique in the Southern defense of slavery prior to the Civil War. John C. Calhoun, for example, compared the plantation slaves of the south to the "wage slaves" of the north, and found the condition of the former to be superior due to the "patriarchal mode" of labor in which sick and elderly slaves were provided for by the plantation master. He also posited a necessary conflict between labor and capital, and suggested that the arrangement of slavery avoided "the disorders and dangers resulting from this conflict."[99] George Fitzhugh repeated and extended the arguments of Calhoun, stating in his *Sociology for the South* that the competitive system encourages selfish virtues and gives "the lamb to the wolf to take care of."[100] Equality rights, Fitzhugh argued, "is but giving license to the strong to oppress the weak. It begets the grossest inequalities of condition. Menials and day laborers are and must be as numerous as in the land of slavery." "The men of property," he continued, "are masters of the poor; masters with none of the feelings, interests, or sympathies of masters; they employ them when they please, and for what they please, and may leave them to die in the highway, for it is the only home to which the poor in free countries are entitled."[101]

In contrast, Abraham Lincoln and the Republican party made free labor the basis of their platform. As Eric Foner has written, "the concept 'free labor' lay at the heart of the Republican ideology, and expressed a coherent social outlook, a model of the good society. Political antislavery was not merely a negative doctrine, an attack on southern slavery and the society built upon it; it was an affirmation of the superiority of the social system of the north—a dynamic, expanding capitalist society, whose achievements and destiny were almost wholly the result of the dignity and opportunities which it offered the average laboring man."[102] This free labor outlook was the necessary correlate of the founding principles expressed in the Declaration of Independence. Still, Foner argues that the antebellum conception of labor concentrated on "the independent farm and small shop" and viewed economic independence as the primary goal of labor, not wealth. Thus wage-labor was not viewed as free labor, even if it was a necessary step to independence.[103] In this context, it might seem that industrial capitalism with its dependence upon wage labor and its concentration of capital was opposed to the earlier conception of free labor.[104] Certainly industrialization involved large changes in the economic system, but not in any way that fundamentally undermined the original understanding of property rights, especially with respect to welfare provisions, and the social relations that followed from those property rights.

King advocated the "realization of equality," and pointed to the vast disparity in incomes between rich and poor as a sign of injustice. But King seems to misunderstand the Declaration's teaching on equality. As Lincoln said in his speech on *Dred Scot*:

> [The authors of the Declaration] did not intend to declare all men equal in *all respects*. They did not mean to say they were equal in color, size, intellect, moral developments, or social capacity. They defined with tolerable distinctness in what respects they did consider all men created equal—equal in "certain inalienable rights, among which are life, liberty, and the pursuit of happiness."

The mere discrepancy in material goods is not evidence of injustice. Indeed, the founders understood that the protection of equal rights would result in unequal distributions of goods. As Madison wrote in *Federalist* 10, "From the protection of different and unequal faculties of acquiring property, the possession of different degrees and kinds of property immediately results."[105] It is this connection of property to the natural faculties that makes the protection of property rights most just. James Wilson wrote in his *Lectures on Law (1791)* that "When we say, that all men are created equal; we mean not to apply this equality to their virtues, their talents, their dispositions, or their acquirements. In all these respects, there is, and it is fit for the great purposes of society that there should be, great inequality among men." "But," he continued, "however great the variety and inequality of men may be with regard to virtue, talents, taste, and acquirements; there is still one aspect, in which all men in society, previous to civil government, are equal. With regard to all, there is an equality in rights and in obligations; there is that 'jus aequum,' that equal law, in which the Romans placed true freedom. The natural rights and duties of man belong equally to all. . . . These laws prohibit the wisest and the most powerful from inflicting misery on the meanest and most ignorant; and from depriving them of their rights or just acquisitions." "By these laws," he continued, "rights, natural or acquired, are confirmed in the same manner, to all; to the weak and artless, their small acquisitions, as well as to the strong and artful, their large ones. If much labour employed entitles the active to great possessions, the indolent have a right, equally sacred, to the little possessions, which they occupy and improve."[106] The distinctive nature of this inequality is that it depends in large part upon natural differences that are not heritable. Thus Tocqueville noticed on his visit to America that while disparity of wealth was ever present, it switched hands rapidly.

> It is not that in the United States, as everywhere, there are no rich; indeed I know no other country where love of money has such a grip on men's hearts or where stronger scorn is expressed for the theory of permanent equality of property. But wealth circulates there with incredible rapidity, and experience shows that two successive generations seldom enjoy its favors.[107]

It is strange that in all his statements on natural and inalienable rights, King hardly ever mentions property as one of those rights. This fact is especially striking when one considers the central importance of property rights to the American founders.[108] When King does mention property, he says things such as the following:

> I am aware that there are many who wince at the distinction between property and persons—who hold both sacrosanct. My views are not so rigid. A life is sacred. Property is intended to serve life, and no matter how much we surround it with rights and respect, it has no personal being. It is part of the earth man walks on; it is not man.[109]

According to King, to treat a person as mere means "is to depersonalize the potential person and desecrate what he is."[110] According to social gospel theorist Walter Rauschenbusch, this explained the evil of capitalism: "It is unchristian as long as Men are made inferior to Things, and are drained and used up to make profit."[111] King inherits this understanding when he says that "the economy must become more person-centered than property-and-profit centered," where "human worth is not measured by the value of the dollar." The fact that men are created in the image of God required the abolition of poverty. He argued that because of the "profound moral fact" that the person is "of infinite metaphysical value," it followed that "we cannot be content to see men hungry, to see men victimized with ill-health, when we have the means to help them."[112]

King partly echoed Abraham Lincoln here. In a letter to Henry Pierce Lincoln noted the irony in the fact that "the Jefferson party," which was formed "upon their supposed superior devotion to the *personal* rights of men, holding the rights of *property* to be secondary only, and greatly inferior" was most like the Republican party. He contrasted the "democracy of today," which held that the liberty of one man was "absolutely nothing, when in conflict with another man's right of *property*," with the Republicans who were "both the *man* and the *dollar*, but in cases of conflict, the man *before* the dollar."[113] But King did not mean the same thing as Lincoln, for in opposing slavery Lincoln believed in the equal right "to eat the bread, without leave of anybody else, which his own hand earns."[114] To be forced to work for the bread of another, Lincoln argued, was the very definition of slavery. Thus it is somewhat false to contrast the natural right to property with the rights of persons; property (properly understood) is an *extension* of the person. As Philip Kurland and Ralph Lerner write, "The bald opposition between human rights and property rights is asserted commonly enough today but would have been largely unintelligible to the Founders."[115] According to Locke, "Though the earth and all inferior Creatures be common to all men, yet every Man has a *Property* in his own *Person*. This no Body has any Right to but himself. The *Labour* of his Body, and the *Work* of his Hands, we may say, are properly his."[116] The rights of the person are inviolable, and are not derived from any previous rights. In words which King (and Kant) would approve, Locke writes:

> For Men being all the Workmanship of one Omnipotent, and infinitely wise Maker; All the servants of one Sovereign Maker, sent into the World by his order and about his business, they are his Property, whose Workmanship they are, made to last during his, not one another's pleasure.[117]

Thus, for Locke and others, to violate the property rights of another is to violate his liberty and thus his person. It is to reduce him to slavery. It was precisely for this reason that the Civil Rights Act of 1866 was the first piece of Congressional legislation passed pursuant to the Thirteenth Amendment prohibiting slavery. That act had as its first objective to provide "the same right . . . to make and enforce contracts, to sue, be parties, and give evidence, to inherit, purchase, sell, hold, and convey real and personal property." In other words, it saw the protection of property as a natural extension of the rights of persons.[118]

While the Declaration does not specifically mention the right to property, it is clear that such a right is implied in the right to the pursuit of happiness. The two were combined in the Virginia Declaration of Rights of 1776 and numerous other state constitutions, and in his first Inaugural Address President Thomas Jefferson (who authored this part of the Declaration) declared the sum of good government to be "a wise and frugal government, which shall restrain men from injuring one another, which shall leave them otherwise free to regulate their own pursuits of industry and improvement, and shall not take from the mouth of labor the bread it has earned."[119] One finds this sentiment expressed throughout the revolutionary era, both in popular writings and documents, and also in the host of laws that increased property rights by abolishing primogeniture and entail and establishing property in "fee simple," the most liberal law regarding land ownership.[120]

Critique of King's Understanding: Welfare

To be sure, this right to property in the founder's view was not unlimited. It was always understood that a certain sum of money in the form of taxes could be required by the government to support legitimate governmental purposes. Also, certain "police powers" in the states to protect the safety, health, morals, and general welfare of the public had always been acknowledged.[121] While the legitimate extent of those powers has been something of a controversy, particularly after the Fourteenth Amendment and the rise of the "Lochner era," there was general agreement that laws should be designed in a way that property is protected and self-reliance is encouraged.

Early advocates of democratic capitalism in America were not so naïve as to believe in a perfect correlation between virtue and material prosperity. They understood that poverty could be caused by a number of factors other than vice, such as disability, old age, temporary shifts in the market, etc. Those subject to such circumstances were provided for. As Tocqueville observed of the first Puritan settlers in America: "Clearly they had a higher and more comprehensive conception of the duties of society toward its members than had the lawgivers of Europe at that time, and they imposed obligations upon it which were shirked elsewhere. There was provision for the poor from the beginning in the states of New England."[122] And as Thomas G. West has demonstrated, "From the earliest colonial days, local governments took responsibility for their poor."[123]

What is critical about the traditional system of welfare in America is that it discriminated between those in genuine need, and those who merely refused to work through laziness or vice. Through a variety of policies the system sought to make citizens and families as self-sufficient, self-reliant, and self-respecting as possible. King's proposals, like much modern welfare policy, neglect or deny this distinction.

This discriminating welfare policy was fully compatible with natural rights protections. According to Locke, natural rights fit into a framework of "the Law of Nature and Nature's God" which obliges men, among other things, to care for one another when their own preservation is not in conflict. Indeed, Locke quotes with approval the maxim of "the Judicious Hooker" that justice and charity are derived from the natural equality of men.[124] Charity, according to Locke, "gives every Man a Title to so much out of another's Plenty, as will keep him from extreme want, where he has no means to subsist otherwise."[125]

Critique of King's Understanding: Personalism

But even if the founder's conception of liberalism provided that those in need be cared for, this still does not address the heart of King's claim. King translated the Declaration through the lens of his personalist philosophy. In doing so he sought to provide an interpretation of the Declaration which supported his understanding both of racial discrimination and of political economy. He was aware that the latter was not rooted in the Constitution. "We have left the realm of constitutional rights and we are entering the area of human rights."[126] He believed that the nation required a "new mode of thinking," and that it was "wasting and degrading human life by clinging to an archaic way of thinking."[127] His most succinct moral statement of political economy was that it "must become more person-centered than property-and-profit-centered." According to him, capitalism is based upon "the profit motive," which "encourages a cut-throat competition and selfish ambition that inspires men to be more concerned about making a living than about making a life."[128] He based this judgment on the biblical and Kantian elements of his personalism.[129]

> Deeply rooted in our religious heritage is the conviction that every man is heir to a legacy of dignity and worth. Our Judeo-Christian tradition refers to this inherent dignity of man in the Biblical term "the image of God." "The image of God" is universally shared in equal portions by all men. There is no graded scale of essential worth. Every human being has etched in his personality the indelible stamp of the Creator. Every man must be respected because God loves him. The worth of the individual does not lie in the measure of his intellect, his racial origin or his social position. Human worth lies in relatedness to God. An individual has value because he has value to God. Whenever this is recognized, "whiteness" and "blackness" pass away as determinants in a relationship and "son" and "brother" are substituted. Immanuel Kant said that "all men must be treated as *ends* and never as *mere* means."[130]

It's not clear what King meant by this statement, or what more it requires of the economy than the abolition of poverty. As suggested above, the founders would have argued that the free-market was a person centered economy insofar as it protected property rights and supported free labor, but this "personalism" was not understood in a way that excluded the legitimate pursuit of profit. It is true the good of the person is not the direct object of a free market economy, but it is the primary justification for such an economy, not only because it corresponds most to natural justice (as suggested above), but also because it seems to work most favorably to the good of persons indirectly. Adam Smith's "discovery" that self-interest might serve humanity better than benevolence—"It is not from the benevolence of the butcher, the brewer, or the baker, that we expect our dinner, but from their regard to their own interest"[131]—was simply a logical inference from the evident fact that human beings care most for what is their own. The unleashing of this self-interest in the free market, while bringing certain dangers, is also responsible for the tremendous increase in the standard of living witnessed in the last several centuries. And here is the paradox and the conundrum for King and others: The free market has done more to eliminate poverty than any other economic system or benevolent association.[132] It more than anything else makes the elimination of poverty even a possibility. But attempting to abolish poverty through massive state intervention might undermine the very conditions that gave the abolition of poverty the appearance of a reachable goal in the first place.

Moreover, while King's personalist formulation does not give explicit direction on how goods ought to be distributed in a regime, it does seem to minimize the natural (i.e., particular) differences responsible for their diverse distribution in a democratic republic. King seems to understand personalism to mean that because natural differences are not essential to personhood, they ought to be disregarded in distributions of material and economic goods.[133] But this argument does not necessarily follow from personalism. Personalism only seems to require that *arbitrary* differences be ignored. It is only with a Kantian understanding of moral reason that King's argument might be made, although Kant did not make it. Kant's *moral* ethic was not intended to be the standard for political right.[134] Indeed, the very nature of Kant's moral ethic is that it cannot be imposed from without, which would result in heteronomy rather than autonomy. Thus Kant's understanding of politics is based not upon personalism, but upon a version of classical liberalism which supported free trade and commerce as much as the American founders.[135] Though there is some ambiguity from Kant on this point, it is fair to say that he realized that human nature could not be relied upon to realize such lofty principles as the categorical imperative. King, on the other hand, seems to believe that personalism had full political implications making extensive demands on the state.[136] But even if personalism demands a complete political articulation, it's not clear that it would demand the kind of welfare state King advocated. This is especially true if property rights are an extension of the person, as suggested above. King seems to assume that dignity will flow from the mere possession of material goods, rather than from the work which gives people the satisfaction that they have exercised their reason and will to provide these goods for themselves.[137]

Conclusion

As Croly suggested above, progressivism depends upon a belief in human perfectibility. This fact alone should have caused King to reconsider his economic program. As pointed out in an earlier chapter, this was one area where King favored the orthodox over the liberal anthropology. He asserted that "a persistent civil war rages within all of our lives" and that "there is some good in the worst of us and some evil in the best of us." He claimed that "the tendency on the part of some liberal theologians to see sin as a mere 'lay of nature' which will be progressively eliminated as man climbs the evolutionary ladder seems . . . quite perilous."[138] This realist anthropology, which he shared with the founders, should have tempered his expectations of politics. As noted earlier, the founder's anthropology was rooted in a Christian biblical tradition which, if experience wasn't sufficient, constantly reminded them of the prevalence of "original sin." This fact of original sin set boundaries to the expectations of politics, providing a moderate and fundamentally anti-millenarian and antiprogressive realism to the foundation of American political justice.[139] Instead, as it will be argued in the next chapter, King turned the presumed consequences of this anthropological fact on its head and made it the basis for aggressive civil disobedience to counteract human recalcitrance.

As James Madison wrote in *Federalist* 10, there are only two methods for curing the mischiefs of faction, "the one, by destroying the liberty which is essential to its existence, the other by giving to every citizen the same opinions, the same passions, and the same interests." Madison concluded:

> It could never be more truly said than of the first remedy that it was worse than the disease. Liberty is to faction what air is to fire, an aliment without which it instantly expires. But it could not be a less folly to abolish liberty, which is essential to political life, because it nourishes faction than it would be to wish the annihilation of air, which is essential to animal life, because it imparts to fire its destructive tendency.

In other words, given human nature as it is, self-interest must somehow be used as part of a less than perfect solution. Such was the revolutionary American solution to the problem of politics. Still, such practical considerations can be found even in classical political thought. For example, Aristotle criticizes Socrates' arrangement that all property be held in common because it "would give rise to many resentments."

> For if they turn out to be unequal rather than equal in the work and in the gratifications deriving from it, accusations against those who can gratify themselves or take much while exerting themselves little must necessarily arise on the part of those who take less and exert themselves more . . . Dividing [care of possessions] will cause them not to raise these accusations against one another, and will actually result in improvement, as each applies himself to his own.[140]

Though it cannot withstand the careful scrutiny of a perfect standard of justice, the choice the founders made was the best possible choice for protecting human liberty and easing human suffering given the limiting conditions of human nature. But this was a choice King's prophetic soul could not tolerate. Still, his criticism has served to remind Americans that their arrangement is not perfect, but only a remote approximation thereunto. He has thereby helped to rescue them from the kind of destructive complacency encouraged by the arrangement. The founders were aware of this danger. They understood that the unlimited quest for material comfort and economic prosperity posed a threat to the virtues necessary for liberty. Thomas Jefferson in one of his more pessimistic reveries expressed this worry in his *Notes on the State of Virginia*. "From the conclusion of this war we shall be going down hill," he wrote. "It will not then be necessary to resort every moment to the people for support. They will be forgotten, therefore, and their rights disregarded. They will forget themselves, but in the sole faculty of making money, and will never think of uniting to effect a due respect for their rights." Jefferson then suggested that the very prosperity promised by the American arrangement would be its downfall. "The shackles, therefore, which shall not be knocked off at the conclusion of this war, will remain on us long, will be made heavier and heavier, till all our rights shall revive or expire in convulsion."[141]

Alexis de Tocqueville echoed this worry in *Democracy in America*. It was his primary concern that the genius which drove democratic capitalism would result in the constricted self-interest called individualism, leading to centralized administration and despotism. Individualism, according to Tocqueville, is "a calm and considered feeling which disposes each citizen to isolate himself from the mass of his fellows and withdraw into the circle of family and friends; with this little society formed to his taste, he gladly leaves the greater society to look after itself."[142] Tocqueville believed that this dangerous tendency was successfully combated in America by two factors: local self-government and an education in religion.

With respect to this last point, King served a vital function in America by warning against the seductive dangers of prosperity and reminding Americans of the proper hierarchy of values on which that prosperity depended. But his declamation also moved from warning against dangers to a diatribe against the system itself. In this movement King departed from the Declaration of Independence and from his better judgment about the limitations and possibilities of human nature, compromising his effectiveness as a national leader.

Notes

1. In Franklin, 277-78. King's change of emphasis closely followed that of his

close friend and sometime advisor Bayard Rustin. See Bayard Rustin, "From Protest to Politics: The Future of the Civil Rights Movement." *Commentary* 39:2 (February 1964): 25-31.

2. King, *Stride*, 90.
3. King, *Why*, 23.
4. King, *Why*, 23.
5. Carson and Holloran, *Knock*, 210.
6. King, *Where*, 7. It's not clear that King ever resolved the question of whether black poverty was caused by the economic system, or by racism.
7. See the appendix to King, *Where*, in which King treats each of these in turn. See also Mergione Pitre, "The Economic Philosophy of Martin Luther King, Jr." *Review of Black Political Economy* 9 (Winter 1979). I will not focus on these recommendations here, except insofar as they serve to illustrate King's larger plans and ideas for fighting poverty.
8. King, *Where*, 162-64. Even with this recommendation, King continued to advocate reforms in education, employment, and housing. See his proposals in *Where*, 193-202.
9. King, *Where*, 162.
10. King, *Why*, 136-41. Interestingly, the idea of a guaranteed income originated with libertarian economist Milton Friedman. It began to receive serious attention when it became increasingly clear that the War on Poverty would not suffice. For a criticism of the various proposals, see Sar Levitan, "The Pitfalls of the Guaranteed Income" *The Reporter* 36 (18 May 1967): 12-15. The National Council of Churches proposed a guaranteed income in 1968. See Olasky, *The Tragedy of American Compassion* (Washington, D.C.: Regnery Publishing, Inc., 1992), 179. The guaranteed income was also experimented with in the 1970s in the form of a negative income tax, and failed miserably. See George Gilder, *Wealth and Poverty* (New York: Basic Books, 1981), 118-19. King added several conditions to the guaranteed income which were not part of the original idea: (1) The income "must be pegged to the median income of society, not at the lowest levels of income;" and (2) "the guaranteed income must be dynamic; it must automatically increase as the total social income grows." These conditions, according to King, would ensure that the program was secure and effective. King, *Where*, 164-65.
11. King, *Why*, 136. Whitney Young of the Urban League first proposed something like the same plan King was advocating. See Young, *To Be Equal*.
12. See Belz, *Abraham Lincoln*, 205-9. See also Eric Foner's judgment of this approach to the Freedmen's Bureau in *Reconstruction*, 279.
13. *Goldberg v. Kelly* (397 U.S. 254, 1970). See Justice Brennan in a dissent written in 1989: "Just as common-law notions no longer define the 'property' that the Constitution protects, see *Goldberg v. Kelly*, neither do they circumscribe the 'liberty' that it guarantees. On the contrary, 'liberty' and 'property' are broad and majestic terms . . . " *Michael H. v. Gerald D.*, 491 U.S. 110 (1989).
14. "Face to Face" television news interview (28 July 1967), in Washington, *Testament*, 409.

15. Quoted in Pitre, "The Economic Philosophy," 194. Pitre attributes this quote to the "I Have a Dream" speech, which is a curious error.

16. To see why this is the case, consider that the usual argument made for transforming welfare entitlements into property rights is that all rights (including so-called natural rights) are a creation of government, and thus subject to the same deliberative scrutiny. For the most trenchant defense of this position, see Cass Sunstein, *The Partial Constitution* (Cambridge, Mass.: Harvard University Press, 1993). Richard Epstein claims to have found substantive support for this limitation on the power to tax in the eminent domain clause of the Constitution. See Richard Epstein, *Takings: Private Property and the Power of Eminent Domain* (Cambridge, Mass.: Harvard University Press, 1985), 263-305. Indeed, Epstein claims that the whole welfare state is unconstitutional. *Takings*, 306-29. His analysis is theoretically sound, but it does not sufficiently consider the historical meaning of the terms of the clause as it was written. It thus fails to account for the kinds of social welfare that were regarded as legitimate by the founders.

17. King, *Where*, 164.

18. See Lee Rainwater and William L. Yancey, *The Moynihan Report and the Politics of Controversy: a Trans-action Social Science and Public Policy Report* (Cambridge and London: The M.I.T. Press, 1967).

19. King, *Where*, 107. See Gilder, *Wealth and Poverty*, 73-74.

20. King, *Stride*, 203. See also his address on the dignity of family life delivered at Abbott House, Westchester County, New York on October 29, 1965, which can be found in Rainwater and Yancey, *The Moynihan Report*, 402-9. It would seem that King's ideas on the family were considerably influenced by The Moynihan Report. See King, *Where*, 104-9. However, his emphasis on the importance of family, and the damage done to the family by economic instability precedes the report by six years.

King believed that the "causes for the present crisis [in the family]" are cultural and social. King, *Where*, 107-8. Yet his recommendations for meeting the crisis of family disintegration in Negro ghettos are almost exclusively economic, making his arguments somewhat circular. Moreover, he seems to underestimate the real disadvantages of poor family life. For example, he suggests (*Where*, 193) that "the job of the school is to teach so well that family background is no longer an issue." Virtually every study, however, shows a strong relationship between family life and achievement at school. On the significance of connecting economic policy to citizen formation, see Michael J. Sandel, "America's Search for a New Public Philosophy." *The Atlantic Monthly* (March 1996): 57-74. Sandel traces the historical rise of the "procedural republic" in which economic concerns of prosperity and fairness are divorced from concerns for civic virtue. By embracing Keynesian economics, Sandel believes, Americans have abandoned the "formative ambition."

21. See for example Allan Carlson, *From Cottage to Work Station: The Family's Search for Social Harmony in the Industrial Age* (San Francisco: Ignatius Press, 1993), and *The New Agrarian Mind: The Movement Toward Decentralist Thought in Twentieth Century America* (New Brunswick. Transaction Publishers, 2000).

22. West, *Vindicating*, 70.

23. King, *Where*, 155.

24. King, *Stride*, 222. This is similar to a statement made by Frederick Douglas: "What we, the colored people, want is character, and this nobody can give us. It is a thing we must get for ourselves. We must labor for it. It is gained by toil—hard toil. Neither the sympathy nor the generosity of our friends can give it to us . . . It is attainable; but we must attain it, and attain it each for himself. I cannot for you, and you cannot for me. . . .We must get character for ourselves, as a people. A change in our political condition would do very little for us without this. . . . Industry, sobriety, honesty, combined with intelligence and a due self-respect, find them where you will, among black and white, must be looked up to—can never be looked down upon. In their presence, prejudice is abashed, confused and mortified." Quoted in Storing, *What*, 171-72.

25. King, *Where*, 126.

26. King, *Where*, 157.

27. King makes this same point in *Stride*, 211. Consider also the words of Frederick Douglas: "It is evident that we can be improved and elevated only just so fast and far as we shall improve and elevate ourselves. We must rise or fall, succeed or fail, by our own merits. . . . Character is the important thing, and without it we must continue to be marked for degradation and stamped with the brand of inferiority," Storing, *What*, 41-46.

28. Washington, *Testament*, 149.

29. Washington, *Testament*, 148-50. One is reminded of the words of Booker T. Washington writing about an address he gave before the National Education Association: "In this address I said that the whole future of the Negro rested largely upon the question as to whether or not he should make himself, through his skill, intelligence, and character, of such undeniable value to the community in which he lived that the community could not dispense with his presence. I said that any individual who learned to do something better than anybody else—learned to do a common thing in an uncommon manner—had solved his problem, regardless of the colour of his skin, and that in proportion as the Negro learned to produce what other people wanted and must have, in the same proportion would he be respected," Washington, *Up From Slavery*, 202. And at another point in that book he writes: "My experience is that there is something in human nature which always makes an individual recognize and reward merit, no matter under what color of skin merit it is found. The individual who can do something that the world wants done will, in the end, make his way regardless of race." *Up From Slavery*, 154-55.

30. King, *Where*, 43-44.

31. Thomas Sowell, *Civil Rights: Rhetoric or Reality?* (New York: Quill William Morrow, 1984), 79-82. Moynihan in his report also noted the success of black middle class families.

32. See Epstein, *Forbidden*. See also Sowell, *Civil Rights*, 112-14.

33. For a general treatment of this point, see Sowell, *Civil Rights*, passim. In a more recent work Sowell argues that this same pattern is found not only in America, but around the world. See Thomas Sowell, *Race and Culture: A World View* (New York: Basic Books, 1994).

34. King, *Where*, 162-63.

35. King, *Where*, 87.

36. Most Americans believed the essential work of the civil rights movement completed with the passage of the Civil Rights Act of 1965 (with the possible exception of fair housing legislation, which came in 1968). For an interesting treatment of this see Willmoore Kendall, "The Civil Rights Movement and the Coming Constitutional Crisis," and "What Killed the Civil Rights Movement," in Willmoore Kendall, *Contra Mundum*, ed. Nellie D. Kendall (Lanham, Md.: University Press of America, 1971), 362-85, 457-68.

37. King, *Where*, 4. The same argument was made by Bayard Rustin in 1964 ("From Protest"), who also used the term "the realization of equality." See also Lyndon B. Johnson's address to Howard University, 4 June 1965, "To Fulfill These Rights" in Rainwater and Yancey, *The Moynihan Report*, 125-132.

38. King, *Where*, 17.

39. King, *Where*, 130.

40. King, *Where*, 130. See also Washington, *Testament*, 58.

41. King, *Where*, 165.

42. King, *Where*, 133-34. Earlier King had said that the American Negro does not want to reject America, he "wants in" on the American dream. While he believed in America, and its system of justice, he also sought for the "higher man" and the "more noble expression of the ideal." King, *Where*, 65, 133-34.

43. King, *Where*, 186.

44. King, *Where*, 133.

45. King, *Where*, 95.

46. King, *Where*, 130.

47. King, *Where*, 166. Lyndon B. Johnson bore the standard for this War against Poverty. See his remarks at the University of Michigan, 22 May 1964, where he introduces the Great Society. King was by no means alone in believing both that poverty could be abolished simply by applying the financial resources, and that the Vietnam War was the reason this step was not being taken. See for example Steven Alsop, "After Vietnam—Abolish Poverty?" *The Saturday Evening Post* (17 Dec. 1966): 12. See also Olasky, *Tragedy*, 174-75.

48. This letter is treated in Garrow, *Bearing*, 418-22.

49. Of course, rhetorically, King could have recommended his changes without making a radical critique of the existing system, as did LBJ, whose recommendations were hardly less radical than King's.

50. Of course, Malcolm viewed the solution to the problem much differently than King.

51. See Garrow, *Bearing*, 475-526.

52. See for example, the last chapter in Garrow, *Bearing*. It is perhaps safer to say that King was an advocate of "democratic socialism." See Pitre, "The Economic Philosophy," 191.

53. King, *Strength*, 103-4.

54. King, *Strength*, 69-70.

55. King, *Where*, 130. Of course, this plea is very different from that offered by Black Nationalists like Malcolm X.

56. See FDR, "Annual Message to Congress," 11 January 1944, in Basil Rauch, ed., The Roosevelt Reader (New York: Holt, Rinehart, 1957), 347.

57. Rauch, The Roosevelt Reader, 347.

58. Samuel Rosenman, ed., *The Public Papers of Franklin D. Roosevelt*, vol. 5 (New York: Random House, 1938), 231-232.

59. For a summary of this scholarship see Jennifer Nedelsky, *Private Property and the Limits of American Constitutionalism: The Madisonian Framework and its Legacy* (Chicago: The University of Chicago Press, 1990), 203-76.

60. See for example Rawls, *Theory*, and Nedelsky, *Private Property*, passim.

61. Ackerman, *We*, 227.

62. Franklin Roosevelt, a great admirer of Woodrow Wilson, also fits quite comfortably in the progressive school. One finds in his speeches a continued and striking effort to innovate the principles of the American founding while at the same time expressing that innovation in traditional terminology. Thus his "economic Bill of Rights" (see above) referring to the Constitutional Bill of Rights, and his comparison of the Revolution of 1776 against political tyranny with the new Revolution against "economic royalists." See his "Acceptance of Renomination for the Presidency," 27 June 1936, in Rosenman, *Public Papers and Addresses of Franklin D. Roosevelt*, vol. 5, 231-34.

63. See also J. Allen Smith, *The Spirit of American Government* (Cambridge Mass.: Belknap Press of Harvard University, 1965); John Dewey, *Liberalism and Social Action* (Canada: Capricorn Books, 1963); Woodrow Wilson, *The New Freedom: A Call For the Emancipation of the Generous Energies of a People* (New York: Doubleday, Page & Company, 1913).

64. See especially King, *Where*, chapter 3.

65. Herbert Croly, *The Promise of American Life* (Boston: Northeastern University Press, 1989; first published in 1909), 3.

66. Croly, *The Promise*, 11.

67. Croly, *The Promise*, 6.

68. Croly, *The Promise*, 6.

69. Croly, *The Promise*, 22. Later Croly says: "Our first experiment in democratic political and economic organization was founded partly on temporary conditions and partly on erroneous theories. A new experiment must consequently be made; and the great value of this new experiment would derive from the implied intellectual and moral emancipation. Its trial would demand both the sacrifice of many cherished interests, habits and traditions for the sake of remaining true to a more fundamental responsibility and a much larger infusion of disinterested motives into the economic and political system." Croly, *The Promise*, 406.

70. Croly, *The Promise*, 398, 420, 427.

71. Croly, *The Promise*, 270.

72. Croly, *The Promise*, 49-50.

73. Croly, *The Promise*, 81.
74. Croly, *The Promise*, 22.
75. "The ultimate end is the complete emancipation of the individual, and that result depends upon his complete disinterestedness. He must become interested exclusively in the excellence of his work; and he can never become disinterestedly interested in his work as long as heavy responsibilities and high achievements are supposed to be rewarded by increased pay." Croly, *The Promise*, 417.
76. Croly, *The Promise*, 409.
77. Croly, *The Promise*, 81.
78. Croly, *The Promise*, 77.
79. Croly, *The Promise*, 400.
80. Croly, *The Promise*, 453.
81. Wilson, *The New Freedom*, 48.
82. See Arthur S. Link, ed., *Papers of Woodrow Wilson*, vol. 5 (Princeton: Princeton University Press, 1966), 559-63.
83. Wilson, *The New Freedom*, 48-49.
84. See the final two paragraphs from Lincoln's Lyceum Address, which share the same architectural terms and imagery.
85. King, *Where*, 84.
86. See King, *Where*, 81. Consider also Wilson's career.
87. On King's personalism see Smith & Zepp, *Search*, 99-118, and Ansbro, *Martin Luther King, Jr.*, 71-109.
88. "Remarks at the University of Michigan," 22 May 1964.
89. Commencement Address at Howard University: "To Fulfill These Rights," 4 June 1965.
90. In Meier, *Black Protest Thought*, 446.
91. Meier, *Black Protest Thought*, 450.
92. Meier, *Black Protest Thought*, 447.
93. Meier, *Black Protest Thought*, 453.
94. Meier, *Black Protest Thought*, 453.
95. See William Julius Wilson, *The Truly Disadvantaged: The Inner City, the Underclass, and Public Policy* (Chicago: University of Chicago Press, 1987) and William Julius Wilson, *When Work Disappears: The World of the New Urban Poor* (New York: Alfred A. Knopf, 1997).
96. See criticisms of Wilson's argument in Myron Magnet, *The Dream and the Nightmare: The Sixties' Legacy to the Underclass* (New York: William Morrow and Company, Inc., 1993), 60-67.
97. See for example John Kenneth Galbraith, *The Affluent Society* (Boston: Houghton Mifflin Company, 1958) and *The New Industrial State* (Boston: Houghton Mifflin Company, 1967). See also Michael Harrington, *The Other America: Poverty in the United States*, rev. ed. (New York: Random House, 1990). This book was very influential on John F. Kennedy, who initiated discussions about the War on Poverty shortly before his death. For a critical historical account of the development of this

critique, see Olasky, *Tragedy*. A more recent treatment, Cass Sunstein, *Partial*, holds that laissez-faire capitalism is unjust because it represents a false perception of neutrality, called "status-quo neutrality." According to Sunstein, the free market itself is not a reflection of the natural order of things, but a creation by law.

98. Detailed critiques of many of these assumptions are abundant. See, for example, Gilder, *Wealth and Poverty*; Michael Novak, *The Spirit of Democratic Capitalism* (Lanham, New York: Madison Books, 1991; first published by Simon and Schuster, 1982); Myron Magnet, *The Dream and the Nightmare*; and West, *Vindicating*.

99. Eric L. McKitrick, ed., *Slavery Defended: The Views of the Old South* (Englewood, N.J.: Prentice Hall, 1963), 14.

100. McKitrick, *Slavery*, 36-37.

101. McKitrick, *Slavery*, 39.

102. Eric Foner, *Free Soil, Free Labor, Free Men: The Ideology of the Republican Party Before the Civil War* (New York: Oxford University Press, 1970), 11.

103. Foner, *Free Soil*, 16-17.

104. This is also the argument of Bellah in *Broken Covenant*.

105. Jennifer Nedelsky claims that the inequality which lies at the root of the Madisonian framework is itself unjust, and thus an inadequate foundation for liberalism. See Jennifer Nedelsky, *Private Property*.

106. James Wilson, "Of Man, as a Member of Society," Lectures on Law (1791) in *The Works of James Wilson*, ed. Robert Green McCloskey (Cambridge: Belknap Press of Harvard University Press, 1967).

107. Alexis de Tocqueville, *Democracy in America*, ed. J. P. Mayer (New York: Harper & Row, 1966; Anchor Books, Doubleday & Co., 1969) 54. See in general his discussion of the importance of inheritance laws for democracy, 51-56.

108. See chapter 2, "Property Rights," in West, *Vindicating*.

109. *Trumpet of Conscience*, quoted in Washington, *Testament*, 649.

110. King, *Where*, 97.

111. Rauschenbusch, *Christianity*, 328.

112. Rauschenbusch, *Christianity*, 180.

113. Lincoln, Fehrenbacher, ed., *Speeches*, vol. 2, 18.

114. Lincoln, Fehrenbacher, ed., *Speeches*, vol. 1, 512.

115. Kurland and Lerner, *The Founder's Constitution*, vol. 1, 577.

116. Locke, *Second Treatise*, ch. 5.

117. Locke, *Second Treatise*, ch. 2.

118. See Carl F. H. Henry, "Christian Perspective on Private Property," in Samuel Blumenfeld, *Property in a Human Economy* (LaSalle, Ill.: Open Court Press, 1974), 23-46.

119. See also his letter to Pierre Samuel Dupont de Nemours, 24 April 1816, Mansfield, *Thomas*, 81-83. For a discussion of this point see West, *Vindicating*, 38-40, and Paul Rahe, *Republics Ancient and Modern* (Chapel Hill: The University of North Carolina Press, 1994; originally published in one hard cover volume, 1992), 17-20.

120. See for example, Kurland and Lerner, *The Founder's Constitution*, vol. 1, chapter 16, 577-604. On colonial changes to feudal law, Jonathan R.T. Hughes, *The*

Governmental Habit: Economic Controls from Colonial Times to the Present (New York: Basic Books, 1977).

121. See Hughes, *Habit*.
122. Tocqueville, *Democracy*, 44-45.
123. West, *Vindicating*, 132. For a general discussion of the early American understanding of welfare see 131-45.
124. Locke, *Second Treatise*, ch. 2.
125. Locke, *Second Treatise*, ch. 4. Richard Epstein criticizes Locke's religious account of property rights. See Epstein, *Takings*, 10-11. For reasons I cannot develop here, I believe that Locke's divine account is critical. In brief, Epstein's equation does not provide for those scenarios in which first possession is not combined with labour. In other words, he does not account for the injustices of that regime whose land is allowed to lie fallow in aristocratic estates to the detriment of nonowners. Locke's common ownership account gives an effective basis to the principle that property is necessarily connected with labour. See West, *Vindicating*, 43-48.
126. King, *Where*, 130. See also Washington, *Testament*, 58.
127. King, *Where*, 165.
128. King, *Strength*, 103. His criticism of democratic capitalism is common, and has been popular at least since Rousseau.
129. See Ansbro, *Martin Luther King, Jr.*, 71-76.
130. King, *Where*, 97.
131. Adam Smith, *An Inquiry into the Nature and Causes of the Wealth of Nations*, eds. R. H. Campbell and A. S. Skinner (Indianapolis, Ind.: Liberty Fund, 1981), 26-27.
132. Indeed, the very effort to "abolish poverty" carries a tone and reflects the kind of technological mind-set that supports the freemarket.
133. This understanding of personalism, imagined as a "veil of ignorance," forms the basis of John Rawls' political project. See Rawls, *A Theory of Justice*.
134. Thus the adaptation of Rawls can only conditionally be called "Kantian." See Epstein's critique of Rawls in *Takings*, 338-44.
135. See for example "On the Common Saying 'This May Be True in Theory, But It Does Not Apply in Practice,'" especially 73-86, and also 258-259 in Hans Reiss, *Kant: Political Writings*, trans. H. B. Nisbet (Cambridge, Mass.: Cambridge University Press, 1970, 1991).
136. See King, "The Ethical Demands for Integration," in Washington, *Testament*, 118-19, where he associates the Declaration with personalism. While he is speaking in this passage about segregation, he applies the same terminology to economic questions. King would have done well to read another "personalist," Max Scheler, who was a contemporary of Rauschenbusch, yet drew opposite conclusions from his personalism and especially his Christianity. In his exceptional work *Resentiment*, Scheler attempts to refute Nietzsche's association of socialism and humanism with Christianity as forms of resentment. According to Scheler: "the greatest mistake would be to interpret the Christian movement on the basis of dim analogies with certain forms of the modern social and democratic movement. Jesus is not a kind of popular

hero and social politician, a man who knows what ails the poor and the oppressed, an enemy of Mammon in the sense that he opposes capitalism as a form of social existence. Christianity does not contain the germ of modern socialist and democratic tendencies and value judgments." Max Scheler, *Resentiment* (Milwaukee, Wis.: Marquette University Press, 1994), 86. Scheler also took exception to traditional natural right terminology.

137. See Olasky, *Tragedy*, 6-42.

138. Carson, *The King Papers*, vol. 2, 137.

139. King partially acknowledged this when he wrote about integration that "The ultimate solution to the race problem lies in the willingness of men to obey the unenforceable. Court orders and federal enforcement agencies are of inestimable value in achieving desegregation, but desegregation is only a partial, though necessary, step toward the final goal which we seek to realize, genuine intergroup and interpersonal living. . . . True integration will be achieved by men who are willingly obedient to unenforceable obligations." King, *Where*, 101-2.

140. Aristotle, *The Politics*, book 2, ch. 5 (1263a10-30).

141. Query 17 in Harvey C. Mansfield, Jr., ed., *Thomas Jefferson: Selected Writings* (Wheeling, Ill.: Harlan Davidson, 1979).

142. Tocqueville, *Democracy*, 502.

Chapter Five

Civil Disobedience

King's Conception of Nonviolent Direct Action

Today in America the name Martin Luther King, Jr., and the principle of civil disobedience have become almost inseparable. Although he did not originate the idea or the practice of civil disobedience, King gave to it, for better or worse, an unparalleled legitimacy in the American order. At least part of the explanation for this influence rests in the fact that for King civil disobedience was only part of what he preferred to call "nonviolent direct action." For King nonviolent direct action was not merely a *method*, it was an *end* in itself. It was *the* solution to the problems of modern man, the "weapon unique in history, which cuts without wounding and ennobles the man who wields it. It is the sword that heals."[1]

In his first book King listed the fundamental components of nonviolent direct action.[2] First, it is "active" and not passive. Second, "it does not seek to humiliate the opponent, but to win his friendship and understanding." "The aftermath of nonviolence is the creation of the beloved community, while the aftermath of violence is tragic bitterness." Third, it is "directed against the forces of evil rather than against persons who happen to be doing the evil." Fourth, it is characterized by "a willingness to accept suffering without retaliation, to accept blows from the opponent without striking back." Fifth, it avoids "violence of the spirit." "At the center of nonviolence stands the principle of love." By love King meant *agape*, disinterested, creative, community-building love. In his sermon before the Montgomery bus boycott King stated that "Love must be our regulating ideal."[3] King explained that "*agape* is love seeking to preserve and create community." Finally, King maintained that nonviolence "is based on the conviction that the universe is on the side of justice." "Whether we call it an unconscious process, an impersonal Brahman, or a Personal Being of matchless power and infinite love, there is a creative force in this universe that works to bring the disconnected aspects of reality into a harmonious whole."[4]

Thus nonviolence for King constituted a comprehensive vision of the world. At the very heart of this vision was what King called *agape* love. Next to the dignity of man in King's order of justice comes the principle of *agape*.[5]

King described *agape* as a "disinterested love" in which the individual seeks not his own good but the good of his neighbor (I Cor. 10:24)." *Agape* for King meant "loving others *for their own sakes*," and thus it "makes no distinction between friend and enemy."[6] For King *agape* is not a passive love, it is "love in action." The action *agape* seeks is to create community. "*Agape* is love seeking to preserve and create community," he wrote.

> It is insistence on community even when one seeks to break it. *Agape* is willingness to sacrifice in the interest of mutuality. *Agape* is a willingness to go to any length to restore community. It doesn't stop at the first mile, but it goes the second mile to restore community. It is a willingness to forgive, not seven times, but seventy times seven to restore community. The cross is the eternal expression of the length to which God will go in order to restore broken community. The resurrection is a symbol of God's triumph over all the forces that seek to block community. The Holy Spirit is the continuing community creating reality that moves through history. He who works against community is working against the whole of creation . . .[7]

King strongly protested against Nietzsche's characterization of love as a passive device of the weak to oppress the strong, insisting instead that love properly understood is active, and "a potent instrument for social and collective transformation."[8] Love and power, he argued, are intrinsically connected: "Power without love is reckless and abusive and love without power is sentimental and anemic. Power at its best is love implementing the demands of justice. Justice at its best is love correcting everything that stands against love."[9]

Although King did not completely respond to Nietzsche's arguments, he did defend a more robust conception of love.[10] But his attempt to combine it with nonviolent direct action was not without difficulty. Perhaps one of the best criticisms of this attempt was expressed in Reinhold Niebuhr's *Moral Man and Immoral Society*. Although it was published when King was only two years old, this work would exert a considerable influence on King.[11] In the penultimate chapter of that book Niebuhr identified and criticized many of the points King embraced. Although he maintained that nonviolent action "offers the largest opportunities for a harmonious relationship with the moral and rational factors in social life,"[12] he denied that nonviolence was based upon persuasion and love and pointed to its coercive elements.[13] King himself knew that nonviolence relied upon coercion, and that there was not a significant victory he achieved that did not ultimately require force for its implementation. This contrast between the claims and reality of nonviolent direct action caused many critics of King to label him a hypocrite. As will be seen below, King himself seemed to embrace this more realistic appraisal of nonviolence in the latter part of his career. Suspicious of absolute claims, Niebuhr evaluated nonviolence on its pragmatic merits and found it "a particularly strategic instrument for an oppressed group which is hopelessly in the minority and has no possibility of developing sufficient power to set against its oppressors."[14]

King's Pacifism

But because he viewed nonviolence in strategic terms, Niebuhr was not a pacifist. He recognized that justice on occasion requires violent resistance. King, on the other hand, identified himself as a pacifist, though he was not consistent in his position. For example, he allowed for defensive violence, such as "the right to defend one's home and one's person when attacked"[15] especially "against assault by . . . lawless night riders."[16] He also argued that the use of police force was occasionally necessary and legitimate. In a striking statement, rare for its kind, King defended the legitimate use of force in Oxford, Mississippi: "As a devotee of nonviolent discipline," he wrote, "I am also a pacifist. Though I regret the use of force in the Mississippi situation, nevertheless, in my humble judgment, it was necessary and justifiable." He distinguished between police power and war power. "Whereas I abhor the use of arms and the thought of war, I do believe in the intelligent use of police power. Though a pacifist, I am not an anarchist. Mississippi's breakdown of law and order demanded the utilization of a police action to quell the disorder and enforce the law of the land." He also stated the conditions for just use of force. "Armed force that intelligently exercises the police power, making civil arrests in which full due process is observed, is not functioning as an army in military engagement, so I feel the presence of troops in Oxford, Mississippi, is a police force seeking to preserve law and order rather than an army engaging in destructive warfare."[17] Because "the destructive power of modern weapons eliminates even the possibility that war may serve any good at all," King maintained that "war is obsolete."[18] He claimed that a "so-called limited war will leave little more than a calamitous legacy of human suffering, political turmoil and spiritual disillusionment."[19] Thus King advocated nonviolence as a possible strategy for dealing with international conflict.

It is reasonable to expect that King might oppose a particular war for particular reasons. The costs he saw in the Vietnam War—both in the way it was fought and in the reasons for which it was fought—were real, and his opposition to the war was therefore understandable, if occasionally excessive. (His designation of America as "the greatest purveyor of violence in the world today"[20] seems particularly unreasonable.) One can even appreciate his warning against an attitude he called "militarism," which seeks to resolve every conflict with violence, which is tragic and should always be used only as a last resort. But it is very difficult to see how King would concede the need for police power to resolve domestic conflict and yet *on principle* oppose the use of military power to resolve international conflict. This inconsistency is especially difficult to understand considering King's experience in the south, where every victory was the result of federal force, of at least the threat of federal force. Clearly *agape* as nonviolence was no match against violence in these circumstances. And if King's personal experience in the south was not enough, memory of the pacification of Hitler's Germany should have reminded King of the intransigence of human nature, and of the dangers of "peace at any cost."

On the domestic scene, however, conditions were good for a nonviolent campaign. In a prophetic paragraph that may have influenced King, Niebuhr wrote:

> The emancipation of the Negro race in America probably waits upon the adequate development of this kind of social and political strategy. It is hopeless for the Negro to expect complete emancipation from the menial social and economic position into which the white man has forced him, merely by trusting in the moral sense of the white race. It is equally hopeless to attempt emancipation through violent rebellion.[21]

Niebuhr concluded his chapter by observing that "There is no problem of political life to which religious imagination can make a larger contribution than this problem of developing nonviolent resistance." He saw superior possibilities in the method. "The discovery of elements of common human frailty in the foe and concomitantly, the appreciation of all human life as possessing transcendent worth, creates attitudes which transcend social conflict and thus mitigate its cruelties. It binds human beings together by reminding them of the common roots and similar character of both their vices and their virtues."[22] While King ultimately denied the legitimacy of Niebuhr's arguments on nonviolence, it is intriguing to consider the ways in which King fulfilled Niebuhr's prophetic prescription.

For King *agape* also required a proper interior disposition. Nonviolent protesters at Montgomery were required to take a pledge to "ten commandments," which included daily meditation on the teachings and life of Christ, daily prayer, sacrifice, service, restraint from violence, and a constant disposition of love."[23] In making this requirement King hoped to balance "two apparent irreconcilables," militancy and nonviolence, with "strong affirmation of the Christian doctrine of love.[24] Christian love was the thread, according to King, that allowed militancy to be woven into moderation. Without Christian love, he suggested, human beings cannot be relied upon to channel their thirst for justice in moderate yet effective ways. Without diminishing the importance of law, King also conceded that "Genuine integration will come when men are obedient to the unenforceable." According to him, "Such obligations are met by one's commitment to an inner law, written on the heart. Man-made laws assure justice, but a higher law produces love."[25] And what would be the source of that higher law? King did not make *agape* contingent upon Christian faith understood as a gift from God. Nevertheless, he made clear in his speeches and writings that the full realization of justice depends upon *agape*, and that *agape* depends upon belief in a provident God. "We must depend upon religion and education to alter the errors of the heart and mind."[26] This necessary condition for the realization of the Dream is often ignored by King scholars.

There has been considerable debate over the historical origins of King's more developed thinking on nonviolence and civil disobedience.[27] Some historians suggest that it came from his intellectual journey, others that it was a result of his experience in Montgomery, and still others that it came from the influence of certain associates, like CORE leader Bayard Rustin.[28] According to the usually careful Kenneth Smith and Ira Zepp, Jr., "The evidence suggests that King did not fully embrace the tenets and implications of nonviolent resistance until *after* the Montgomery bus boycott and his trip to India."[29] Curiously, Smith and Zepp cite King's article "My Trip to the Land of Gandhi," written in 1959, as their evidence. However, King wrote "Pilgrimage to Nonviolence" before that trip, indicating that his thinking was already developed by this time.

In any event, the primary concern of this essay is not on the origins of King's understanding of civil disobedience, nor with the political dimensions of *agape* which have been discussed earlier. The purpose of this essay is to consider King's arguments from an historical and constitutional perspective.

Civil Disobedience, Natural Law, and Constitutionalism in the American Political Tradition

King repeatedly argued that civil disobedience was part of the American understanding of justice. Speaking to the American Jewish Committee in 1965 he stated that "no one can scorn nonviolent direct action or civil disobedience without canceling out American history." He then traced the history of civil disobedience in the American tradition.

> The first nonviolent direct action did not occur in Montgomery. Its roots go back to the American Revolution and the boycott against British tea, culminating in the Boston Tea Party. It was the favorite weapon of the suffragette movement when women had to fight for their right to vote. It was a technique the trade unions employed to organize the mass production industries. Many here tonight can recall the events of the thirties, when federal court injunctions crippled and stifled union organization. Even a Wagner Act could not facilitate a breakthrough. When the now historic sit-down strikes burst forth in 1937, a new national attitude congealed. Through the Congress of the In-

dustrial Organizations a new major movement was born.[30]

King might also have pointed to the precedent for nonviolent direct action in civil rights activities. Years before the Montgomery Bus Boycott, civil rights activists like Glenn Smiley, Bayard Rustin, and James Lawson had been promoting Gandhi's tactics of nonviolence as a way to address race problems in America. Two of their organizations, the Fellowship of Reconciliation (FOR) and the Congress of Racial Equality (CORE) had sponsored the first "freedom ride" in 1947, fourteen years before the memorable "freedom rides" of 1961.

In an address delivered to the New York Bar Association in 1965 King suggested a comparison between the civil rights protests and the American Revolution: "Would it not be altogether fitting," he said, "if we, who are denied a right to participate in the government of the state, who are brutalized by its police officials, who are deprived of equality before the law, who were the last hired and the first fired, left perishing on the lonely island of poverty in the midst of a vast ocean of material prosperity, whose children are kept illegally segregated in inferior schools, followed the historic example of the Sons of Liberty?"[31]

While King's comparisons lacked precision in their distinctions between the different forms of disobedience (the Boston Tea Party, for example, would have violated King's own method insofar as it was covert and its participants refused to accept the penalty of the law), they provide strong circumstantial evidence of the legitimacy of disobedience in America to what are considered unjust laws.

King also appealed to the Western tradition of political thought, where one finds a long history of what one might loosely call "civil disobedience." He found many examples: Shadrach, Meshach, and Abednego (Daniel 3), the early Christian martyrs, Socrates, Henry David Thoreau, and perhaps most importantly, Mahatma Gandhi.[32] He liked to quote Augustine's famous maxim "it seems an unjust law is no law at all."[33] At other times he cited Scripture ("We must obey God rather than men," Acts 5) and St. Thomas Aquinas.

The Augustinian tradition, however, while distinguishing between just and unjust laws, was very cautious about advising disobedience, and only required it when the law made demands directly contrary to the Divine Law. And while it rarely required noncompliance, resistance or rebellion was out of the question, because "all authority comes from God"(Romans 13). Traditional Christian political thought, informed by an understanding of original sin, was resigned to some degree of injustice, and recognized that political perfection was not to be found in this life, in the Earthly City, but in the heavenly City of God. The resister's only options were to flee the regime or face martyrdom.[34]

Liberal thought, in modifying the purposes of government, while retaining, and even emphasizing the distinction between just and unjust laws, is less reticent about the principles of obedience to political authority. One finds in John Locke's *Second Treatise* the first defense of revolution, a defense which later exerts its influence in America through the Declaration of Independence. According to the formula of the Declaration, "whenever government becomes destructive of these ends (i.e., the security of natural rights), it is the right of the people to alter or to abolish it, and to institute new government." What one does *not* find in the Declaration is a defense of disobedience to legitimate authority.[35] The alternatives seem to be simple: obedience or revolution. The defense of disobedience, however, does seem to be implied in the principles of just government, and the practice of America bears this out. The issue, however, is complicated in the American political order by the Constitution and the principle of federalism.

In the same speech to the Jewish Committee referred to above, King claimed that the Negroes had not yet employed civil disobedience. According to him, "civil disobedience in its authentic historical form involves defiance of fundamental national law," and this the Negro had not yet done. "The Negro today, when he marches in the streets, is not practicing civil disobedience because he is not challenging the Constitution, the Supreme Court, or the enactments of Congress. Instead he seeks to uphold them. He may be violating local municipal ordinances or state laws, but it is these laws which [contradict] basic national law. Negroes by their direct action are exposing the contradiction."[36]

This, however, was not King's regular argument. In fact, in his most famous defense of civil disobedience, the "Letter From Birmingham Jail," *he does not even mention it*, implicitly leading the reader to believe that civil disobedience is indeed taking place in Birmingham, contrary to his claim above. Part of the explanation might rest in the fact that the Letter was addressed to clergymen, but it is difficult to see how his argument would not have been made stronger by pointing out that he and his followers were not breaking law, but merely following fundamental national law.

It is not easy to refute the argument that obedience to the fundamental national law takes priority over obedience to local or state law. Constitutional supremacy is declared in the fifth article of the Constitution, and has been repeatedly affirmed by American institutions and practices. Most of the civil rights demands behind the protests of the 1950s and early 1960s were affirmed in the Constitution, and thus most of the protesters were ultimately vindicated in the courts. King's relative silence about the Constitutional defense of disobedience to local ordinances and state laws reveals some difficulties. It is quite possible that his repeated recourse to higher law arguments when Constitutional arguments were sufficient had the negative and unintended effect of undermining respect for the fundamental principles of the regime in two important respects. First, through silence about the Constitutional arguments citizens may become inclined to believe that the normal recourse to justice in the regime, especially to the Constitution, is ineffective. Second, citizens may begin to require a perfect identity between the Constitution and natural law, and thus *expect* a perfect conformity not just between the Constitution and law, but between natural law and human law.

Regarding the second point, King is right in citing St. Thomas Aquinas as an authority for the argument that unjust laws are those which do not conform to the natural law. Responding to the question "Whether Every Human Law Is Derived from the Natural Law?" St. Thomas writes:

> As Augustine says (*De Lib. Arb.* i. 5), *that which is not just seems to be no law at all*: wherefore the force of a law depends on the extent of its justice. Now in human affairs a thing is said to be just, from being right, according to the rule of reason. But the first rule of reason is the law of nature, as is clear from what has been stated above (Q. 91, A. 2 *ad* 2). Consequently every human law has just so much of the nature of law, as it is derived from the law of nature. But if in any point it deflects from the law of nature, it is no longer a law, but a perversion of law.[37]

But this does *not* mean that the reverse is true, that any regime which does not perfectly conform to the natural law is unjust. In the very next question St. Thomas, asking "Whether It Belongs to the Human Law to Repress All Vices," answers in the negative. He writes:

> Laws imposed on men should . . . be in keeping with their condition, for, as Isidore says (*Etym.* V. 21), law should be *possible both according to nature, and according to the customs of the country.* . . . Now human law is framed for a number of human beings, the majority of whom are not perfect in virtue. Wherefore human laws do not forbid all vices, from which the virtuous abstain, but only the more grievous vices, from which it is possible for the majority to abstain; and chiefly those that are to the hurt of others, without the prohibition of which human society could not be maintained: thus human law prohibits murder, theft and suchlike.[38]

Unlike King, St. Thomas made a careful distinction between natural law and human law. Regarding the latter, he recognized in human law the legitimate modifications to the perfect realization of natural law required in applying the principles of justice to particular circumstances. What may be *wrong* in a perfect world, might be permitted (and even required) by law in an imperfect world.

While King shared with St. Thomas an understanding of natural law he lacked the necessary distinction between natural law and human law that makes genuine politics possible. One might compare St. Thomas' statement above with one from King:

It has been affirmed that any change in present conditions would mean going against the "cherished customs" of our community. But if the customs are wrong we have every reason in the world to change them. The decision which we must make now is whether we will give our allegiance to outmoded and unjust customs or to the ethical demands of the universe. As Christians we owe our ultimate allegiance to God and His will, rather than to man and his folkways.[39]

In this case, King was undoubtedly correct in challenging the discriminatory customs of Montgomery. This is especially true because they were in violation of the Constitution. But not every custom and folkway can be held up to "the ethical demands of the universe" with the same rigor. For one reason, those demands are not always clearly discernible, and secondly, they may not always apply to the circumstances at hand.[40] According to St. Thomas Aquinas, while the first principles of the natural law are clear, they are also quite general, and thus require a careful application of the practical reason. Moreover, the practical reason differs in a critical way from the speculative reason. Notice St. Thomas' careful distinctions:

> The speculative reason . . . is differently situated . . . from the practical reason. For, since the speculative reason is busied chiefly with necessary things, which cannot be otherwise than they are, its proper conclusions, like the universal principles, contain the truth without fail. The practical reason, on the other hand, is busied with contingent matters, about which human actions are concerned: and consequently, although there is necessity in the general principles, the more we descend into matters of detail, the more frequently we encounter defects.

St. Thomas then continues:

> Accordingly then in speculative matters truth is the same in all men, both as to principles and as to conclusions: although the truth is not known to all as regards the conclusions, but only as regards the principles which are called common notions. But in matters of action, truth or practical rectitude is not the same for all, as to matters of detail, but only as to the general principles: and where there is the same rectitude in matters of detail, it is not equally known to all.[41]

In contrast to St. Thomas, King repeatedly depicts the natural law as universal, comprehensive, clear, inflexible, and unchanging, more like the categorical imperative of Kant than classical natural law theory. In one of his early sermons which has now become famous he asserted that "there are moral laws of the universe, just as abiding as the physical laws."[42] In this regard, John

Ansbro makes an interesting comparison of King to Gandhi. According to Ansbro, while Gandhi acknowledged that he had not yet found the Truth for which he was seeking, King "arrived at a system of definite philosophical and theological convictions about the nature of God, human nature, the direction of history, the mission of the Christian Church, and the role of the state in social reform. Unlike Gandhi, after his formal studies King did not pursue answers to ultimate questions, but rather was seeking the social implementation of the ultimate truths he had already accepted."[43]

The confusion in King's thinking about the natural law should not undermine his very important critique of modern relativism. It is a truth too often forgotten or neglected that the natural right to liberty for the founders was not a right to license; that in their understanding liberty is governed by a law of nature. It is also true that there are some things which are always right or wrong regardless of circumstance, but such things are very few, and only serve as the foundation for real political work. Nor is the comparison of King to St. Thomas intended to imply that all of King's decisions were imprudent. To the contrary, in a number of instances King exercised prudence and moderation, often in the face of significant pressure to take a more radical position.[44] Finally, the comparison does not deny that the regime, including the Constitution, is accountable to a higher law.

What it does do is suggest the political limitations of King's philosophy. Had he the opportunity to study Plato's *Republic* with the care he desired, he would have learned the difficulties faced by the Philosopher King in breaking the chains of opinion, moving outside the cave, gazing upon the source of all goodness, knowledge, and beauty, and then returning to the cave to paint what he has seen into the regime. The comparison emphasizes the danger of *replacing* the Constitution with natural law or other higher law arguments, for it is precisely in its adaptation of the higher law to the human condition that Constitutional government becomes so compelling, and also so fragile. The need for such an adaptation seems to be recognized and provided for in the Declaration of Independence itself, which states that "Prudence, indeed, will dictate that Governments long established should not be changed for light and transient causes."

One might take exception to the use of St. Thomas Aquinas here as a representative of American principles of justice, especially when it is recalled that St. Thomas defended the superiority of church authority in political affairs, a defense the American founders would have abhorred. While Aquinas' direct influence on America is admittedly difficult to establish, the extent of his indirect influence is beyond question. His exposition of natural law, consisting of a comprehensive synthesis of classical and Christian thought, quickly became classic, and exerted a tremendous influence on subsequent natural law theorists. One such theorist was Thomas Hooker, whose *Of the Laws of Ecclesias-*

tical Polity, published in 1594, was one of the most influential works on natural law in American thought.[45] But it is telling that King himself refers to Aquinas, and not Hooker, in his "Letter from Birmingham Jail."

But apart from the historical connection to St. Thomas' thought, it seems the founders accepted his understanding of the distinction between natural law and human law, and thus were willing to strive for the greatest good possible under the circumstances. But this fact, which indicates that the Constitution and natural law are not identical, while providing for certain problems poses others in its wake.

The Limits of Constitutionalism

What is to be done when the Constitution itself, the fundamental law, either sanctions injustice, or fails to provide justice? A clear example of the former can be found in the provisions for slavery in the Constitution, which made the Constitution itself contradictory by explicitly providing due process protections for persons on the one hand (Fifth Amendment), and at the same time implicitly violating rights of persons by recognizing the right of some persons to property in other persons. The latter right was made explicit in Taney's decision in *Dred Scot*, exacerbating the conflict between the states, and providing evidence for Lincoln's claim that state laws forbidding slavery might one day be declared unconstitutional.[46]

The problems caused by these provisions were exacerbated in the Fugitive Slave Act of 1850, which was never ruled unconstitutional. While the previous arrangements for returning runaway slaves were unpleasant to advocates of liberty, the Fugitive Slave Act was particularly odious because it required northern acquiescence in perpetuating what many of them considered to be a grossly unjust institution. The north could no longer justify its uneasy conscience by pointing out that slavery was limited to the south and thus beyond northern control. But in the end, it was not the moral purists of the north who sought to destroy the Union, but the self-interested slaveholders of the south.[47]

Interestingly, King, in the speeches referred to at the beginning of this chapter, does not mention the massive resistance to the Fugitive Slave Act, which occurred when Americans were confronted with a clear contradiction in their principles and practice of justice.[48] The act was bitterly challenged by many in the north, and resulted in many and various reflections on the extent of political obligation to unjust laws. According to some the act was unconstitutional, and hence invalid and undeserving of cooperation. For others the Act merely reinforced their belief that the entire Constitution had become corrupt and invalid.[49] While not everyone in the north responded to or resisted the law in the same way, few contested the justice of the Underground Railroad and other illegal clandestine operations which sought to aid runaway slaves.

But the Constitutional compromise with slavery is unique, and one is extremely hard-pressed to find another such example of flagrant incongruity between the principles of justice and the Constitution. It is important to remember the limited objectives of government in a liberal regime. Justice according to the Declaration consists in the protection of natural rights within a regime based upon the consent of the governed. It does not require government to secure the perfection of human nature (as in the classical understanding), or even all the conditions within which that perfection can take place (LBJ liberalism). Zeal for perfect justice must be tempered by the limitations imposed by respect for the liberty of persons. While there are some things no person has a right to do (such as violate the natural rights of another person), there may be some things, however right and proper, that no person can be required to do by law. One might recall the answer St. Thomas More gives in Robert Bolt's play *A Man For All Seasons* to his zealous future son-in-law Roper who would "cut down every law in England" to get at the devil:

> MORE: (Roused and excited) Oh? (Advances on Roper) And when the last law was down, and the Devil turned round on you—where would you hide, Roper, the laws all being flat? This country's planted thick with laws from coast to coast—man's laws, not God's—and if you cut them down—and you're just the man to do it—d'you really think you could stand upright in the winds that would blow then? (Quietly) Yes, I'd give the Devil benefit of law, for my own safety's sake.[50]

Bolt's More is not saying here that law is not accountable to a higher standard. Indeed, he will eventually suffer death at the hands of the state rather than violate his own conscience. But More does point out the fact that the safest and most just way to combat injustice is through law, however awkward and unwieldy it may be (it even gives the devil the "benefit of the law"!). While it may not guarantee perfect justice, the law is necessary because of the imperfections of human knowledge and judgment.

Young Abraham Lincoln took a similar position. In his "Address to the Young Men's Lyceum" delivered in 1838, Lincoln sharply criticized "the increasing disregard for law which pervades the country." While he was objecting to various displays of mob law and vigilante justice (which would include lynching) his argument applies to any challenges to the rule of law. He was willing to concede that on certain occasions mob rule was more just, "abstractly considered." But he warned that disobedience to the laws would encourage a general disregard for the laws, and that the way would subsequently be paved for the destruction of the regime by "men of sufficient talent and ambition." To counteract the tendency toward mob violence Lincoln recommended a "political religion" of the nation which would instill reverence for the law, a civil religion which his own magnificent rhetoric served to reinforce and which largely influenced King's own career. This exhortation to obedience did not make Lincoln a legal positivist. He told his audience that "bad laws, if they exist, should be repealed as soon as possible, still while they continue in force, for the sake of example, they should be religiously observed." Of course, some argue that Lincoln himself violated the fundamental law when he served as President by calling a blockade, calling up troops and suspending the write of *habeas corpus*. But these actions were taken in response to considerable demands of necessity, and should not take away from his general observations.

The Constitution is law. Besides the usual protections it provides to persons, it also can be a vehicle to achieve greater justice through consent by the process of amendment. Thus, while nothing in the Constitution prevented women from voting, the nineteenth amendment secured them this right. The process of amendment may be long and tiresome, but this serves as much to prevent imprudent or unjust changes to the Constitution as wise and just ones. As long as the normal vehicles are open for Constitutional change, disobedience to the fundamental law for the sake of a higher law becomes questionable.

King's Argument in the "Letter from Birmingham Jail"

As stated above, King's usual defense of civil disobedience took the form of a higher law versus human law argument. This in spite of the fact that in his whole career of civil disobedience he only disobeyed a federal law or court order once, in Birmingham, for which he eventually served time in jail.[51] His most comprehensive argument of this nature is found in his "Letter from Birmingham Jail."[52] There he began by distinguishing between just and unjust laws, citing Augustine's maxim that "an unjust law is no law at all." The difference between the two rests in the fact that a just law "squares with the moral law or the law of God. An unjust law is a code that is out of harmony with the moral law." He referred to St. Thomas Aquinas to clarify his position that "an unjust law is a human law that is not rooted in eternal and natural law." He then attempted to set forth principles for determining whether a human law squares with the natural law. His general argument was that "any law that degrades human personality is unjust." This general argument is followed by several particular arguments. The first argument sounded like Justice Warren's decision in *Brown*: "segregation distorts the soul and damages the personality." In the next argument, using the language of Martin Buber, he suggested that "segregation substitutes an 'I-it' relationship for the 'I-thou' relationship, and ends up relegating persons to the status of things." Finally he cited Paul Tillich as an authority for the statement that "sin is separation."

King's assertions are of questionable validity because they are either too general, or because the premises are not stated. He simply might have said that because laws of segregation are based upon an arbitrary distinction between persons, they are unjust. Perhaps because he realized the precarious validity of his previous arguments, he attempted to become more "concrete." According to him, "An unjust law is a code that a majority inflicts on a minority that is not binding on itself. This is difference made legal." While he properly recognized here the principle of "rule of law," he again failed to state a premise, for nearly all legislation could fit into the category of "difference made legal." The question is whether the difference made legal is related to a reasonable and just object. To exclude black citizens from voting merely because of their color is unjust. To exclude those who cannot read from voting is not. The latter distinction has a relation to its object (the need for voting citizens to be educated) that the former lacks.

He next argued that "an unjust law is a code inflicted upon a minority which that minority had no part in enacting or creating because they did not have the unhampered right to vote." His argument again contains an unstated premise. Although he never treats the right to vote from the perspective of the needs of the regime (and this to his detriment) it is doubtful he would have advocated the right of children to vote, or that laws made for their benefit under such conditions were for this reason unjust. His implied premise seems to be that laws which arbitrarily exclude citizens from participating in government are unjust, and if these are his premises, his arguments are valid. His final example of unjust laws are those which are just on the surface, but which are executed in an arbitrary fashion. Here again, he correctly identifies an instance of injustice.

Although there are some differences, the substance of King's arguments can be found in St. Thomas Aquinas. In the *Summa Theologica*, in answer to the question whether human law binds a man in conscience, St. Thomas wrote that "Laws framed by man are either just or unjust. If they be just, they have the power of binding in conscience, from the eternal law whence they are derived. Now laws are said to be just, both from the end, when, to wit, they are ordained to the common good, and from their author, that is to say, when the law that is made does not exceed the power of the lawgiver, and from their form, when, to wit, burdens are laid on subjects, according to the equality of proportion and with a view to the common good." It followed then for Aquinas that unjust laws are the reverse of these. That is, they violate these principles in end, authority, or form. "Laws may be unjust in two ways: first, by being contrary to human good, through being opposed to the things mentioned above: either in respect of the end, as when the authority imposes on his subjects burdensome laws, conducive, not to the common good, but rather to his own cupidity or vainglory; or in respect of the author, as when a man makes a law that goes beyond the power committed to him; or in respect of the form, as when burdens are imposed unequally on the community . . . The like are acts of violence rather than laws; because, as Augustine says, *a law that is not just, seems to be no law at all.*" St. Thomas concluded that unjust laws "do not bind in conscience, except perhaps in order to avoid scandal and disturbance, for which cause a man should even yield his right, according to Math. 5. 40:41: *If a man . . . take away thy coat, let go they cloak also unto him; and whosoever will force thee once mile, go with him other two.*"[53] Thus for St. Thomas the decision to disobey the law (except in cases where the law requires violations of Divine Law) is always one of prudence. The threat of scandal or disturbance might require obedience to otherwise unjust laws.

After distinguishing between just and unjust laws King attempted to show that disobedience to unjust laws is valid. According to him, there were at least three conditions necessary for valid civil disobedience: "One who breaks an unjust law must do it *openly, lovingly* . . . and with a willingness to accept the penalty." Thus King could say that his protests, rather than undermining law and order, expressed "the very highest respect for law."

Here it should be pointed out that, in contrast to Thoreau's self-righteous and individualistic justification for civil disobedience, King's justification is political and ultimately concerned with the good of the regime. This political justification of civil disobedience allowed King to be prudent about choosing when and where to practice it, and also allowed him to acknowledge valid exercises of violence in nonpolitical circumstances.

Nonviolent Direct Action as a Mode of Civil Discourse

It is the political nature of civil disobedience which provided King his greatest benefits as well as his greatest problems. What for Augustine and St. Thomas is considered from the perspective of obedience to one's conscience under the guidance of prudent concern for public order, becomes for King (as it was for Gandhi and others) a routine method for pursuing political change. Indeed, one of King's first acts after the success of Montgomery was to help found SCLC (the Southern Christian Leadership Conference) which had as its primary purpose the advocacy of political change in the south through nonviolent direct action. This continued to be his primary aim until the end of his life.[54] But how does one make disobedience to laws one considers unjust a regular part of the regime?

This seeming contradiction has its defenders. According to Hannah Arendt, civil disobedience, in origin and substance, is a particularly American phenomenon which ought to become a regular part of the regime.[55] She came to this conclusion by comparing civil disobedience to the system of "free associations" described by Tocqueville: "It is my contention that civil disobedients are nothing but the latest form of voluntary association, and that they are thus quite in tune with the oldest traditions of the country."[56] Arendt believed that in the case of civil disobedience, instead of individuals contesting the laws and customs of the community, "we are dealing with organized minorities, who stand against assumed inarticulate, though hardly 'silent,' majorities." In addition, "these majorities have changed in mood and opinion to an astounding degree under the pressure of the minorities."[57] Thus Arendt expressed hope that somehow the regime would design a way to accommodate civil disobedience into its regular institutional framework.[58]

Her misunderstanding or misuse of Tocqueville aside, Arendt's encouragement of civil disobedience betrays a surprising and dangerous superficiality in political understanding. Routine disobedience to laws can only result in a loss of respect for the laws and for the regime. While the initial motivation may be noble, human nature is such that those with less noble motives may take advantage of the circumstances for their own advantage. This process was evident in the race riots of the 1960s. What may have begun as a protest against a particular form of injustice, inevitably became an opportunity for theft and gratuitous violence with impunity. In fact, many have attributed the race riots of the 1960s to King's irresponsible use of civil disobedience.[59] They have pointed out the high expectations given by leaders of the movement to its participants, as if legal equality would instantly result in social and economic equality, and to the implicit threats of violence which always rested behind King's more successful campaigns of nonviolence.[60] Whether or not a direct causal relation can be found, it ought to be clear that no regime in which citizens are encouraged to disobey laws with which they disagree can long survive.[61]

Arendt was concerned that traditional Constitutional provisions were inadequate to secure the rights of minorities.[62] One should appreciate the fact that the framers of the Constitution were aware of the problem, however, and took deliberate steps to deal with it within the context of free government. According to Madison, the problem of majority faction was "the great desideratum by which alone this form of government can be rescued from the opprobrium under which it has so long labored and be recommended to the esteem and adoption of mankind."[63] This same problem of how to combine two potentially contradictory things, the protection of natural rights and consent, can be found in the Declaration. "The great object" of inquiry, according Madison, was "to secure the public good and private rights against the danger of [majority] faction, and at the same time to preserve the spirit and form of popular government." Madison's primary solution to the problem of majority tyranny (apart from a written Constitution itself) rested in five "improvements" in the science of politics: "the regular distribution of power into distinct departments"; "the introduction of legislative balances and checks"; "the institution of courts composed of judges holding their offices during good behavior"; the representation of the people in the legislature by deputies of their own election"; and finally "THE ENLARGEMENT OF THE ORBIT within which such systems are to revolve, either in respect to the dimensions of a single State, or to the consolidation of several smaller States into one great Confederacy." According to him, this last arrangement would multiply the passions, opinions, and interests of Americans in such a way that effective majority rule could only exist on the basis of compromise and coalition. Writing on this federal arrangement, Publius said that "Whilst all authority in it will be derived from and dependent on the society, the society itself will be broken into so many parts, interests and classes of citizens, that the rights of the individuals, or of the minority, will be in little danger from interested combinations of the majority . . . In the extended republic of the United States, and among the great variety of interests, parties, and sects which it embraces, a coalition of a majority of the whole society could seldom take place on any other principles than those of justice and the general good."[64] While these solutions may not be perfect, one should appreciate the complexity of a problem that eludes perfect resolution. With such an appreciation, the Constitutional solution appears quite sound.

Not only is regular disobedience dangerous; so is indiscriminate disobedience to all forms of injustice. What works for one circumstance may utterly fail in another. The early protests of the movement had the right conditions for success. This is not to diminish the courage of those who risked their safety, security, and even their lives, to achieve change. It is rather to compliment the leaders who understood the needs of the time. When Blacks were denied the franchise, they were denied the primary mechanism for change in a democracy. Civil disobedience was their only recourse. But once those victories had been won, the place of civil disobedience as a vehicle of political change ought to have been left behind and substituted with the hard work of liberty in a Constitutional democracy.

King himself recognized some of the limits of civil protest. In an essay written in 1966 he wrote: "When the idea is a sound one, the cause a just one, and the demonstration a righteous one, change will be forthcoming. But if any of these conditions are not present, the power for change is missing also."[65] King should have known that in politics soundness of an idea is relative to the circumstances to which it must be applied. This is especially true of circumstances as complicated as issues of political economy.

King's Use of Nonviolent Direct Action in the Second Phase

King's attempts to apply civil disobedience to the issues of political economy were imprudent and bound to fail. And yet he continued to do so up until his death. Thus in his last book, writing on the economic and social issues treated in the last chapter he said "The question that now divides the people who want radically to change that situation is: can a program of nonviolence—even if it envisions massive civil disobedience—realistically expect to deal with such an enormous, entrenched evil?" "I intended to show that nonviolence will be effective," he continued, "but not until it has achieved the massive dimensions, the disciplined planning, and the intense commitment of a sustained, direct-action movement of civil disobedience on a national scale."[66]

At the time he died King was planning a massive, nonviolent poor people's campaign in Washington which through tactics of civil disobedience would force the government to achieve his goals of political economy.[67] In this campaign poor people from across America would come to Washington, D.C. and build a shantytown outside the city from which they would launch their protests (perhaps in imitation of the famous Bonus March of the '20s). As one part of this plan, King confessed that "as a last resort" he would be forced "to bring the Government machinery to a halt by using human barricades to block bridges and highways."[68]

King tried to bring out the parallels of this protest to earlier civil rights protests. "This [Washington demonstration] will be an attempt to bring a kind of Selma-like movement, Birmingham-like movement, into being, substantially around the economic issues. Just as we dealt with the social problem of segregation through massive demonstrations, and we dealt with the political problem—the denial of the right to vote—through massive demonstrations, we are now trying to deal with the economic problems—the right to live, to have a job and income—through massive protest. It will be a Selma-like movement on economic issues."[69]

Yet he was aware of one critical difference. The earlier strategy had been fourfold: First, demonstrators would take their protest to the streets; second, racists would unleash violence; third, Americans "in the name of decency" would demand federal intervention and legislation, and finally the administration would intervene and initiate remedial legislation.[70] Under the new circumstances the third part of the strategy (and thus the fourth part of the strategy) could not be relied upon. No longer would there be a majority of Americans sympathetic to his cause pressuring the administration for intervention and legislation. This new condition called for new tactics: "We must formulate a program, and we must fashion the new tactics which do not count on government good will, but instead serve to compel unwilling authorities to yield to the mandates of justice."[71]

It is at this point that one begins to sense that King is taking his plans for nonviolence too far. In the first place, there is no unjust law which is being protested or resisted. In the second place, the legitimacy of his demands is questionable. There is certainly not the clear contrast between natural law and human law that one finds in the case of segregation, nor is there a local violation of Constitutional provision. Finally, by seeking to *force* legislation from Congress, King is violating basic democratic principles, and threatening to transform political deliberation by elected representatives into a politics (not to say tyranny) of compulsion. If, as King liked to point out, a majority of Americans supported his economic proposals, then why was his protest even necessary? In disregarding political forms for achieving results (tearing down the laws to get at the devil) he disregarded the very basis of the political order.

Another comment should be made regarding the third point above. In his early defense of civil disobedience, King speaks in sympathetic tones for segregationists who themselves were merely the victims of blindness, and he emphasized the capacity of civil disobedience to persuade and convert the opponent by lovingly confronting him with his evil. This conversion would result in redemption and reconciliation, the aftermath of which would be "the beloved community." But he also acknowledged that "no one gives up his privileges without strong resistance."[72] This last observation came to dominate his later rhetoric. Later in his career his tone became increasingly cold, intolerant, and confrontational, and his emphasis was placed on force rather than persuasion. Thus in his "Letter from Birmingham Jail" exhortations to love are replaced with the observation "that freedom is never voluntarily given by the oppressor; it must be demanded by the oppressed." The coercive character of nonviolent protest is frankly stated: "Nonviolent direct action seeks to create such a crisis and foster such a tension that a community which has constantly refused to negotiate is *forced* to confront the issue."[73]

But can force be the foundation for healing, reconciliation, and love (especially when that force is called "love")? On the contrary, is it not often a vehicle for bitterness, resentment, and hatred? How could King expect a "beloved community" to be established under such conditions? Hardly a single victory was won in the south without the intervention of the federal government, and when King began to challenge it also, he expected a result the likelihood of which was contrary to both his reason and experience.

The difficulty of making civil disobedience a regular means of achieving justice can be gauged by the comments of Michael Dyson, who in referring to the explosion of nonviolent protest movements against abortion in the late 1980s criticizes the way "King's patriotic example of religiously based political activism and civil disobedience has recently been co-opted and sometimes twisted in the grasp of the religious and militant right."[74] In particular Dyson objects to the activities of groups like Operation Rescue who seek to apply the principles of nonviolence to abortion by peacefully blocking the entrances to abortion clinics. He quotes the founder of Operation Rescue, Randall Terry, who claimed that Operation Rescue was simply imitating the methods of King, a national hero. Dyson's objections to Terry's arguments are weak, however. First he criticizes the "extremists in the rescue movement" who have "resorted to bombing abortion clinics and murder doctors who perform abortions as a violent measure of deterrence."[75] It is unbelievable that Dyson would resort to the very same arguments that were regularly launched at King without noticing the glaring contradiction. Dyson does little to conceal the ideological motivation for his disapproval of Rescue.

> Where the civil rights movement struggled to gain constitutional rights that were being unjustly denied to millions of black citizens, the antiabortion rescue movement aims to deny the constitutional rights of women to exercise reproductive choice. In such a light, the brand of civil disobedience practiced by the antiabortion rescue movement is morally flawed; it lacks a compelling ground of justification that respects the human dignity of its opponents.[76]

It is difficult to say where King would have stood on the question of abortion, but certainly a strong case can be made that the same person who held such high regard for the state of motherhood, who disdained the violence against innocent women and children in Vietnam, and who expressed great compassion for the poor and disadvantaged would not have forgotten the most defenseless persons of all, the unborn.[77] Indeed, King might have viewed abortion as another example of the way in which a capitalist economy transforms "persons into things," depriving them of their dignity as beings "created in the image and likeness of God." Dyson suggests that whereas Rescue seeks to impose a legal prohibition on a women's right to choose, the civil rights movement merely sought the legal protection of constitutional rights for blacks. This formulation of the problem is disingenuous and begs the question. Certainly civil rights activists were seeking to restrict the rights of southerners to "choose" segregation, were they not? As Lincoln regularly pointed out to Stephen Douglas, "choice" alone is not sufficient for justice. In the end, Dyson's argument comes down to this: He approves of King's use of civil disobedience because he believes segregation was wrong, and he opposes the use of civil disobedience by Operation Rescue because he believes abortion is right. What Dyson doesn't consider is how this approach can resolve the nation's most pressing problems. On matters over which there is deep national disagreement civil disobedience cannot be a safe or effective means of resolution.

Conclusion

In sum, the following general observations can be made about King's position on civil disobedience. First, his distinction between just and unjust laws finds support in the Declaration and in the entire Western tradition of political thought. Second, disobedience to unjust laws under certain circumstances is legitimate and just. Third, because of Constitutional supremacy, disobedience to unconstitutional laws and ordinances is legitimate and just. Fourth, segregation laws were unconstitutional and unjust, and therefore deserving of disobedience. Thus King's early protests were valid and even commendable in securing greater justice in America.

There are, however, some questionable elements to King's understanding. First, his usual defense of civil disobedience focused on higher law arguments at the expense of the Constitution. This had the effect of minimizing the perceived effectiveness of the Constitution in securing justice and of replacing it with natural law. But the natural law cannot be the absolute standard for political justice in the sense of providing immediate practical guidance. It requires the application of prudence to the particular circumstances. King's understanding of natural law was deficient insofar as it did not provide for the natural right grounded in prudence that makes natural law effective. Second, King's demands for justice went beyond those required by the Declaration. Third, in attempting to force these changes, King was undermining self-government.

One may conclude from this that King's defense and practice of civil disobedience were quite in line with American principles and practice, and that they served as a legitimate and powerful force for providing Constitutional protection to blacks in the south. However, one should also appreciate the latent tension in King's arguments resulting from a deficient understanding of natural law and its relationship to Constitutional government. This misunderstanding became particularly manifest in his later years, when he placed unrealistic expectations upon the power of civil disobedience to produce social and political change.

Notes

1. King, *Why*, 26.
2. See King, *Stride*, 102-7.
3. King, *Stride*, 62.
4. Nonviolence for King did not require (though it perhaps encouraged) the com-

prehensive state of being practiced and encouraged by Gandhi. Gandhi, however, exhibited striking pragmatism. See Ved Mehta, "Gandhiism Is Not Easily Copied," The *New York Times Magazine* (9 July 1961): 8-11.

5. According to Ansbro, King resolved a potential conflict between *agape* and the dignity of the human person. See Ansbro, *Martin Luther King, Jr.*, 1-36.

6. We will not treat here whether King's conception of *agape* is consistent with his personalism, or the other problems connected with King's conception of *agape*. For a critical treatment see Hanes Walton, Jr., *The Political Philosophy of Martin Luther King, Jr.* (Westport, Conn.: Greenwood, 1971), 77-102. For a point by point response to Walton, see Ansbro, *Martin Luther King, Jr.*, 276-78, footnote 193.

7. King, *Stride*, 105-6.

8. See King, *Stride*, 96-97. For a similar critique of Nietzche's conception, see Scheler, *Resentiment*.

9. King, *Where*, 37.

10. By calling love "weak," Nietzsche did not mean that it was ineffective. To the contrary it was his position that Christian love exercised an enormous power over Western civilization. He only meant to say that the power of love was directed against the naturaly strong, intelligent, and beautiful in favor of the weak, stupid, and ugly.

11. King, *Stride*, 97-99.

12. Reinhold Niebuhr, *Moral Man and Immoral Society; A Study in Ethics and Politics* (New York: Scribener, 1960), 251.

13. Niebuhr, *Moral Man*, 240.

14. Niebuhr, *Moral Man*, 252.

15. King, *Where*, 55.

16. "Nonviolence: The Only Road to Freedom," in Washington, *Testament*, 56.

17. King, "Who Is Their God?" 210. For more on this see Smith and Zepp, *Search*, 94-97.

18. King, *Where*, 183.

19. King, *Where*, 184.

20. King, *Where*, 233.

21. Niebuhr, *Moral Man*, 252.

22. Niebuhr, *Moral Man*, 254-55.

23. See King, *Why*, 63-64.

24. King, *Stride*, 60.

25. Washington, *Testament*, 123.

26. King, *Stride*, 198.

27. See for example the first chapter of Garrow, *Bearing*, on the origins of King's understanding. Compare this with King's own account in "Pilgrimage to Nonviolence" two different versions of which can be found in King, *Stride*, 90-107, and King, *Strength*, 146-54. See also Meier, "On the Role of Martin Luther King"; Harlan, "Thoughts on the Leadership of Martin Luther King, Jr." in Albert and Hoffman, *We Shall Overcome*, 59-68.

28. See Garrow, *Bearing*, chapter 1; Ansbro, *Martin Luther King, Jr.*, 110-62.

29. Smith and Zepp, *Search*, 17.

30. "Address to the American Jewish Committee," transcribed from the recording *Dr. Martin Luther King, Jr.: In Search of Freedom* (Mercury SR 61170), quoted from excerpt in David R. Weber, *Civil Disobedience in America: A Documentary History* (Ithaca, New York: Cornell University Press, 1978), 220. See also "The Civil Rights Struggle in the United States Today," in *The Record of the Association of the Bar of the City of New York* 20:5 (May,1965), 3-19.

31. "The Civil Rights Struggle in the United States Today," *The Record of the Association of the Bar of the City of New York* (May 1965), 14.

32. Gandhi's eclectic philosophy is difficult to generalize, but the Western influences which he inherited through his British education are clear. A list of his influences includes John Ruskin, Leo Tolstoy, Henry David Thoreau, and Jesus. See, however, Smith and Zepp, who maintain that "his thought was essentially Indian and all of his basic ideas can be found in the Indian religious tradition." Smith and Zepp, *Search*, 49.

33. Augustine, *De Libertas Arbitrio*, i. 5.

34. For an excellent treatment of Augustine's understanding of political authority, see Herbert Deane, *The Political and Social Ideas of St. Augustine* (New York: Columbia University Press, 1963), especially 146-52. See also Ansbro, *Martin Luther King, Jr.*, chapter 4.

35. Although see John Locke, *A Letter Concerning Toleration*, ed. James H. Tully (Indianapolis: Hackett, 1983), 48: "But some may ask, What if the Magistrate should enjoyn any thing by his Authority that appears unlawful to the Conscience of a private Person? I answer, That if Government be faithfully administered, and the Counsels of the Magistrate be indeed directed to the publick Good, this will seldom happen. But if perhaps it do so fall out: I say, that such a private Person is to abstain from the Action he judges unlawful; and he is to undergo the Punishment, which it is not unlawful for him to bear."

36. Locke, *A Letter*, 220. See also Weber, 211-12; Garrow, *Bearing*, especially 401-7, in which he gives an account of King's dilemma. See Jaffa, "Martin Luther King, Jr. Remembered." Jaffa supports King's argument above (that King did not violate the law), but he does not seem to be aware that King made it.

37. *Summa Theologica* 1-2 q95, a2, corpus.

38. *Summa Theologica* 1-2, q96,a2.

39. King, *Stride*, 117.

40. King always depicts the natural law as clear, absolute, and unchanging. For a clear example, see one of King's early sermons, "Rediscovering Lost Values," in Carson, *The King Papers*, vol. 2, 248-56. See also the telling comparison of King to Gandhi in Ansbro, *Martin Luther King, Jr.*, 140.

41. *Summa Theologica* 1-2 q94, a4.

42. "Rediscovering Lost Values," in Carson, *The King Papers*, vol. 2, 248-56. In fairness to King, in the sermon he does not give those laws concrete expression.

43. Ansbro, *Martin Luther King, Jr.*, 140.

44. See chapter 4, section E above. This appears to pose problems for my argument above that King lacked a conception of natural law flexible enough for political

life. Perhaps it was only in King's rhetoric that natural law was so inflexible, and that in practice he was willing to accommodate his thought to conditions for the accomplishment of greater goods. While there seems to be some truth to this, two points should be noticed: (1) I am unaware of any place where King gives a theoretical defense of prudence, such as that contained in the Declaration; (2) it seems clear that his increasingly inflexible natural law rhetoric was not successful, and alienated him from the mainstream of the civil rights movement.

45. See Kirk, *Roots,* 238-47. See also the many references to Hooker in John Locke, *Second Treatise.*

46. See Fehrenbacher, *Slavery,* especially chapter 1. See also Jaffa, with Bruce Ledewitz, *Original Intent and the Framers of the Constitution: A Disputed Question* (Washington, D.C.: Regnery Gateway, 1993).

47. I believe that Lincoln's First Inaugural Address makes this point clear.

48. He does mention the abolition movement in other places, though I am aware of no place where he makes any extensive parallels. See for example, "Love, Law and Civil Disobedience" in Washington, *Testament,* 50.

49. See Weber, 99-175.

50. From Robert Bolt, *A Man For All Seasons* (New York: Vintage Books, 1960).

51. King, *Why,* 68-75; Garrow, *Bearing,* 240-47, 579-80.

52. For an earlier expression of the ideas contained in the letter, see "Love, Law and Civil Disobedience," in Washington, *Testament,* 43-53. See also James A. Colaiaco, "The American Dream Unfulfilled: Martin Luther King, Jr. and the 'Letter From Birmingham Jail,'" *Phylon* 45:1 (Spring 1984): 1-18.

53. *Summa Theologica,* 1-2, q96,a4.

54. See his essay "Showdown for Nonviolence," in Washington, *Testament,* 64-72, which was published after his death.

55. Hannah Arendt, *On Revolution* (New York: Viking Press, 1963), 83.

56. Arendt, *Revolution,* 96.

57. Arendt, *Revolution,* 98-99.

58. Arendt, *Revolution,* 101-2.

59. See for example Lionel Lokos, *House Divided: The Life and Legacy of Martin Luther King, Jr.* (New Rochelle, New York.: Arlington House, 1968).

60. See for example Marvin Meyer, "The Violence of Nonviolence," National Review, 20 April 1965, 327. Meyer recognizes that civil disobedience in some cases is justified, but he denies that it can be justified in a Constitutional order. For a response to Meyer and others see James A. Colaiaco, "Martin Luther King, Jr. and the Paradox of Nonviolent Direct Action," *Phylon* 47:1 (Spring 1986): 16-28.

61. For more on this theme one should read carefully Aristotle's *Politics,* 2.8; *Federalist* 49; and Lincoln's "Address to the Young Men's Lyceum."

62. See her general discussion in Arendt, *Revolution,* 82-102. For a more contemporary discussion of majority tyranny, especially in the context of race, see Lani Guinier, *Tyranny of the Majority* (New York: The Free Press, 1994).

63. *Federalist* 10.

64. *Federalist* 51.

65. "Nonviolence: The Only Road to Freedom," in Washington, *Testament*, 59.
66. *Trumpet*, quoted in Washington, *Testament*, 648, 650.
67. See King, *Trumpet*, chapter 4; Garrow, Bearing, chapter 11.
68. Quoted in Ansbro, *Martin Luther King, Jr.*, 145.
69. "Showdown for Nonviolence," Washington, *Testament*, 65.
70. See Martin Luther King, Jr., "Behind the Selma March," *Saturday Review* 48 (3 April 1965): 16.
71. Quoted in Garrow, *Bearing*, 581.
72. King, *Stride*, 113.
73. King, *Why*, 79 (italics mine).
74. Dyson, *I May Not*, 234.
75. Dyson, *I May Not*, 242.
76. Dyson, *I May Not*, 243.
77. The Rev. Richard J. Neuhaus, who marched with King on numerous occasions and is founder and editor of First Things, maintains that King would have opposed abortion.

Conclusion

The objective of this study has been to offer a critical historical, political, and philosophical reflection on one of America's most remarkable individuals, Martin Luther King, Jr. Because King studies, like most matters in America dealing with race, are so politically charged, it has been difficult to gain perspective on the man whom we have seen fit to honor with a national holiday. But if that holiday is to gain the support in practice that it holds in law, it must become a holiday for all Americans, and not just some. This can only come from robust and candid study of the man honored, a study that attempts to see him from all sides, and not just one.

It is regrettable to observe that this study may be the first to engage in a critical examination of the thought and action of King from a perspective outside that of the liberal establishment. It is equally regrettable to observe the way conservatives—when they have paid attention to King at all—have, by and large, attempted to counteract that liberal bias through selective memory and citation rather than through thorough and truthful examination of King's thought and actions. This study is necessarily incomplete. But if it serves to open up new areas of thoughtful reflection about King and America, it will have succeeded. Yet if the study is incomplete, one thing is for certain: King himself defied facile political categories. He was husband, father, preacher, sinner, statesman, thinker, and activist, all in one. Such a rare and complex individual cannot be the exclusive property of one sect, party, or dogma, not to mention one nation.

Bibliography

Works by Martin Luther King, Jr.

Books

A Knock at Midnight: Inspiration from the Great Sermons of Martin Luther King, Jr. ed. Clayborne Carson and Peter Holloran. New York: Time Warner, 2000.
A Martin Luther King Treasury. Yonkers, New York: Education Heritage, 1964.
The Measure of a Man. Philadelphia: Christian Education Press, 1959.
Strength to Love. Philadelphia: Fortress Press, 1981.
Stride Toward Freedom. New York: Harper & Row, 1958; reprint, San Francisco: HarperSanFrancisco, 1986.
The Trumpet of Conscience. New York: Harper & Row Publishers, 1963.
Where Do We Go from Here: Chaos or Community. Boston: Beacon Press, 1968.
Why We Can't Wait. New York: Harper & Row, 1964; reprint, New York: Mentor, 1964.

Articles

"Behind the Selma March," *Saturday Review* 48 (3 April. 1965): 16.
"The Civil Rights Struggle in the United States Today." *The Record of the Association of the Bar of the City of New York.* 20:5 (May 1965): 3-19.
"Who is their God?" *The Nation* (13 Oct. 1962): 209-13.

Other

Carson, Clayborn and Kris Shepard, ed. *A Call to Conscience: The Landmark Speeches of Dr. Martin Luther King, Jr.* New York: Warner Books, 2001.
Carson, Clayborne, ed. *A Knock at Midnight: Inspiration from the Great Sermons of Reverend Martin Luther King, Jr.* New York: Warner Books, 2000.
———, ed. *The Papers of Martin Luther King, Jr.* vol. 1-4 (Work in progress). Berkeley: University of California Press, 1994.
Washington, James M. *A Testament of Hope: The Essential Writings and Speeches of Martin Luther King, Jr.* New York: Harper San Francisco, 1991.

Works about Martin Luther King, Jr.

Books

Albert, Peter J., and Ronald Hoffman. *We Shall Overcome: Martin Luther King, Jr., and the Black Freedom Struggle.* New York: Da Capo Press, 1993.

Ansbro, John J. *Martin Luther King, Jr.: The Making of a Mind.* Maryknoll, New York: Orbis Books, 1982.

Baldwin, Lewis. *There is a Balm in Gilead: The Cultural Roots of Martin Luther King, Jr.* Minneapolis: Fortress Press, 1992.

———. *To Make the Wounded Whole: The Cultural Legacy of Martin Luther King, Jr.* Minneapolis: Fortress Press, 1992.

Bennett, Lerone. *What Manner of Man.* Chicago: Johnson, 1964.

Branch, Taylor. *Parting the Waters: America in the King Years, 1954-1963.* New York: Simon and Schuster, 1988.

———. *Pillar of Fire: America in the King Years, 1963-1965.* New York: Simon and Schuster, 1998.

Calloway-Thomas, Carolyn, and John Louis Lucaites, eds. *Martin Luther King, Jr., and the Sermonic Power of Public Discourse.* Tuscaloosa: University of Alabama Press, 1993.

Cone, James H. *Martin and Malcolm and America: A Dream or a Nightmare.* New York: Orbis, 1991.

Fairclough, Adam. *To Redeem the Soul of America: The Southern Christian Leadership Conference and Martin Luther King, Jr.* Athens: University of Georgia Press, 1987.

Garrow, David. *Bearing the Cross: Martin Luther King, Jr. and the Southern Christian Leadership Conference.* New York: Vintage Books, 1988.

———. *The FBI and Martin Luther King, Jr.: From "Solo" to Memphis.* New York: W. W. Norton, 1981.

———. *Protest at Selma: Martin Luther King, Jr., and the Voting Rights Act of 1965.* New Haven and London: Yale University Press, 1978.

Howard-Pitney, Dean. *Afro-American Jeremiad: Appeals for Justice in America.* Philadelphia: Temple University Press, 1990.

Lewis, David. *King: A Critical Biography.* New York: Praegen, 1970.

Lischer, Richard. *The Preacher King: Martin Luther King, Jr. and the Word That Moved America.* New York: Oxford University Press, 1995.

Lokos, Lionel. *House Divided: The Life and Legacy of Martin Luther King, Jr.* New Rochelle, N.Y.: Arlington House, 1968.

Miller, Keith. *Voice of Deliverance: The Language of Martin Luther King, Jr., and Its Sources.* New York: Free Press, 1992.

Oates, Stephen B. *Let the Trumpet Sound: A Life of Martin Luther King, Jr.* New York: Harper & Row, 1982.

Pappas, Theodore. *Plagiarism and the Culture War: The Writings of Martin Luther King, Jr. and Other Prominent Americans.* New York: Hallberg Publishing, 1998.

Reddick, Lawrence. *Crusader without Violence: A Biography of Martin Luther King, Jr.* New York: Harper & Brothers, 1959.

Scott, Robert L, and Brockriede, Wayne, eds. *The Rhetoric of Black Power*. New York: Harper & Row, 1969.
Smith, Ervin. *The Role of Personalism in the Development of the Social Ethics of Martin Luther King, Jr.* Ph.D. diss., Northwestern University, 1976.
Smith, Kenneth L., and Ira G. Zepp. *Search for the Beloved Community: The Thinking of Martin Luther King, Jr.* Valley Forge, Penn.: Judson Press, 1974.
Walton, Jr., Hanes. *The Political Philosophy of Martin Luther King, Jr.* Westport, Conn.: Greenwood, 1971.
Wiggins, William H. *O Freedom! African-American Emancipation Celebrations*. Knoxville: University of Tennessee Press, 1987.

Articles

Baldwin, Lewis V. "Understanding Martin Luther King, Jr. Within the Context of Southern Black Religious History," *Journal of Religious Studies* 13:2 (Fall 1987): 1-26.
Bennett, Lerone, Jr. "The Real Meaning of the King Holiday." *Ebony*, January 1986, 31.
Bennett, William J. "The Conservative Virtues of Dr. Martin Luther King." *The Heritage Lectures*. Heritage Foundation, 481.
Bosmajian, Haig. "The Inaccuracies in the Reprintings of Martin Luther King's 'I Have a Dream' Speech." *Communication Education* 31 (April 1982).
Branch, Taylor. "Uneasy Holiday." *The New Republic*, 3 February 1986.
Burns, Stewart. "From the Mountaintop: The Changing Political Vision of Martin Luther King, Jr." *History Teacher* 27 (November 1993): 17-18.
Carson, Clayborne. "Documenting Martin Luther King's Importance—and His Flaws." *Chronicle of Higher Education*, 16 January 1991, A52.
———, with Peter Holloran, Ralph E.Luker and Penny Russell. "Martin Luther King, Jr., as Scholar: A Reexamination of His Theological Writings." *Journal of American History* 78 (June 1991): 98-111.
Colaiaco, James A. "The American Dream Unfulfilled: Martin Luther King, Jr. and the 'Letter From Birmingham Jail.'" *Phylon* 45:1 (Spring 1984): 1-18.
———. "Martin Luther King, Jr. and the Paradox of Nonviolent Direct Action." *Phylon* 47:1 (Spring 1986): 16-28.
Darby, Henry E. and Margaret N Rowley. "King on Vietnam and Beyond." *Phylon* 47 (March 1986): 43-50.
DePlama, Anthony. "Plagiarism Seen by Scholars in King's Ph.D. Dissertation." *New York Times*, 10 November 1990, 1ff.
Fairclough, Adam. "Martin Luther King, Jr. and the War in Vietnam." *Phylon* 45 (January 1984): 19-39.
Garrow, David J. "King's Plagiarism: Imitation, Insecurity, and Transformation." *Journal of American History* 78 (1991): 89.
Jaffa, Harry V. "Martin Luther King, Jr. Remembered." *Public Research Syndicated*. Claremont, Calif., 22 March, 1983.
Lawson, Steven F. "Martin Luther King, Jr., and the Civil Rights Movement." *Georgia Historical Quarterly* (Summer 1987): 243-60.
O'Brien, Michael. "Old Myths/New Insights: History and Dr. King." *History Teacher*

22 (November 1988): 49-65.
Pitre, Mergione. "The Economic Philosophy of Martin Luther King, Jr." *Review of Black Political Economy* 9 (Winter 1979).
Smith, Kenneth L. "The Radicalization of Martin Luther King, Jr.: The Last Three Years." *Journal of Ecumenical Studies* 26 (September 1989): 270-88.
Steinkraus, Warren E. "Martin Luther King's Personalism and Nonviolence." *Journal of the History of Ideas*. 30:1 (January-March 1973): 97-111.
Waldman, Peter. "To Their Dismay, King Scholars Find a Troubling Pattern." *Wall Street Journal*, 9 November 1990, 1ff.

Other

Skene, Gordon. *Great American Speeches, Volume 3—The Dreams, the Inspirations, the Accomplishments*. Santa Monica, Calif.: Rhino Records, 1991. Audiocasette.
King, Dexter. *Our Friend Martin; A Magical Movie Adventure Inspired by the Life of Martin Luther King, Jr.* Philip Jones & DIC Entertainment. CBS Fox Company, 1998. Videocassette.

Works on America, Race, Other

Books

Ackerman, Bruce. *Social Justice and the Liberal State*. New Haven, Conn.: Yale University Press, 1980.
———. *We the People: Foundations*. Cambridge, Mass.: The Belknap Press of Harvard University Press, 1991.
Amos, Gary T. *Defending the Declaration: How the Bible and Christianity Influenced the Writing of the Declaration of Independence*. Brentwood, Tenn.: Wolgemuth & Hyatt, 1989.
Anastaplo, George. *Abraham Lincoln: A Constitutional Biography*. Lanham, Md.: Rowman & Littlefield, 1999.
———. *The Constitution of 1787: A Commentary*. Baltimore, Md.: The Johns Hopkins University Press, 1989.
Andrews, Joan. *I Will Never Forget You: The Rescue Movement in the Life of Joan Andrews*. San Francisco: Ignatius Press, 1989.
Arendt, Hannah. *On Revolution*. New York: Viking Press, 1963.
Aristotle. *The Politics*, trans. Carnes Lord. Chicago: The University of Chicago Press, 1984.
Arkes, Hadley. *Beyond the Constitution*. Princeton: Princeton University Press, 1990.
Arnhart, Larry. *Aristotle on Political Reasoning: A Commentary on the 'Rhetoric.'* De Kalb, Ill.: Northern Illinois University Press, 1981.
Aronoff, Myron J., ed. *Political Anthropology, Volume 3: Religion and Politics*. New Brunswick and London: Transaction Books, 1984.
Augustine. *The City of God*, trans. Henry Bettenson. London: Penguin Books, 1984.
Bailyn, Bernard. *The Ideological Origins of the American Revolution*. Cambridge:

Belknap Press of Harvard University Press, 1967.
Barton, David. *The Myth of Separation: What is the Correct Relationship between Church and State?* Aledo, Tex.: WallBuilder Press, 1989.
Basler, Roy, ed. *Abraham Lincoln: His Speeches and Writings.* One volume edition. World Publishing Co., 1946.
Bell, Derrick A., Jr. *Race, Racism and American Law,* 2d edition. Boston and Toronto: Little, Brown and Company, 1980.
Bellah, Robert N. *The Broken Covenant: American Civil Religion in Time of Trial.* New York: The Seabury Press, 1975.
———. *Thomas Jefferson: Selected Writings.* Harvey C. Mansfield, Jr. Wheeling, Ill.: Harlan Davidson, 1979.
Belz, Herman. *Abraham Lincoln, Constitutionalism, and Equal Rights in the Civil War Era.* New York: Fordham University Press, 1998.
———. *Emancipation and Equal Rights; Politics and Constitutionalism in the Civil War Era.* New York: W. W. Norton and Co., 1978.
———. *Equality Transformed: A Quarter-Century of Affirmative Action.* New Brunswick: Transaction Publishers, 1991.
Bercovitch, Sacvan. *The American Jeremiad.* Madison: The University of Wisconsin Press, 1978.
Berman, Daniel M. *It Is So Ordered: The Supreme Court Rules on School Segregation.* New York: W. W. Norton & Co., 1966.
Bickel, Alexander. *The Morality of Consent.* New Haven, Conn.: Yale University Press, 1989.
Blumenfeld, Samuel. *Property in a Humane Economy.* LaSalle, Ill: Open Court Press, 1974.
Bolt, Robert. *A Man For All Seasons.* New York: Vintage Books, 1960.
Boorstin, Daniel. *An American Primer.* New York: New American Library, 1968.
Bork, Robert H. *Slouching Towards Gomorrah: Modern Liberalism and American Decline.* New York: Regan Books, 1996.
Bradford, M. E. *A Better Guide than Reason: Studies in the American Revolution.* LaSalle, Ill.: Sherwood Sugden & Co., 1979.
———. *Original Intentions on the Making and Ratification of the United States Constitution.* Athens, Ga.: The University of Georgia Press, 1993.
Brown, Robert E. *Charles Beard and the Constitution: A Critical Analysis of "An Economic Interpretation of the Constitution."* New York: Norton, 1965.
Calhoun, John C. *Union and Liberty: The Political Philosophy of John C. Calhoun.* ed. Ross M. Lence. Indianapolis, Ind.: Liberty Fund, 1992.
Carlson, Allan. *From Cottage to Work Station: The Family's Search for Social Harmony in the Industrial Age.* San Francisco: Ignatius Press, 1993.
———. *The New Agrarian Mind: The Movement Toward Decentralist Thought in Twentieth Century America.* New Brunswick: Transaction Publishers, 2000.
Craycraft, Kenneth R. *The American Myth of Religious Freedom.* Dallas: Spence Publishing, 1999.
Croly, Herbert. *The Promise of American Life.* Boston: Northeastern University Press, 1989; first published in 1909.
Curtis, Michael Kent. *No State Shall Abridge.* Durham, N. C.: Duke University Press, 1986.

de Alvarez, Leo Paul, ed. *Abraham Lincoln, the Gettysburg Address, and American Constitutionalism.* Irving, Tex.: The University of Dallas Press, 1976.
Deane, Herbert. *The Political and Social Ideas of St. Augustine.* New York: Columbia University Press, 1963.
Dewey, John. *Liberalism and Social Action.* New York: Capricorn Books, 1963.
Diamond, Martin. *As Far as Republican Principles Will Admit.* ed. William Schambra. Washington, D.C.: The AEI Press, 1992.
Douglass, Frederick. *The Life and Writings of Frederick Douglass.* 4 volumes. ed. Philip Foner. New York: International Press, 1955.
D'Souza, Dinesh. *The End of Racism.* New York: The Free Press, 1995.
Du Bois, W. E. B. *The Souls of Black Folk.* New York: A Penguin Book, 1989.
Dunning, William A. *Reconstruction, Political and Economic, 1865-1877.* New York: Harper & Row, 1907.
Dworkin, Ronald. *Taking Rights Seriously.* Cambridge, Mass.: Harvard University Press, 1977.
Elkins, Stanley M. *Slavery: A Problem in American Institutional and Intellectual Life.* New York: Universal Library, 1963; University of Chicago, 1959.
Epstein, Richard. *Forbidden Grounds: The Case Against Employment Discrimination Laws.* Cambridge, Mass.: Harvard University Press, 1992.
———. *Takings: Private Property and the Power of Eminent Domain.* Cambridge, Mass.: Harvard University Press, 1985.
Fehrenbacher, Don E., ed. *Abraham Lincoln: Speeches and Writings* (in two volumes). New York: The Library of America, 1989.
———. *The Dred Scott Case: Its Significance in American Law and Politics.* New York: Oxford University Press, 1978.
Foner, Eric. *Free Soil, Free Labor, Free Men: The Ideology of the Republican Party Before the Civil War.* New York: Oxford University Press, 1970.
———. *A Short History of Reconstruction.* New York: Harper & Row, 1990.
———. *Reconstruction: America's Unfinished Revolution.* New York: Harper & Row, 1988.
Franklin, John Hope and August Meier, eds. *Black Leaders of the Twentieth Century.* Urbana, Chicago, London: University of Illinois Press, 1982.
Franklin, John Hope and Isidore Starr. *The Negro in 20th Century America: A Reader on the Struggle for Civil Rights.* New York: Vintage Books, 1967.
Galbraith, John Kenneth. *The Affluent Society.* Boston: Houghton Mifflin Company, 1958.
———. *The New Industrial State.* Boston: Houghton Mifflin Company, 1967.
Gates, Henry Louis, Jr., and Cornel West. *The Future of the Race.* New York: Alfred A. Knopf, 1996.
Genovese, Eugene D. *Roll Jordan Roll; the World the Slaves Made.* New York: Vintage Books, 1976; Random House, 1972.
———. *Southern Front: History and Politics in the Culture War.* Columbia, Mo.: University of Missouri Press, 1995.
———. *The Southern Tradition: The Achievement and Limitations of an American Conservatism.* Cambridge: Harvard University Press, 1994.
Gilder, George. *Wealth and Poverty.* New York: Basic Books, 1981.
Glazer, Nathan. *Affirmative Discrimination: Ethnic Inequality and Public Policy.* New

York: Basic Books, 1975.
Goldwin, Robert, ed. *100 Years of Emancipation*. Chicago: Rand McNally Co., 1964.
Graham, Hugh. *The Civil Rights Era: Origins and Development of National Policy, 1960-1972*. New York: Oxford University Press, 1990.
Guinier, Lani. *Tyranny of the Majority*. New York: The Free Press, 1994.
Gutman, Herbert G. *The Black Family in Slavery and Freedom, 1750-1925*. New York: Vintage Books, 1977.
Halbwachs, Maurice. *On Collective Memory*, trans. J. Ditter, Jr. and Vida Yazdi Ditter. New York: Pantheon Books, 1998.
Harrington, Michael. *The Other America: Poverty in the United States*, rev. ed. New York: Random House, 1990.
Harris, Richard and Sidney M. Milkis, eds. *Remaking American Politics*. Boulder, San Francisco, and London: Westview Press, 1989.
Harris, William C. *With Charity for All: Lincoln and the Restoration of the Union*. Kentucky: The University of Kentucky Press, 1997.
Hart, Benjamin. *Faith and Freedom: The Christian Roots of American Liberty*. Dallas: Lewis and Stanley, 1988.
Hill, Herbert and James E. Jones, eds. *Race in America: The Struggle for Equality*. Madison: The University of Wisconsin Press, 1993.
Hofstadter, Richard. *The American Political Tradition & the Men Who Made It*. New York: Vintage Books, 1974; Alfred A. Knopf, 1948.
Horwitz, Robert, ed. *The Moral Foundations of the American Republic*. Charlottesville: University Press of Virginia, 1977.
Hughes, Jonathan R. T., *The Governmental Habit: Economic Controls from Colonial Times to the Present*. New York: Basic Books, 1977.
Hyneman, Charles S., and Donald Lutz. *American Political Writing During the Founding Era: 1760-1805*, in two volumes. Indianapolis, Ind.: Liberty Fund, 1983.
Jaffa, Harry V. *Crisis of the House Divided: An Interpretation of the Issues of the Lincoln-Douglas Debates*. Chicago: The University of Chicago Press, 1959, 1982.
———. *Equality and Liberty: Theory and Practice in American Politics*. New York: Oxford University Press, 1965.
———. *How to Think About the American Revolution: A Bicentennial Celebration*. Durham, N.C.: Carolina Academic Press, 1978.
———. *A New Birth of Freedom: Abraham Lincoln and the Coming of the Civil War*. Lanham, Md.: Rowman and Littlefield, 2000.
———, with Bruce Ledewitz. *Original Intent and the Framers of the Constitution: A Disputed Question*. Washington, D.C.: Regnery Gateway, 1993.
Jones, William R. *Is God a White Racist? A Preamble to Black Theology*. New York: Anchor Press/Doubleday, 1973.
Kendall, Willmoore, and George Cary. *The Basic Symbols of the American Political Tradition*. Baton Rouge: Louisiana State University Press, 1970.
———. *Contra Mundum*. ed. Nellie D. Kendall. Lanham, Md.: University Press of America, 1971.
Kennedy, George. *On Rhetoric: A Theory of Civic Discourse*. New York: Oxford University Press, 1991.
Kennedy, Randall. *Race, Crime and the Law*. New York: Vintage Books, 1997.

Kesler, Charles, ed. *Saving the Revolution: The Federalist Papers and the American Founding*. New York: The Free Press, a Division of Macmillan, 1987.

Kirk, Russell. *The Roots of American Order*. Washington, D.C.: Regnery Gateway, 1991.

Kull, Andrew. *The Color-Blind Constitution*. Cambridge, Mass.: Harvard University Press, 1992.

Kurland, Philip B., and Ralph Lerner. *The Founder's Constitution*. Chicago: University of Chicago Press, 1987.

Lawler, Peter Augustine. *The Restless Mind: On the Origin and Perpetuation of Human Liberty*. Lanham, Md.: Rowman & Littlefield, 1993.

———. *Tocqueville's Defense of Human Liberty: Current Essays*, ed. Peter Augustine Lawler. New York: Garland, 1993.

Levine, Lawrence W. *Black Culture and Black Consciousness: American Folk Thought from Slavery to Freedom*. New York: Oxford University Press, 1977.

Levinson, Sanford. *Constitutional Faith*. Princeton: Princeton University Press, 1988.

Link, Arthur S., ed. *Papers of Woodrow Wilson*. Princeton: Princeton University Press, 1966.

Locke, John. *A Letter Concerning Toleration*. ed. James H. Tully. Indianapolis, Ind.: Hackett Publishing, 1983.

Lovell, John Jr. *Black Song: The Forge and the Flame. The Story of How the Afro-American Spiritual was Hammered Out*. New York: The Macmillian Company, 1972.

Magnet, Myron. *The Dream and the Nightmare: The Sixties' Legacy to the Underclass*. New York: William Morrow and Company, 1993.

Manent, Pierre. *Tocqueville and the Nature of Democracy*, trans. John Waggoner. Lanham, Md.: Rowman & Littlefield, 1996.

Mansfield, Jr., Harvey C. *The Taming of the Prince: The Ambivalence of the Modern Executive Power*. Baltimore: The Johns Hopkins University Press, 1989.

———. *Thomas Jefferson: Selected Writings*. Harvey C. Mansfield, Jr. Wheeling, Ill.: Harlan Davidson, 1979.

McDonald, Forrest. *Novus Ordo Seclorum: The Intellectual Origins of the Constitution*. Lawrence, Kans.: The University Press of Kansas, 1985.

McKitrick, Eric L. ed. *Slavery Defended: The Views of the Old South*. Englewood, N.J.: Prentice Hall, 1963.

McPherson, James M. *Abraham Lincoln and the Second American Revolution*. New York: Oxford University Press, 1991.

———. *We the People*. Chicago: University of Chicago Press, 1958.

Meier, August, and Eliot Rudwick. *Along the Color Line: Explorations in the Black Experience*. Urbana, Ill.: University of Illinois Press, 1976.

Melzer, Arthur M., Jerry Wienberger, and M. Richard Zinman, eds. *Multiculturalism and American Democracy*. Lawrence: University Press of Kansas, 1998.

Meyers, Marvin, ed. *The Mind of the Founder: Sources of the Political Thought of James Madison*. London: University Press of New England for Brandeis University Press, 1973; revised ed. 1981.

Mitchell, Paul, ed. *Race Riots in Black and White*. Englewood Cliffs, N.J.: Prentice-Hall, 1970.

Morgan, Edmund S. *The Puritan Dilemma: The Story of John Winthrop*. Boston and

Toronto: Little, Brown, and Company, 1958.

Moses, Wilson Jeremiah. *Black Messiahs and Uncle Toms: Social and Literary Manipulations of a Religious Myth*. University Park and London: Pennsylvania State University Press, 1982.

Muncy, Mitch, ed. *The End of Democracy?: A Celebrated First Things Debate, With Arguments Pro and Con*. Dallas, Tex.: Spence Publishing, 1997.

Murray, Charles. *Losing Ground: American Social Policy, 1950-1980*. New York: Basic Books, 1984.

Murray, John Courtney. *We Hold These Truths: Catholic Reflections on the American Proposition*. New York: Sheed & Ward, 1960.

Nedelsky, Jennifer. *Private Property and the Limits of American Constitutionalism: The Madisonian Framework and its Legacy*. Chicago: The University of Chicago Press, 1990.

Neibuhr, Reinhold. *An Interpretation of Christian Ethics*. New York: Harper Brothers, 1935.

———. *Moral Man and Immoral Society; A Study in Ethics and Politics*. New York: Scribener, 1960.

Niebuhr, Richard. *The Kingdom of God in America*. New York: Harper, 1959.

Novak, Michael. *The Spirit of Democratic Capitalism*. Lanham, New York: Madison Books, 1991; first published by Simon and Schuster, 1982.

O'Brien, David. *Constitutional Law and Politics, Volume Two: Civil Rights and Liberties*, 2d ed. New York: W. W. Norton & Company, 1995.

Obst, Lynda R., ed. *The Sixties*. New York: Random House/Rolling Stone Press, 1977.

Olasky, Marvin. *The Tragedy of American Compassion*. Washington, D.C.: Regnery Publishing, Inc., 1992.

Palm, Daniel C., ed. *On Faith and Free Government*. Lanham, Md.: Rowman & Littlefield, 1997.

Pangle, Thomas. *The Ennobling of Democracy: The Challenge of the Postmodern Age*. Baltimore and London: The Johns Hopkins University Press, 1992.

———. *The Spirit of Modern Republicanism: The Moral Vision of the American Founders and the Philosophy of Locke*. Chicago: The University of Chicago Press, 1988.

Panichas, George A., ed. *Modern Age: The First Twenty-Five Years*. Indianapolis, Ind.: Liberty Press, 1988.

Pocock, J. G. A. *The Machiavellian Moment: Florentine Political Thought and the Atlantic Republican Tradition*. Princeton, N. J.: Princeton University Press, 1975.

Rahe, Paul. *Republics Ancient and Modern*. Chapel Hill: The University of North Carolina Press, 1994.

Rainwater, Lee, and William L. Yancey. *The Moynihan Report and the Politics of Controversy: a Trans-action Social Science and Public Policy Report*. Cambridge and London: The M. I. T. Press, 1967.

Rakove, Jack, ed. *Interpreting the Constitution: The Debate over Original Intent*. Boston: Northeastern University Press, 1990.

Ransom, John Crowe and others. *I'll Take My Stand: The South and the Agrarian Tradition*. Baton Rouge: Louisiana State University Press, 1980; Harper & Brothers, 1930.

Rauch, Basil, ed. *The Roosevelt Reader*. New York: Holt, Rinehart, 1957.

Rauschenbusch, Walter. *Christianity and the Social Crisis*. Louisville, Ky.: Westmin-

ster/Knox Press, 1991.
Rawls, John. *A Theory of Justice*. Cambridge, Mass.: The Belknap Press of Harvard University Press, 1971.
Reiss, Hans. *Kant: Political Writings*. trans. H. B. Nisbet. Cambridge: Cambridge University Press, 1970, 1991.
Risen, James, and Judy L. Thomas. *Wrath of Angels: The American Abortion War*. New York: Basic Books, 1998.
Rorty, Richard. *Achieving America: Leftist Thought in Twentieth Century America*. Cambridge, Mass.: Harvard University Press, 1998.
———. *Contingency, Irony, Solidarity*. Cambrige, Mass.: Cambridge University Press, 1989.
Rosenman, Samuel, ed., *The Public Papers of Franklin D. Roosevelt*. New York: Random House, 1938.
Sandel, Michael J. *Democracy's Discontent: America in Search of a Public Philosophy*. Cambridge, Mass.: Belknap Press of Harvard University Press, 1996.
Schaeffer, Francis. *A Christian Manifesto*. Westchester, Ill.: Crossway Books, 1981.
Scheler, Max. *Resentiment*. Milwaukee: Marquette University Press, 1994.
Shain, Barry Allan. *The Myth of American Individualism: The Protestant Origins of American Political Thought*. N.J.: Princeton University Press, 1994.
Smith, Adam. *An Inquiry into the Nature and Causes of the Wealth of Nations*. eds. R. H. Campbell and A. S. Skinner. Indianapolis, Ind.: Liberty Fund, 1981.
Smith, J. Allen. *The Spirit of American Government*. Cambridge: Belknap Press of Harvard University Press, 1965.
Smith, Rogers. *Civic Ideals: Conflicting Visions of Citizenship in U.S. History*. New Haven: Yale University Press, 1997.
———. *Liberalism and American Constitutional Law*. Cambridge Mass.: Harvard University Press, 1985.
Sowell, Thomas. *Civil Rights: Rhetoric or Reality?* New York: Quill William Morrow, 1984.
———. *Race and Culture: A World View*. New York: Basic Books, 1994.
Steele, Shelby. *The Content of Our Character: A New Vision of Race in America*. New York: St. Martin's Press, 1990.
———. *A Dream Deferred: The Second Betrayal of Black Freedom in America*. New York: HarperCollins, 1998.
Storing, Herbert J. *Toward a More Perfect Union*. ed. Joseph M. Bessette. Washington, D.C.: The AEI Press, 1995.
———. *What Country Have I: Political Writings by Black Americans*. New York: St. Martin's Press, 1970.
Strauss, Leo. *Natural Right and History*. Chicago: The University of Chicago Press, 1953; paperback 1965.
Sunstein, Cass. *The Partial Constitution*. Cambridge, Mass.: Harvard University Press, 1993.
ten Broek, Jacobus. *Equal Under Law*. rev. ed. New York: Collier Books, 1965.
Thurow, Glen. *Abraham Lincoln and American Political Religion*. Albany, New York: State University of New York Press, 1976.
Thurow, Sarah Baumgartner, ed. *Constitutionalism in Perspective: The United States Constitution in Twentieth Century Politics*. vol. 3 of *Constitutionalism in America*.

Dallas: University of Dallas Press, 1988.
Tocqueville, Alexis de. *Democracy in America*, ed. J. P. Mayer. New York: Harper & Row, 1966; Anchor Books, Doubleday & Co., 1969.
Tuck, Brian. *Natural Rights Theories: Their Origin and Development*. Cambridge, Mass.: Cambridge University Press, 1979.
Ture, Kwame and Charles V. Hamilton. *Black Power: The Politics of Liberation*. New York: Vintage Books, 1992; New York: Random House, 1967.
Tuveson, Ernest Lee. *Redeemer Nation: The Idea of America's Millenial Role*. Chicago: The University of Chicago Press, 1969; Midway Reprint, 1980.
Van Woodward, C. *The Strange Career of Jim Crow*. London: Oxford University Press, 1966; 2d. rev. ed.
Voegelin, Eric. *The New Science of Politics*. Chicago: The University of Chicago Press, 1952.
Warren, Robert Penn. *The Legacy of the Civil War*. Lincoln, Nebr.: University of Nebraska Press, 1961.
Washington, Booker T. *Up From Slavery*. N. Y.: Carol Publishing Group Edition, 1993.
Weaver, Richard M. *The Ethics of Rhetoric*. Regnery/Gateway, 1953; Davis, Calif.: Hermagoras Press, 1985.
———. *Ideas Have Consequences*. Chicago: The University of Chicago Press, 1948.
Weber, David R. *Civil Disobedience in America: A Documentary History*. Ithaca, New York: Cornell University Press, 1978.
West, Cornel. *Race Matters*. New York: Vintage Books, 1994.
West, Thomas G. *Vindicating the Founders: Race, Sex, Class, and Justice in the Origins of America*. Lanham, Md.: Rowman & Littlefield, 1997.
Williams, Juan. *Eyes on the Prize: America's Civil Rights Years 1954-1965*. New York: Penguin Books, 1988; Viking Penguin 1987.
Wills, Garry. *Lincoln at Gettysburg: The Words that Remade America*. New York: Simon and Schuster, 1992.
Wilson, James. *The Works of James Wilson*. ed. Robert Green McCloskey, 2 vols. Cambridge, Mass.: Belknap Press of Harvard University Press, 1967.
Wilson, William Julius. *The Truly Disadvantaged: The Inner City, the Underclass, and Public Policy*. Chicago: University of Chicago Press, 1987.
———. *When Work Disappears: The World of the New Urban Poor*. New York: Alfred A. Knopf, 1997.
Wilson, Woodrow. *The New Freedom: A Call for the Emancipation of the Generous Energies of a People*. New York: Doubleday, Page & Company, 1913.
Wood, Gordon S. *The Creation of the American Republic 1776-1789*. Chapel Hill: The University of North Carolina Press, 1969.
Woodson, Carter G. *Negro Orators and Their Orations*. Washington, D.C.: The Associated Publishers, 1925.
Young, Whitney. *To Be Equal*. New York: McGraw Hill, 1964.
Zuckert, Michael P. *Natural Rights and the New Republicanism*. Princeton, N. J.: Princeton University Press, 1994.
———. *The Natural Rights Republic: Studies in the Foundation of the American Political Tradition*. Notre Dame, Ind.: Notre Dame University Press, 1996.

Articles

Ackerman, Bruce. "Constitutional Politics/Constitutional Law." *Yale Law Journal* 99:3 (December 1989): 453-547.
Alsop, Stewart. "After Vietnam—Abolish Poverty?" *The Saturday Evening Post*, 17 December, 1966 12.
Avins, Alfred. "The Equal Protection of the Laws: The Original Understanding." *New York Law Forum* 12:5 (Fall 1966): 385-429.
———. "Freedom of Choice in Personal Service Occupations: Thirteenth Amendment Limitations on Antidiscrimination Legislation." *Cornell Law Quarterly* 49:2 (Winter 1964): 228-56.
———. "Incorporation of the Bill of Rights: The Crosskey-Fairman Debates Revisted." *Harvard Journal on Legislation* 6:1 (November 1968): 1-26.
Bellah, Robert. "Civil Religion in America." *Deadalus*, vol. 96 (Winter 1967) 1-21.
Belz, Herman. "The Civil War Amendments to the Constitution: The Relevance of Original Intent." *Constitutional Commentary* 5:115 (Winter 1988) 115-141.
———. "Comments on 'Equality as a Constitutional Concept.'" *Maryland Law Review* 47:1 (Fall 1987) 28-37.
Bickel, Alexander M. "The Original Understanding and the Segregation Decision." *Harvard Law Review* 69:1 (November 1955): 1-65.
Bryner, Gary. "Congress, Courts, and Agencies: Equal Employment and the Limits of Policy Implementation." *Political Science Quarterly*. 96:3 (Fall 1981) 411-30.
Epstein, Richard A. "The Proper Scope of the Commerce Clause." *Virginia Law Review* 73: 1443-55.
Erler, Edward J. "Sowing the Wind: Judicial Oligarchy and the Legacy of *Brown v. Board of Education*." *Harvard Journal of Law and Public Policy*. 8:3 (Summer 1985): 399-426.
Eskridge, William N. "Dynamic Statutory Interpretation." *University of Pennsylvania Law Review* 135:6 (July 1987) 1479-555.
Finkelman, Paul. "Prelude to the Fourteenth Amendment: Black Legal Rights in the Antebellum North." *Rutgers Law Journal* 17:3 & 4 (Spring & Summer 1986): 415-482.
Fish, Stanley. "Mission Impossible: Settling the Just Bounds Between Church and State." *Columbia Law Review* 97:8 (December 1997): 2255-333.
Frank, John P., and Robert F. Munro. "The Original Understanding of 'Equal Protection of the Laws.'" *Columbia Law Review* 50:2 (February 1950): 131-69.
Frantz, Laurent B. "Congressional Power to Enforce the Fourteenth Amendment Against Private Acts." *Yale Law Journal* 73:1352-1384.
Glazer, Nathan. "A Breakdown in Civil Rights Enforcement?" *The Public Interest* (Winter 1971):108-15.
Graham, Howard J. "The Early Antislavery Backgrounds of the Fourteenth Amendment." *Wisconsin Law Review* 610 (1950).
Graham, Hugh Davis. "On Riots and Riot Commissions: Civil Disorders in the 1960's." *The Public Historian* 2:4 (Summer 1980) 7-27.
Harrison, John. "Equality, Race, Discrimination and the Fourteenth Amendment." *Constitutional Commentary* 13:3 (Winter 1996): 243-55.
———. "Reconstructing the Privileges and Immunities Clause." *Yale Law Journal*

101:7 (Winter 1992): 1385-474.
Kennedy, Randall. "Suspect Policy." *New Republic*, 13 September 1999, 30-36.
Klarman, Michael. "Brown: Originalism, and Constitutional Theory: A Response to Professor McConnell." *Virginia Law Review* 81:7 (October 1995): 1881-936.
———. "Constitutional Fact/Constitutional Fiction: A Critique of Bruce Ackerman's Theory of Constitutional Moments." *Stanford Law Review* 44:3 (February 1992): 759-88.
Levitan, Sar. "The Pitfalls of the Guaranteed Income." *The Reporter* 36 (18 May 1967): 12-15.
Maltz, Earl. "Originalism and the Desegregation Decisions—A Response to Professor McConnell." *Constitutional Commentary* 13:3 (Winter 1996): 223-31.
———. "Reconstruction without Revolution: Republican Civil Rights Theory in the Era of the Fourteenth Amendment." *Houston Law Review* 24:2 (March 1987): 221-79.
———. "'Separate But Equal' and the Law of Common Carriers in the Era of the Fourteenth Amendment." *Rutgers Law Journal* 17:3 and 4 (Spring & Summer 1986): 553-68.
Mansfield, Jr., Harvey C. "Returning to the Founders: the Debate on the Constitution." *The New Criterion* 12:1 (September 1993): 48-54.
Marshall, Thurgood. "Reflections on the Bicentennial of the United States," *Harvard Law Review* 101:1 (November 1987): 1-5.
McConnell, Michael. "The Forgotten Constitutional Moment." *Constitutional Commentary* 11:1 (Winter 1994): 115-44.
———. "The Fourteenth Amendment: A Second American Revolution or the Logical Culmination of the Tradition?" *Loyola of Los Angeles Law Review* 25:4 (June 1992): 1159-76.
———. "Originalism and the Desegregation Decisions." *Virginia Law Review* 81:4 (May 1995): 947-1140.
———. "The Originalist Justification for Brown: A Reply to Professor Klarman." *Virginia Law Review* 81:7 (October 1995): 1937-56.
———. "Segregation and the Original Understanding: A Reply to Professor Maltz." *Constitutional Commentary* 13:3 (Winter 1996): 233-41.
Mehta, Ved. "Gandhiism is not Easily Copied." *The New York Times Magazine*, 9 July 1961, 8-11.
Mendelson, Wallace. "From Warren to Burger: The Rise and Decline of Substantive Equal Protection." *The American Political Science Review* 66 (December 1972): 226-1233.
Meyer, Frank S. "Principles and Heresies." *National Review*, 20 April 1965, 327.
Meyers, Marvin. "The Violence of Nonviolence." *National Review*, 20 April 1965, 327.
Moreno, Paul. 'Racial Classifications and Reconstruction Legislation." *The Journal of Southern History*. Vol. 61, No. 2 (May 1995).
Neuhaus, Richard J. "Contract, Covenant, and the Beginning of the 'American Century.'" *First Things*. 107:73-76 (November,2000).
Rustin, Bayard. "From Protest to Politics: The Future of the Civil Rights Movement." *Commentary* 39:2 (February 1964): 25-31.
Sandel, Michael J. "America's Search for a New Public Philosophy." *The Atlantic Monthly* (March 1996): 57-74.

Schnapper, Eric. "Affirmative Action and the Legislative History of the Fourteenth Amendment." *Virginia Law Review* 71:5 (1985): 753-98.

Schwartz, Barry. "Social Change and Collective Memory: The Democratization of George Washington." *American Sociological Review* 56 (April 1991): 221-36.

Silberman, Lawrence. "The Road to Racial Quotas." *The Wall Street Journal*, 11 August 1977.

Tierney, Brian. "Origins of Natural Rights Language: Texts and Contexts, 1150-1250." *History of Political Thought* 10:4 (Winter 1989), 625-46.

Tussman and ten Broek, "The Equal Protection of the Laws." *Californian Law Review* 37: 341 (1949).

Zinn, Howard. "The Force of Nonviolence." *The Nation* 204, 17 March 1962, 227-33.

Zuckert, Michael P. "Congressional Power Under the Fourteenth Amendment—The Original Understanding of Section Five." *Constitutional Commentary* 3:1 (Winter 1986): 123-56.

———. "Completing the Constitution: The Fourteenth Amendment and Constitutional Rights." *Publius* (Spring 1992): 69-91.

———. "Completing the Constitution: The Thirteenth Amendment." *Constitutional Commentary* 4:2 (Summer 1987): 259-83.

Index

Abernathy, Ralph, 9
affirmative action, 2, 19, 60; King's advocacy of, 63–65, 77–80; by Freedmen's Bureau, 90
AFL-CIO, Political Action Committee of, 76
agape, 46, 125–29
Akerman, Bruce, 33, 53n16
Amos, 15, 16, 28n68
Ansbro, John, xxi, 134
Aquinas, Thomas, 38, 49–50, 130, 132–34; and the American founding, 58n91, 134–35; in the "Letter from Birmingham Jail," 137–38
Arendt, Hannah, 139, 140, 148, 156
Aristotle, xviii, 21, 113; on equality, 49-50; on rhetoric, xxi-xxiii, 8, 24n31, 24n33, 25n42, 25n45
Augustine, 49, 137, 139; on obedience to the laws, 130–32

Baldwin, Lewis, xix
Beloved Community, xiii, 41
Belz, Herman, 12, 65
Bennett, Lerone, Jr., xvi
Bible, xiii, xxi, 2
Bill of Rights, xiv, xxi, 2, 99, 119n62
Bill of Rights for the Disadvantaged, 90, 99
black power, 64, 80
Board of Education v. Tinnon, 70
Bolt, Robert, 136
Bork, Robert, 34
Bradford, M. E., 11
Brown v. Board of Education, 62, 65–69, 79, 86n86, 137

Calhoun, John C., 11, 106
Calloway-Thomas, Carolyn, xix
capitalism, 98, 100, 107–10, 111, 114
Carmichal, Stokely, 97
Christianity, 54n34, 123n136; influence of on King's thought, xvi, xxvin30, 16, 44–46
church, 44, 46, 134. *See also* Christianity
civil disobedience, 61, 98, 144–45; in the American political tradition, 129–37; King's conception of, 125–29; in "Letter from Birmingham Jail," 137–39; as a mode of civil discourse, 139–44
civil religion, xii–xiii, xviii, xxii, xxvin30, 9, 16, 38–42, 46, 54n37, 136–37. *See also* religion
Civil Rights Act of 1866, 67, 72, 109
Civil Rights Act of 1875, 66–74, 83n42
Civil Rights Act of 1964, 2, 60, 64, 75–79, 80n5, 83n42
Civil Rights Cases, 71–73
Civil War, xv, 69, 102, 106
Committee on Fair Employment Practice, 7
communism, 31, 98
communitarianism, 46–51
Congress of Racial Equality, 76, 130
Constitution, xiii, xxi, 27n65, 34, 54n25; and civil disobedience, 129, 131–35, 140–45, 148n60; and discrimination, 65–80, 82n34, 83n42, 83n45, 86n77; in the "I Have a Dream" speech, 1, 10–13;

in King's "Appeal to the President," 60–65; and King's personalism, 111; and King's political economy, 89, 95–96, 115n13, 116n16; limits of, 135–37; and Lincoln, 13, 26n50; and progressivism, 99–106; and religion, 40–48
covenant, xiii, 20, 25, 41
Croly, Herbert, 100–4, 112, 119n69

Declaration of Independence, xiii–xvi, 73, 80; in the "Appeal to the President," 64; and civil disobedience, 131, 145; and civil religion, 38–39; and discrimination, 65–69; on equality and property, 106-9; in the "I Have a Dream" speech, 11, 13, 16, 18, 22; and King's personalism, 31–32, 36, 111, 122–23n136; and King's political economy, 89–90, 114; liberalism of, 34, 36, 48–50, 51, 53n18; and minority rights, 140; and progressivism, 55n43, 99–106; prudence in, 134–36, 147–48n44
discrimination, xiii, 3, 22n10, 24n25, 28n81, 59–80, 80n5, 83n42, 84n55, 87n91, 97; and the free market, 106; in the "I Have a Dream" speech, 13, 15, 19, 22; and King's personalism, 111; and the March on Washington, 7–8; and poverty, 89–95; in Roosevelt's Executive Order, 7
Douglas, Stephen, 11, 40, 144,
dream, the American Dream, xiii–xvi, 18, 19, 22; King's Dream, 31–33, 35, 50–51, 59, 80, 89, 99, 100, 129. *See also* "I Have a Dream" speech
Du Bois, W. E. B., 21, 22, 29, 158
Dworkin, Ronald, 33, 53, 158
Dyson, Michael E., xii, xiii, xxi, xxiv, xxv, xxvii, 2, 23, 82, 143,
144, 149

Eisenhower, Dwight D., 6
Emancipation Proclamation, 7, 11–13, 16, 26n50, 27n63, 27n65, 59
equality, 27n63, 49–50, 62, 63, 66–70, 83n42, 107, 111, 113; created equal, xi, xiii, 11, 18, 31, 43, 104, 107; equal opportunity, xiv, 73, 99; equal rights, 60, 68, 85n75, 107, 109; separate but equal, 68–69, 81n16, 83n45
equal protection clause, 60, 62, 67–72, 78, 79, 83–84n51, 85n75

Fair Housing Act of 1968, 79
family, King's ideas on, 91–99, 114, 116n20, 117n31
FECP. *See* Committee on Fair Employment Practice
Fellowship of Reconciliation, 130
Fitzhugh, George, 106
Foner, Eric, 82n33, 106–7
founding fathers, xiv, xv, xvi, 18
Fourteenth Amendment, 60, 62, 66–78, 80n5, 81n10, 83n45, 84n51, 85nn74–75, 110
framers, xvi, 12, 36, 140
Franklin, Benjamin, 39, 93
Frantz, Laurent B., 66, 83n45
Fugitive Slave Act of 1850, 135

Gandhi, xvi, xxvin30, 2, 15, 129, 130, 134, 139, 145n4, 147n32, 147n40
Garrow, David, xviii, xxvin28, 1, 8, 17
God, xiii, 16–17, 20, 31, 36, 51, 74, 108, 110, 136, 28n73; and civil religion, 39–40, 48–51, 54n34; in the Declaration of Independence, 36–37, 39, 54n34; King's references to; xi, 5, 14, 16, 21, 31, 32, 33, 35, 40–46, 54n24, 56n66, 60, 96, 104, 111, 126, 130, 133, 134, 137, 144

Graham, Hugh Davis, 76–77
Great Society, 104, 118n47
guaranteed income, 90, 94, 115n10
Harding, Vincent, xii–xiii, xxviin39
Harlan, John, 72–73
Heschel, Abraham, xi
Himes, Carl Wendall, Jr., xii
Hobbes, Thomas, 37, 58n91
Hooker, Thomas, 110, 134–35, 148n45
human rights, 33, 53n16, 60, 95, 109, 111

I Have a Dream speech, xii–xxii, 1–22, 24n26, 28n78, 28n81, 51, 62, 89
Isaiah, 20, 28n73

Jaffa, Harry V., xxiiin6, 26–27n51, 28n76, 58n94, 147n36, 148n46
Jefferson, Thomas, 34, 37, 49, 86n83, 108, 109, 114,
jeremiad, xii–xv, xviii, xxivn14, 14, 21, 42
Jews, 20, 92, 94
John the Baptist, 20, 43
Johnson, Lyndon B., 27n63, 63, 82n23, 104, 118n47, 118n49, 136
Jones, James E. Jr., 77–79,

Kant, 33, 45, 47, 49, 109, 111–12, 122n134, 133
Kendall, Willmoore, 118n36
Kennedy, John F., 6, 8, 12, 59, 60, 61, 79, 121n97
King federal holiday, xi–xvii, xxvin34, 1–3, 39
Kull, Andrew, 76, 87n91
Kurland, Philip, 109

Law of Nature. *See* Natural Law
Lerner, Ralph, 109,
"Letter from Birmingham Jail," xxi, 2, 24n23, 36, 74, 131, 135, 137–39, 143
Levison, Stanley, xxviin34, 97

liberalism, xxii, 9, 79, 111–13, 121n105, 136; foundations of in American and in King, 31–51, 53n16, 53n18, 56n66, 56n77, 58n91, 58n96
Lincoln, Abraham, xi–xiii, xxiiin5, 1, 2, 4, 11–22, 26–27nn50–51, 27n59, 28n76, 34, 40, 51, 106–9, 120n54, 135–37, 144, 148n47
Lischer, Richard, 28n78, 41–42
Locke, 48–49, 57n81, 58n91, 58n96, 109–10, 122n125, 131, 147n35
love, 5, 15, 36, 38, 45, 46, 48, 51, 54n26, 64, 108, 125–26, 128, 143, 146n10. *See also agape*
Lucaites, John Louis, xix, 9

Madison, James, 34, 37–38, 41, 107, 113, 121n105, 140
Malcolm X, 14–15, 97, 119n55
March on Washington, xv, 1, 7, 23n1, 79, 91, 98
Mayflower Compact, 20
McConnell, Michael, 66–70, 72, 73, 83–84n51, 85n77, 86n85
McPherson, James B., 12
Meier, August, 6, 23–24n17, 146
MIA. *See* Montgomery Improvement Association
Miller, Keith, xix–xx, 4
Montgomery boycott, xxvn27, 29n90, 71, 81n14, 97, 125, 128, 129, 130, 133, 139
Montgomery Improvement Association, 5–6, 23n16, 28n69
Moses, Wilson, xxiv, 4–5
Moynihan Report, 91–92, 116n20

NAACP. *See* National Association for the Advancement of Colored People
National Association for the Advancement of Colored People, 62, 76, 81n16
National Urban League, 18, 28n81, 76, 90

natural law, 33, 48, 58n91, 74–75, 129, 132–37, 143, 145, 147n40, 147–48n44
natural rights, 32, 40, 47–51, 55n43, 58n91, 79, 100–2, 104, 107, 110, 116n16, 131, 136, 140
New Deal, 76, 79, 87n90, 100
Niebuhr, Reinhold, 126, 127–28
Nietzsche, Friedrich, 122–23n130, 126, 146n10
nonviolent direct action. *See* civil disobedience

O'Brien, Michael, xviii
Oates, Stephen B., xx, xxvn27
Operation Breadbasket, 63
Operation Rescue, 143–44

Parks, Rosa, xvi, 6
personalism, 31–32, 36, 46, 47, 74, 104, 120n87, 122n133, 122–23n136, 146n6; critique of King's understanding of, 111–12
Plato, xiii, xx, 12, 17, 22, 29n88, 134
Plessy v. Ferguson, 62, 72–73, 81n16
political economy, xiv, 22, 89–114, 115n7, 141, 142
poverty, xiii, xxii, 13, 20, 22, 23n10, 59, 63, 80, 110–12, 122n132, 130; King on the nature and causes of, 89–98, 115nn6–7, 118n47; summary of King's ideas on, 105–6, 108. *See also* War on Poverty
preferential treatment. *See* Affirmative Action
property, 19, 47–50, 67, 71, 74, 90, 96, 99, 111; critique of King's understanding, 106–9; redistribution of, 90; rights, 34, 90, 96, 100, 104, 110–13, 115n13, 116n16, 122n125, 135
Publius, 38, 55n42, 141,

racism, xii, xv, xvii, xxii, 2, 3, 20, 23n10, 76–77, 94, 96, 106, 115n6

Randolph, A. Philip, 7
Rauschenbusch, Walter, 28n71, 44–45, 103, 108, 122–23n136
Rawls, John, 33, 53n16, 122nn133–34
Reagan, Ronald, xi, 1, 23n1, 78
Reconstruction, 7, 65–69, 73, 77, 82n33, 86n77
Reddick, Lawrence, xxvn27, 10, 25n42
religion, 16, 19, 34, 35, 38–39, 52n4, 55n43, 57–58n77; establishment of, 40; King's ideas on, 41–46, 48, 51, 103, 114, 129. *See also* civil religion
rhetoric, xii, xv, xviii, xix, xxii, xxviin42, 1–2, 4–9, 14, 23n13, 23n16, 24n31, 24n33, 26n48, 39–42, 97, 100, 118n49, 137, 143, 147–48n44
Riverside Address, 2
Roosevelt, Franklin D., 7, 99–100, 103–4
Roosevelt, Theodore, 61, 119
Rorty, Richard, 33, 53n16
Rousseau, 33, 122n128
Rustin, Bayard, 104–5, 115–15n1, 118n37, 129, 130

Sandel, Michael, 33–34, 47, 116n20,
Satyagraha, 15
Schnapper, Eric, 77–78
segregation, 32, 35, 42, 79, 92, 123n139; in the "Appeal to the President," 59–62, 86n85; and *Brown v. Board of Education,* 62, 64–68; history of, 66–67, 69–70, 73, 76, 83n42, 83n45, 83–84n51, 86n85; and King's Dream, xiii, xv, 18, 22; in the "Letter from Birmingham Jail," 137–38; and personalism, 74–75, 122–23n136; and preferential treatment, 59, 64; and the two phases of King's career, 3, 6, 13, 19, 22n10, 89–95, 142–45

Selma protest march, 70, 94, 97, 142
Shute, Daniel, 49
slavery, xi, 11–13, 15, 18, 26n50, 27n63, 32, 50, 60, 63, 65, 68, 71–72, 78, 86n85, 87n91, 93–94, 102, 106, 109, 135–36
Smith, Adam, 111
Smith, Kenneth L., xxi, xxvin29, 2, 35, 41, 52n2, 120n87, 129, 146n17, 147n32
SNCC. *See* Student Nonviolent Coordinating Committee
Southern Christian Leadership Conference, xiii, xx, 9, 139
Sowell, Thomas, 93, 117–18n33
Steele, Shelby, 87n104, 93
Stevens, Alexander, 68
Strauder v. West Virginia, 69
Strauss, Leo, 57n81
Stride Toward Freedom, 5
Student Nonviolent Coordinating Committee, 6

Thirteenth Amendment, 71–72, 109
Tocqueville, Alexis, 4, 23n12, 44, 47, 56–57n77, 108, 110, 114, 121n107, 140

Vietnam War, xii, 42, 96, 118n47, 127, 144

virtue, xiii, 6, 22, 38, 39, 45, 47–48, 56n66, 58n91, 86n83, 91–93, 106–7, 110, 114, 116n20, 128, 132
Voegelin, Eric, 28n75, 41
Voting Rights Act of 1965, 2, 79, 94

War on Poverty, 104–5, 115n10, 118n47, 121n97. *See also* poverty
Warren, Earl, 62, 66–67, 86n86, 137
Washington, Booker T., 89, 92–93, 117n29
Washington, George, xi, xxiin4, xxiii–xxivn10, xxvn19, 39
Washington, James, xx
West, Cornel, xv–xvi, xxvin30, 91, 99, 122n119, 122n123
West, Samuel, 48–49
West, Thomas G., 110
Why We Can't Wait, 63
Williams, Juan, 7, 24, 163
Wilson, William Julius, 105, 87n98, 120n96
Wilson, Woodrow, 61, 100–4, 119n62, 120n86
Winthrop, John, 20–21, 29n86
Woodward, C. Vann, 66

Zepp, Ira G., xxi, xxvin29, 35, 41, 52n2, 54, 55, 56, 120, 129, 146, 147

About the Author

Dr. Nathan Schlueter is an Assistant Professor of Political Science and Director of Pre-Law Studies at St. Ambrose University in Davenport, Iowa, where he lives with his wife Elizabeth and two children. He received his Ph.D. in Politics from the Institute of Philosophic Studies at the University of Dallas in 1999. In 2000 Dr. Schlueter received a postdoctoral fellowship with Liberty Fund which enabled him to complete this manuscript. His publications include "Prospero's Second Sailing: A Machiavellian Reading of the Tempest," published in *Shakespeare's Late Plays: Readings in Politics and Literature*, edited by Travis Curtright and Steve Smith (also published by Lexington Books) and "Drawing Pro-Life Lines" (*First Things: A Journal of Religion and Public Life*, October, 2001, no. 116). Dr. Schlueter has presented numerous papers on King's thought and has lectured widely on King.